John Murray Moore

New Zealand

For the Emigrant, Invalid, And Tourist

John Murray Moore

New Zealand
For the Emigrant, Invalid, And Tourist

ISBN/EAN: 9783744743501

Printed in Europe, USA, Canada, Australia, Japan

Cover: Foto ©ninafisch / pixelio.de

More available books at **www.hansebooks.com**

NEW ZEALAND

FOR THE

EMIGRANT, INVALID, AND TOURIST.

NEW ZEALAND

FOR THE

EMIGRANT, INVALID, AND TOURIST.

BY

JOHN MURRAY MOORE,

M.D. Univ. Edin.; M.R.C.S. Eng.; M.D. New Zealand University; F.R.G.S.;
Fell. Royal Bot. Soc. Edin.; Member Royal Med. Soc. Edin.;
Fellow of the Royal Colonial Institute, &c.

Author of
"*The Plants of Scripture*," "*The Poison Oak of California*,"
"*Shakspeare and Euphuism*," *and other Essays.*

'The climate's delicate, the air most sweet,
'Fertile the Isle.'
WINTER'S TALE, III., i.

LONDON:
SAMPSON LOW, MARSTON, SEARLE & RIVINGTON,
LIMITED,
St. Dunstan's House,
FETTER LANE, FLEET STREET.
1890.

[All rights reserved.]

LONDON:
PRINTED BY WILLIAM CLOWES AND SONS, LIMITED,
STAMFORD STREET AND CHARING CROSS.

To
SIR WILLIAM FOX, K.C.M.G., J.P., ETC.,
FORMERLY PREMIER OF NEW ZEALAND,

AND

LADY FOX,
THIS LITTLE BOOK IS DEDICATED, BY PERMISSION, IN
GRATEFUL ACKNOWLEDGMENT OF MUCH KINDNESS,

BY

THE AUTHOR.

PREFACE.

If an apology be deemed necessary for adding another volume to the ever-increasing mass of literature relating to the New Zealand of to-day it must be found in the originality of the scope and plan of chapters ii. and v. of this little book. In these have been set forth with care and original research—fruits of the author's nine years' professional work in the colony—the various Climatic Zones into which New Zealand viewed as a Health-Resort is divisible, which are here classified for the first time; and a fully detailed account of the characters and therapeutic achievements, up to date, of the principal Thermal Springs of the North Island.

The work of accurate investigation and trial of these springs must go on all the time; and it may be many years before a book on the Thermal Springs of New Zealand equal in value, for example, to "Sutro on the Spas of Europe" can be produced. But I venture to hope that this handbook, imperfect as it is, may serve both the medical profession and the public, as a useful introduction to the climatology and balneology of New Zealand. The original title of the work was to have been "Nine Years in New Zealand," and more than half of the MS. was written before the present title was adopted; therefore readers will understand, and, I trust, pardon, any occasional incongruity between the personal and descriptive styles. With a view of rendering the book useful to the three classes of persons specially addressed, each chapter has been made as nearly as possible complete in itself. The emigrant will find chapters i., iv., viii., ix., and xi. suited to his requirements; the invalid will be specially interested in chapters ii., iv., and v.; while the tourist may study the whole book profitably, except the last chapter, which is written for medical men alone.

Perhaps the critics may be reminded that the author is fully conscious of many sins, both of omission and commission, his valid excuse being that the MS. was prepared amid many professional interruptions, and in a provincial city far away from the central offices and libraries where the latest and best information relating to New Zealand is from time to time received.

The legislative and financial problems now being worked out in New Zealand merit more attention from publicists than they receive. If the accomplished author of "Greater Britain"—the book which first inspired me with a desire to visit the colonies—should bring out a new edition, I hope that he will devote a large section to New Zealand.

It seems but fitting that I should here acknowledge with gratitude the renovation of my health, due, under the kind providence of a gracious God, to the health-giving New Zealand air, and that for both my wife and myself. I should express our warmest thanks to our many Auckland friends for all their kindness, sympathy, and generous hospitality during our residence there.

That New Zealand will very soon completely emerge from her financial cloud into the full sunshine of prosperity, and that she will become in time the wealthiest and most influential, as she is now the healthiest and most adventurous colony of the Australasian group, is the confident hope and expectation of

THE AUTHOR.

CANNING STREET, LIVERPOOL.
November 25th, 1889.

CONTENTS.

CHAPTER I.

MIGRATION, EMIGRATION, AND IMMIGRATION.

	PAGE
The Anglo-Saxon race inclined to wander—The colonies and the "globe-trotter"—Centrifugal and centripetal laws of emigration—Necessity of emigration for the British—Restrictions imposed by the United States gives the colonies a chance—New Zealand the best field—Classes of emigrants *not* wanted out there—Who *are* wanted—Who are likely to succeed—Outfit—Various routes to the colony—Ordinary rates of wages—Cost of living	1

CHAPTER II.

THE CLIMATES OF NEW ZEALAND, GENERAL AND LOCAL.

The differences of Australian and New Zealand climates not generally known to consulting physicians—The colonies offer advantages over other health-resorts—General climatology and meteorology of New Zealand—Effects of the mountain ranges and forests—The colony divisible into four climatic zones: 1. North Cape to Napier; 2. Napier to Hurunui; 3. Hurunui to Stewart's Island; 4. Alpine plateau of North Island—Local climatology of Auckland, Whangarei, Napier, Palmerston, Nelson, Picton, Taranaki, Wellington, Christchurch, Dunedin, Queenstown, Invercargill—Cautions to Invalids—General Summary .. 14

CHAPTER III.

THE MAORIS AND THEIR CUSTOMS.

The name, origin, and features of the Maori—Tattooing—Language, with prose and poetical specimens—Rhyme for pronunciation—History of Old New Zealand—Judge

Maning—Causes of their decline—Customs of *tapu, muru, utu*, explained—Ceremonies of *korero, haka, tangi*—Meaning of *mana*—Bishop Selwyn on the Maori character—Old Mohi in " Our Maoris "—Conversions to Christianity—Chivalry in war—Future of the Maori race 39

CHAPTER IV.

AUCKLAND, THE NAPLES OF NEW ZEALAND.

Its position, geographical and commercial importance—The " Corinth of the south "—Third city in Australasia by population—Sheltered Waitemata Inlet—Graving-docks, large and small—Picturesque approach to the city—Public buildings—Grey collection of MSS.—City government—Newspapers—Developments of art, music, science, and literature—Recreations—Amusing anecdote of the parachutist—Ostrich farm—The schoolboy's account of the bird—Observance of Sunday—Acclimatization of fauna (birds, fishes, &c.)—Growth of Auckland during nine years. 57

CHAPTER V.

THE MINERAL SPRINGS OF NEW ZEALAND.

Seventy-three already analyzed—Arranged in five classes—Description of the three oldest spas: Waiwera, Ta Aroha, Rotorua—The new town of Rotorua—Its special arrangements for visitors—Priest's Bath—Madame Rachel—Blue Bath — Pain killer — Lake House Baths — Oil Bath — Wonders of Tikitere—Hot waterfall, " Te Kute "—Diseases cured by the above—Leprosy probably curable by them—The " season " for Rotorua thermal treatment—Advice to the Invalid, the Tourist, and the Invalid-Tourist .. 74

CHAPTER VI.

THE WONDERLANDS OF NEW ZEALAND: EXCURSIONS TO THE HOT LAKES AND TERRACES, AND TO THE WEST COAST SOUNDS.

Excursions to Rotorua *viâ* Tauranga in December, 1880—Tauranga and its sunset—Oropi—Beauty of the forest along the Gorge Road—Ohinemutu—Native " loafers "—Bathing, laundry-work, and cooking *al fresco*—Tikitapu Bush—Visit to Wairoa, Lake Tarawera, and the Terraces

CONTENTS.   xi

                                                                 PAGE
—White Terrace surpasses the Taj Mahal—Geysers and
    fumaroles—Pink Terrace and luxurious bathing—Return
    in canoe down the swift hot stream Kaiwaka—Fate of
    the Tuhourangis—Scenery of the Middle Island: lakes,
    mountains, glaciers, fjords—Lakes Wakatipu, Te Anau, and
    Manapouri—Annual trip by steamship *Tarawera* to the
    West Coast Sounds—My visit in January, 1884—Excel-
    lent arrangements—Port Chalmers—Cuttle Cove—Dusky
    Sound and Mr. Doherty—Spinach discovered by Cook in
    Dusky Sound—Wet Jacket Arm—Hector's theory of the
    formation of these fjords—Caswell Bay and its marble—
    Milford Sound: the Narrows, Mitre Peak, Bowen Falls—
    Ascent of Mitre Peak—Sutherland the explorer—Suther-
    land Falls, 1900 feet—Reischek and his wonderful dog—
    Return to the Bluff and Port Chalmers—Entertainments
    on board   97

                      CHAPTER VII.

           THE VOLCANIC ERUPTION OF MOUNT TARAWERA.

New Zealand a link in the chain of Pacific Ocean volcanoes—
    Principal volcanic eruptions from 1883 to 1886—Upheaval
    of North Island—Great fissure in the earth's crust, running
    south-west to north-east—Taupo volcanic zone: its craters
    and hot springs—The eruption of Mount Tarawera on
    June 10, 1886—Premonitory signs—Results of the erup-
    tion—Loss of life—Deaths of C. A. Haszard, E. A.
    Bainbridge, and Tuhoto—The Wonderland that remains
    —Waiotapu Valley—New Sinter Terraces forming—Pink
    Cauldron and Crow's Nest Geyser of Wairakei—Mount
    Horo-Horo—Lake Taupo—The new grand tour: Te
    Aroha, Rotorua, Ruapehu National Park, to the Upper
    Wanganui   120

                      CHAPTER VIII.

         SELF-GOVERNMENT, AND THE SETTLEMENT OF THE LAND.

History of the colony—Treaty of Waitangi, 1840—Several
    centres of colonization—Changes in the constitution—
    Responsible self-government granted in 1853—Governors
    of New Zealand from 1840 to 1889—Premiers from 1853
    to 1889—Premiers I have known—Beneficent legislation
    —How the Colonial Debt was incurred—Absolute solvency

of the colony—Laws regulating sale, lease, and transfer of Crown lands—Success of perpetual leasing, and of the village settlements—Some previous training necessary for success as a farmer 136

CHAPTER IX.

PUBLIC WORKS AND INSTITUTIONS.

Their growth—Nourished on loans—Reactions and commercial depression—Improving prospects and return of prosperity—Churches—Education: primary, secondary, and university—New Zealand University: its statutes, &c.—Auckland University College—Technical School—Otago Medical School—Lincoln School of Agriculture—The press of New Zealand—Hospitals and asylums—Police and prisons—Public works—Post-office and other Government departments—Telephones—Government insurance—Public trustee—Assignees in bankruptcy—Friendly and building societies—Sailors' Homes and Rests 150

CHAPTER X.

PRODUCTIONS AND INDUSTRIES.

Natural products evolve certain industries—The growth of fifty years—Exports now exceed imports in value—Statistics of the export of wool, meat (frozen and canned), skins and hides, dairy produce, wheat and cereals, timber, kauri gum, gold and silver, other metals, building stone, coal, native flax, fungus, tan bark, petroleum, train-oil—Minor industries—Reasons for the high tariff—Policy of bonuses for new cultures and industries—The workingman of New Zealand and the Chinese—W. N. Blair on labour and capital—Patent law—Inventiveness of New Zealanders—Humane legislation for women and children in factories 178

CHAPTER XI.

SOCIAL LIFE IN NEW ZEALAND.

Its heartiness and unconventionality—Tourist's mistakes and exaggerations—Ups and downs—Ruling forces in society—*Nouveaux riches*—The highest education and culture of

England appreciated by colonial parents—Neighbourly kindness—Fire !—Hospitality—Effects of flesh-eating on character—The " larrikin "—The cures for " larrikinism "—Recreation out of doors : cricket, football, tennis, cycling, volunteering—Indoor amusements: rinking, lectures, chess, Shakspeare and dramatic clubs—Music : concerts, amateur vocalists, professional teacher—A musical colony—Art, Artists, and Art Exhibitions — Literature — Amateur science—Happy and unhappy homes—Drinking customs—" Lambing down "—The slain by drink—New Zealand the country for a true home 197

CHAPTER XII.

PROFESSIONAL EXPERIENCES.

Openings for practice, and prospects of new comers—Age at which to emigrate—Outfit—Registration—Fees in New Zealand—Clubs—Working expenses of practice—Diseases prevalent among the Maoris—Native remedies—Singular mode of resuscitation—Letter from missionary on causes of decrease of natives—Diseases of the colonists—Typhoid fever : cause, prevention, and mortality—The Exanthemata—Diphtheria maligna cases—Poisoning from tinned meat and from Ptomaines—Phthisis pulmonalis—Cases arrested by New Zealand climate—Phthisis laryngea—Bronchitis and cynanche benefited by Auckland climate—Entozoa common—Caries of teeth—No Ague in New Zealand—Case of Katipo bite—Diseases arising from abuse of alcohol and tobacco — Lunacy in New Zealand —Vital statistics—Conclusion 219

LIST OF ILLUSTRATIONS.

Map of New Zealand . . . . *To face Title-page.*
View of Auckland Harbour and North Shore . . . . . . ,, *page* 24
Map of the Hot Lake District . . ,, ,, 97
Map of the West Coast Sounds . . ,, ,, 108
Map of the Taupo Volcanic Zone . . ,, ,, 120

NEW ZEALAND

FOR THE

EMIGRANT, INVALID, AND TOURIST.

CHAPTER I.

MIGRATION, EMIGRATION, AND IMMIGRATION.

The Anglo-Saxon race inclined to wander—The Colonies and the "globe-trotter"—Centrifugal and Centripetal laws of Emigration—Necessity of emigration for the British—Restrictions imposed by the United States give the colonies a chance—New Zealand the best field—Classes of immigrants *not* wanted out there—Who *are* wanted—Who are likely to succeed—Outfit—Various routes to New Zealand—Ordinary rates of wages—Cost of living.

THAT man is a migratory animal is evident from the history of the past, and the development of colonization in the present day. Of all races of mankind the Anglo-Saxon race has shown that a genuine love for home can co-exist with an ardent desire to explore new regions, to conquer the difficulties presented both by the barbarian inhabitant and by Nature, and even to make a new and a permanent settlement in lands far remote from his native soil.

Bound as this great race is, some day, to dominate the civilized world, it behoves the stay-at-home Briton, who, at his comfortable fireside, may read the news of the globe, to keep himself well informed of the characteristics, resources, and progress of that "Greater Britain" upon which the sun never sets.

This is essentially a travelling age; and the Englishman of wealth and culture, who formerly used to confine

B

his excursions to the continent of Europe, now takes bolder and longer flights. He crosses the "herring pond" to the United States and Canada; he rushes down to Cape Colony in eighteen days; in three weeks from leaving London he finds himself in India; and even the far-off Antipodes are becoming known to him. The term "globe-trotter" has been coined to suit him—the origin of this word I leave to Dr. Murray to find out—which admirably conveys the manner of the hasty tourist. Now that "Thomas Cook and Sons" have annexed New Zealand, no great social distinction will attach to the traveller who has "done" that country; but its beauties will become much more extensively known, and they are on such a scale that nothing can vulgarise them.

The "globe-trotter" is sometimes seized with a desire to leave his foggy Albion, and settle for the rest of his days in some balmy Eden of the Southern Pacific, or some Neapolitan-like city, such as Auckland, and when he carries out this idea he seldom regrets his choice.

Feeling grateful to New Zealand for the renovation of my health, which was much broken down in 1879, and having made many careful observations of the meteorology, mineral springs, and various Zones of Climate of that country, I have incorporated these and other results of nine years' experience in this little Handbook for the Emigrant, Tourist, and Invalid. In a work of this scope it is not desirable to enter at length into the native question, colonial history, colonial politics, or debatable problems of political economy. I have only introduced such matters to such an amount as would make the book complete. Such features of social life as are discussed in these pages are treated candidly and impartially, with a sincere desire to

> "Naught extenuate
> Nor aught set down in malice."

It is my conviction, based upon a happy experience, that derives some value from my having resided in the course of my life in three quarters of the world, that there is no country over which our grand old flag waves, where a Briton can make as comfortable a home as he can in New Zealand. If an invalid, he must make a careful selection of the locality; and this work will supply the information needed.

But let us turn to the question of emigration, and the need for it.

In the present day we may clearly distinguish two general laws regulating emigration and immigration—a centrifugal law and a centripetal law. By the force of the former law, the Englishman, a citizen of the greatest maritime empire of all time, is impelled to explore unknown seas and lands, to colonize and to trade in all parts of the world. Geography being now taught in schools more intelligently than of yore, and books of thrilling adventure firing the imagination of youth, boys and girls become familiar with the description of foreign countries, and long to visit them. A love for travel is characteristic of the two great branches of the Anglo-Saxon race; but the Englishman will colonize, while the American merely stays for a time. Germany is now waking up to her need of colonies, incited doubtless by the irresistible power of this Centrifugal Law, which has gained for little England her glorious colonial empire.

On the other hand there is a Centripetal Law, which counterbalances, but only to a slight extent, the Centrifugal Law. When the Briton has prospered in the Colonies, in the United States, or in foreign countries, he often retires to London or to some part of his native country to end his days. Or, not being able to leave the land of his adoption, he sends his sons and daughters "Home" to be educated. Every year a larger number of highly cultured Americans adopt England as their home. The marriage of American ladies with the nobility of England exhibits this centripetal tendency. And it is more and more becoming the fashion for the wealthy Australian to settle in England, become a member of a leading London club, and enter Parliament. Let me here observe that the affectionate and becoming expression "Home" is applied to Great Britain throughout the Australasian colonies. The highest standard of every department of knowledge is supposed to exist at "Home," and I am quite convinced that the colonies are both loyal to the Crown and eager to form their centres of culture upon British models.

Seeing that the area of Great Britain, as it is now parcelled out, is insufficient to support our population, increasing as it does by more than 300,000 persons annually, after allowing for loss by death and by emigration, we must all feel glad that now we recognize emigration to be a *positive necessity* to avert a socialistic revolution, we have a "Greater Britain" beyond the seas, where

> "A man is a man if he is willing to toil,
> And the humblest may gather the fruits of the soil."

It is calculated by A. McDougal of Manchester that at least five and a half millions of our fellow countrymen, above the grade of paupers, live in miserable poverty, huddled together in stifling courts and alleys, living from hand to mouth, and never *sure* of three days' *consecutive* employment. Another alarming but true statement is made by an unexceptionable authority on statistics, viz., that during the last quarter of a century the foreign population of England has increased by 135 per cent. England is now almost the only civilized country that admits all nationalities, whether paupers or not, to settle within her territory, without any restriction whatever. This very large immigration of foreigners has not only lowered the wages (as in the east end of London) of English handicraftsmen to starvation point, but has left and is leaving a large *residuum* of helpless foreign-born paupers to be supported by the poor rates in London, and in the large provincial towns. In some lines of industry, I am informed that the Germans are actually crowding out our own working-men.

The time is come when statesmen and philanthropists

should use all their energies to grapple with these sad facts, and should regard as a means of relief the vast field presented for immigration by our colonies. State-assisted or State-regulated emigration should be considered as already a " burning question." Meantime the Self-help Emigration Societies of London, Liverpool, Manchester, and other cities, are doing a good work, though on a small scale, in the right direction.

I feel strongly that now that the United States is adopting measures restrictive of immigration, which bear more hardly on our own population than on that of other European countries, the time for our colonists to show a generous spirit, and for the imperial Government to reciprocate it, has arrived.

Nothing can strengthen the bonds of love between the mother country and her children more than the settlement in the colonies of steady industrious men and women, who will remain under the same sovereign and the same old flag, and who can never forget that both they and we are of one blood, one language, and, in a broad sense, of one religion. It is in the hope of placing the advantages offered by the picturesque, fertile, and healthy colony of New Zealand before the British public, and of dispelling some erroneous impressions conveyed by mere passing travellers—most of whom commit their crude experiences to print on their return —that I have ventured this little barque upon the ocean of literature.

Apart from a roving spirit and love of adventure, men leave the old country of their own free will only for one cause—"*to better themselves,*" in pocket, health, social or political position, or to work out a new line for themselves in life which they have not attempted before. To a Briton who wishes to remain under his native standard, the Australasian colonies offer a healthier climate than that of India or of the West Indies. New Zealand, moreover, presents a magnificent *choice of climates*—as I shall demonstrate in chapter ii.— in none of which exists either the arctic cold of Canada, or the broiling intense solar heat of the Cape or of

Australia. Statistics show that the land there is the most productive, when tilled, of all the agricultural colonies; and that, while no spot in the whole of the three islands is more than seventy-five miles from the sea, none is more than ten miles from a lake, stream, or river of drinkable water. The emigrant need have no fear of native, coolie, or Chinese cheap labour in New Zealand. The influx of the yellow man has been checked by an impost of £10 per head per annum. The Maoris work for themselves, but seldom for others, and are not fond of manual labour as yet.

On landing in a New Zealand port, the new arrival will scarcely notice anything foreign or 'un-English' around him, except, indeed, the absence of seedy and ragged boys and girls, and out-at-elbows idlers, who in the old country beset the traveller to get money from him by begging or by trivial and unasked attentions. The cheerful, well-fed, well-clothed appearance of working men, women and children is also 'un-English.'

It is well to point out, now that we have arrived at the stage of the desirability of New Zealand for the emigrant, that by the latest private and official sources of information, the only classes of immigrants required in the colony are:—(1) female domestic servants; (2) farmers with capital; (3) agricultural labourers; (4) shepherds and herdmen. No assistance in paying any part of the passage-money is now given by the Government, which is carefully retrenching its expenses. All other trades, occupations, and professions are now so full in the colony that it is difficult for a new arrival to find work.

Certain facts are forgotten sometimes by too eloquent emigration agents; for instance, (1) that the birth-rate in New Zealand is very high, amounting in some years to 38·5 per cent., and that the colony will complete its first half-century in 1890. It follows, as a consequence, that there are hundreds of New Zealand boys and girls, all of very fair education, ready and eager to fill situations, to enter offices, learn trades, and to get into the large Civil Service of the Government, which also practically includes the great Education Department. Lawyers, teachers, clerks, governesses, lady helps, clergymen, artists, and even musicians are not well advised to go out just now to settle in New Zealand. I say "*even* musicians," because all the cities and towns of the colony *are* musical. Clergymen with high testimonials from home can sometimes obtain an appointment, generally of smaller value than that they left in England. Barristers, solicitors, and attorneys are qualified by study and examination within the colony. There is also a theological training college, providing clergymen for the Maoris and the country districts of New Zealand.

No complete medical education has as yet been given in the colony, though the University of New Zealand has the power to confer the degrees of M.B. and M.D., after a course of study and several examinations, equal to those of Edinburgh University. It is said that in four or five years the first undergraduate will be duly qualified for his degree. There are now (1889) 495 medical practitioners on the colonial register, and 107 dentists, the white population being estimated at 610,000. Openings do occur here and there for doctors, and sometimes with a minimum income guaranteed, but they are quickly snapped up. In the Church and in Medicine the colonists prefer men fresh from home; but in other lines the "new chum" has to yield to the man who has had already some colonial experience.

Nor do colonists want any men who have been failures in the old country. They are good-hearted enough to give such a man "another chance," but woe to him if he neglects or misuses it or fails at it altogether! They are sharp and shrewd in judging character, and he does not get another such opening. Smartness and common sense are essential to success in New Zealand. Even an honest and faithful *employé*, if dull and slow, may have to give place to a "smarter" man. But the bright and bracing climate stimulates the faculties of the whole nature of the immigrant, so that he who has been slow, unintelligent, and depressed in England, becomes quick, lively, hopeful, and energetic in the "Britain of the South."

Having seen several disastrous wrecks of men and women shunted, as it were, from England on to this colony, I do not blame New Zealanders for indignantly protesting against the practice that has grown up at home of exiling the family scapegrace or ne'er-do-weel to their country, simply because it is geographically the most distant point he can reach. The colony is not a safe reformatory for the habitual drunkard, gambler, or profligate. Such a man will find boon companions to share his vices so long as he has a shilling to spend. The end is the hospital, the refuge, the asylum, the prison, or the suicide's grave. It is not fair to the honest and hard-working citizens to send among them men who spread a blight around them wherever they wander. The hopefullest of mothers of these prodigal sons should remember that truest of Horatian maxims—

"Cœlum, non animum mutant, qui trans mare currunt."

A young, healthy, single man, of good morals and principles, energetic and ready to "rough it," with a handicraft of some kind at which he is expert, is the type of emigrant that will succeed in New Zealand. If he leaves old England with hope in his bosom, faith in his heart, and love to his fellow-man beaming from his eyes, always ready to do a good turn, handy and hard-working, and skilled in his own particular trade, he will not fail of getting remunerative employment. With a very small capital he can buy land on one of the easy systems described in chapter vii.; he will marry a practical, sensible colonial girl (splendid housewives they make!) and having given his children a free education better than he ever had, will place them out in life much earlier than he could have done in England. The sons that take to farming will have the advantage of knowing how to farm in New Zealand—not by any means the same thing as English farming; and thus a second generation will grow up, industrious, prosperous, and contented.

The poet Campbell had the right idea of this type of emigrant.

> "The pride to rear an independent shed,
> And give the lips we love unborrowed bread;
> To see a world from shadowy forest won,
> In youthful beauty wedded to the sun.
> To skirt our home with harvests widely sown,
> And call the blooming landscape all our own;
> Our children's heritage, in prospect long;
> These are the hopes—high-minded hopes and strong—
> That beckon England's wanderers o'er the brine,
> To realms where foreign constellations shine."

If a man desirous of farming land arrives in the colony with capital, let him put his money into the Government Savings Bank, where it will earn four per cent., and travel up the country, getting employment wherever he can for a few months, until he has gained the necessary experience. Just now numerous "bargains" in the shape of well-improved farms are to be picked up, but as the colony gradually rights itself after the late depression these will be absorbed. The new-comer must be careful not to pay too high a price for an improved farm. The small capitalist, equally with the man who has only a few pounds, will have to work hard upon his land and await results. Crown land for sale is generally remote from towns, and requires clearing, fencing, "burning off," sowing, &c., before any living can be made out of it. The cry of the New Zealand farmer now is, "Oh, that we had cheap labour!" And the agricultural labourers that may go out there should take this hint, so that no Oriental race may gradually creep in; for New Zealand should be kept for the European races to people and possess.

The best time of year for the intending settler to arrive in New Zealand is during the months of September, October, and November for the North Island, and at any time during the summer (November to March) for the Middle (usually but erroneously termed the "South") Island.

His outfit should include a large stock of clothes, his

books, tools, and any labour-saving machines he may have, for there is a high protective tariff in New Zealand. If he contemplates making his abode in Auckland, Napier, or New Plymouth, he should bring lighter clothes, both outer and inner garments, than he would wear in England. For other parts the ordinary English clothes will suffice. For the long summer the helmet is inevitable. Umbrellas and waterproofs should not be forgotten, because of the high price of these articles in the colony. Really good (not half-worn) furniture should also be taken or sent by ship to New Zealand if economy is an object.

We now come to the choice of routes for New Zealand. The old days of a three to six months' sea voyage by sailing ship are drawing to a close, for the two companies who are running large steamers, carrying mails, direct to the colony, carry steerage passengers for the very moderate rate of £16 to £21, giving three liberal meals *per diem*, plenty of cabin space, and landing them in from thirty-seven to forty-four days from port to port. I can bear witness from personal knowledge, having returned to England on the *Tainui*, that the Shaw, Savill, and Albion Company treat this and the other two classes of passengers most generously as to food and accommodation.

1. This company start their steamers, the *Arawa*, *Tainui*, *Ionic*, and *Coptic*, each from 4400 to 5000 tons, on alternate fortnights with those of the New Zealand Shipping Company, the *Aorangi*, *Ruapehu*, *Tongariro*, and *Rimutaka*, all magnificent and fast vessels of 4170 tons. The steamers leave the West India Docks on Thursday and call at Plymouth on the Saturday for mails and passengers. Going out, they all call at Teneriffe (Santa Cruz), Cape Town, and Hobart (Tasmania). On the homeward voyage they visit Rio de Janeiro and Teneriffe. The first-class fare is £63, return £105 and £115, the second-class £40, return £60.

2. Another route is *viâ* the Mediterranean, Suez Canal, Red Sea, and Indian Ocean, by the magnificent steamers of the Orient and the Peninsular and Oriental

companies; the average length of the outward voyage being forty days to Sydney, thence by Union Company of New Zealand steamer, or by the San Francisco mail steamer, four and a half to five days to Auckland. Fares, first-class £63 and £70, second-class £42, steerage seventeen guineas to £22. Travellers who can choose the best season for passing through the Red Sea, say, January and February, and who can take plenty of time, may enjoy this route by stopping at Naples to see Pompeii, &c., or at Port Said to see Alexandria, Cairo, and the Pyramids, and proceeding by the next following steamer (fortnightly) of the line they have selected. There are fewer long stretches of ocean upon this route than on the first one described.

3. Lastly, we have the fast mail route *viâ* New York across the United States by the Union and Central Pacific railroads to San Francisco, thence by American built steamers to Honolulu, Tutuila (Samoa), and Auckland. By this mail I have often received letters on the thirty-fourth day after their despatch from Liverpool. But no one would for choice travel across at this speed. To those tourists who do not regard expense much, who dread sea-sickness, can sleep on the railroad journey, or have friends in the United States, this is the best route. The through fare, first-class, from London or Liverpool to Auckland, Wellington, Dunedin, or Christchurch is £66 to £72, but to this must be added cost of sleeping-car, drawing-room car, and meals on the train, and hotel and carriage expenses. Probably £110 would cover the whole trip. The most agreeable season of the year for this route is, going west, to start in July, August, or September, and, going homewards, to start in March, April, or May.

It is interesting to see that Jules Verne's romance is now a realizable fact, for a traveller can go round the world in eighty days.

As Messrs. Thomas Cook and Sons have now included New Zealand in their excursion scheme, travel to the colony and through it will be simplified and cheapened.

A round-the-world ticket, to go by one route and return by another, can be purchased for £140.

To the visitor I would say further, " obtain and use any good letters of introduction to New Zealand residents that you can get." To the emigrant and intending settler I would say the same, but add, " do not base any hopes of immediate employment upon them."

The following definite official information respecting the wages now prevailing in the colony, the cost of the necessaries of life, of clothing, house-rent, &c., will be found useful by the emigrant.

Wages by the Week, with Board.

	Auckland.	Wellington.	Canterbury.	Otago.
Farm and station hands	12s. to 20s.	15s. to 20s.	12s. to 20s.	15s. to 20s.
Domestic servants	8s. ,, 10s.	8s. ,, 12s.	10s. ,, 15s.	10s. ,, 16s.
Laundresses	12s. ,, 15s.	12s. ,, 14s.	10s. ,, 15s.	10s. ,, 15s.

Wages per Week throughout the Colony, without Board.

Bakers	20s. to 45s.
Butchers	25s. ,, 50s.
Shoemakers	30s. ,, 50s.
Tailors	30s. ,, 40s.

Wages per Day throughout the Colony, without Board.

Blacksmiths	7s. to 12s.
Bricklayers	7s. ,, 12s.
Brickmakers	6s. ,, 8s.
Carpenters	6s. ,, 10s.
Painters	6s. ,, 9s.
Masons	6s. to 10s.
Shipwrights	8s. ,, 12s.
Miners	6s. ,, 12s.
General labourers	5s. ,, 7s.

Cost of Living in New Zealand.

1. House-rent is perhaps the heaviest item in the expenditure of the working man. The rent of a three-roomed cottage (of wood) is about 6s.; of larger houses,

suitable for workmen, from 8s. to 14s. per week in towns; in the country, 4s. to 10s. per week. Furnishing is from seventy-five to 100 per cent. more expensive than at home.

2. Board and lodging may be had in any of the towns for a single adult for 15s., 17s. 6d., or £1 per week.

3. Clothing of the cheaper qualities, most worn by the working classes, is from fifteen to twenty-five per cent. dearer than at home. But the more expensive materials, broadcloth, silk, flannel, &c., are fully thirty to fifty per cent. higher.

4. There are numerous benefit societies, the rules of which provide medical attendance and medicine in sickness free to members. Medical fees and the price of drugs are higher than in England.

5. By means of the building societies a frugal and constantly employed workman or tradesman can, on easy terms, become possessor of a freehold house and allotment in three to seven years.

COST OF PROVISIONS, RETAIL, IN NEW ZEALAND.
(Liable to fluctuations.)

	Auckland.	Wellington.	Christchurch.	Dunedin.
Beef, per lb.	2d. to 6d.	2d. to 6d.	3d. to 6d.	4d. to 6d.
Mutton ,,	1½d. ,, 4d.	1½d. ,, 4d.	1½d. ,, 4d.	2½d. ,, 3½d.
Butter ,,	1/ ,, 1/3	6d. ,, 1/	8d. ,, 10d.	10d. ,, 1/
Cheese ,,	5d. ,, 7d.	4d. ,, 9d.	3d. ,, 6d.	6d. ,, 7d.
Tea ,,	1/10 ,, 2/10	1/6 ,, 3/	1/8 ,, 3/	2/ ,, 3/
Coffee ,,	1/1 ,, 1/10	1/3 ,, 1/8	1/10 ,, 2/	1/8 ,, 1/10
Sugar ,,	3d. ,, 4d.	2d. ,, 4d.	2½d. ,, 4d.	3½d. ,, 4½d.
Bread, per 4-lb. loaf	3½d. ,, 6d.	4½d. ,, 7d.	4d. ,, 5d.	6d.
Milk, per quart	3½d.	4d.	5d.	5d.
Potatoes, per cwt.	4/ ,, 5/	3/ ,, 5/	3/ ,, 5/	5d.
Coal, per ton	25/ ,, 50/	30/ ,, 50/	32/ ,, 42/	30/ to 55/

Firewood varies, according to season of the year, and proximity to forests, from 10s. to £2 per ton.

CHAPTER II.

THE CLIMATES OF NEW ZEALAND: GENERAL AND LOCAL.

Differences of Australian and New Zealand climate not sufficiently recognized by consulting physicians—Advantages of the colonies for the British invalid—General climate of New Zealand—Topography—Meteorology—Effects of mountain ranges and forests—Muggy weather and its antidote—Four subordinate zones of climate: 1. North Cape to Napier; 2. Napier to Hurunui; 3. Hurunui to South Island; 4. Alpine Plateau of North Island—Particular features and suitability to various pulmonary diseases—Auckland, Whangarei, Napier, Palmerston, Nelson, Picton, Christchurch, Dunedin, Invercargill—Cautions to invalids—General summary.

THE previous chapter having been chiefly devoted to the emigrant, we now turn to the interests of the health-seekers, of whom hundreds are now familiarized more or less by personal experience with the bright skies and perpetual sunshine of the Australasian colonies. Travel by the routes we have described being now made both moderate in cost and luxurious in every detail; the horrid *mal-de-mer* having been reduced to its *minimum* by the shortened passage between the ports of call; and hotel accommodation, railway, steamer, and coach facilities having permeated even the wildest parts of such recent acquisitions as New Zealand and Tasmania, the invalid may now regard the former colony as an easily accessible health resort.

Fashionable consultants in my own profession have been in the habit hitherto of sending their consumptive or nerve-exhausted patients to New Zealand or Australia, chiefly for the sake of the voyage. But they have not given sufficient attention to the differences of climate between (1) Australia, Tasmania, and New

Zealand, and (2) between the different districts of the last-mentioned colony. While Australia, as a whole, is a much drier country than New Zealand, less stormy, and therefore more suitable for some forms of consumption, experience shows that it is so violent and sudden a contrast to the English climate as to make the transition injurious to many consumptive and debilitated invalids. The experience during the first few days after landing of a hot wind in Sydney or in Adelaide, or of a "southerly burster" in Melbourne, makes a sick man regret the termination of his ocean voyage. But on the inland mountain plateaux, such as the Darling Downs of Queensland, health is often restored, even in a pronounced case of the second stage of consumption, and life in that dry bracing air, though under a hot sun, becomes enjoyable. It is my duty to lay before my readers, both lay and medical, the observations and conclusions derived from nine years' sojourn as to the Four General Climatic Zones into which New Zealand may be divided for the purposes of the valetudinarian and his advisers.

The British who travel for health become in time tired of foreign countries, and look round the world for a region where pure and bracing or mild air, interesting natives, beautiful scenery, good water for drinking, mineral baths, their accustomed food, convenient excursions, and pleasant society may be enjoyed among people of their own language. All these advantages, together with an unsurpassed climate, are to be found in New Zealand. When tired of the "mistral" or "bise," of the noise and dust of the Riviera, of the demoralizing gaming-tables, and of the parasites who hang on to the visitors at all foreign resorts, the invalid of the future will fly on the wings of steam to the realm of the Southern Cross, and

"By the long wash of Australasian seas,"

will find in New Zealand, at Auckland, the Bay of Islands, Napier, Rotorua, or Nelson, a new world of calm delight, in a balmy yet invigorating atmosphere.

The General Climate of New Zealand.

The three islands forming, with three groups of islets (Auckland Islands, Chatham Islands, Kermadee Islands), the colony of New Zealand extend from north to south through 13° of S. Lat., and from east to west through nearly 13° of E. Long. The colony possesses a coast-line of over 3000 miles, and mountain chains run through all the three islands, North, Middle, and South or Stewart's Island. In the North Island the chief mountains are in the centre and near the east coast; in the Middle Island they are near the west coast; so that the plains of the North and of the Middle Islands are on opposite sides. On glancing at the map, the reader will notice the singular resemblance in figure of the whole colony to Italy reversed, and amputated, as it were, from the continent of Europe. The promontories of Gargano and of Ancona in the older country seem whimsically reproduced in those of Akaroa and of Port Chalmers in the new. The active volcano Vesuvius has its counterpart in Mount Tongariro, and the more recent volcano, Mount Tarawera. The climate of the Auckland provincial district is not unlike that of South Italy and of Sicily. I need not enlarge on other correspondences. The area of the whole colony is 104,000 square miles, about one-sixth less than the entire area of Great Britain and Ireland. As no point in the colony is more than 75 miles from the coast, and as two straits—Cook's Strait, thirteen miles across, and Foveaux Straits, fifteen miles wide, separate the three islands, the climate of the colony, as a whole, is insular, and tolerably equable. It is certainly warmer than that of Great Britain, for it lies within the southern temperate zone. The average temperature for the whole year is, in the North Island, 57°, in the Middle Island, 52°. For the whole colony the mean temperature for the summer is 63°, for the winter 48°, for the spring 55°, and for the autumn 57°. In the northern part of the North Island there is no true spring nor autumn, but only a hot season November to April, inclusive; and a cold and wet season, May to October, inclusive. During three-quarters of the year a healthy man may sleep out of doors with impunity to health, if furnished with simply a blanket and a mackintosh, anywhere in the North Island.

The most important fact for invalids is the smallness of the mean daily range of temperature, which is from 15° to 20° only, showing great equability of climate. Next to this, the average annual rainfall must be studied, for it varies much in different districts, as the following table will show:—

MEAN ANNUAL RAINFALL, FOR EIGHTEEN YEARS, ENDING 1884.
(In inches, omitting decimals.)

North Island.		South Island.	
Auckland	45	Christchurch	25
Taranaki	58	Dunedin	32
Napier	37	Southland	43
Wellington	50	Hokitika	112

The principal towns of New Zealand are all abundantly supplied with good drinking water, whereas the Australian capitals, lying along the edge of a sun-baked continent, often suffer from drought, and have to obtain their potable water from a distance at a large expense. The New Zealand Government has an efficient Meteorological Department, the weather reports being telegraphed every morning at nine o'clock to the chief at Wellington from twenty-five stations at various elevations, and then posted up at all the principal ports and inland towns, together with Captain Edwin's forecasts of the weather, about two-thirds of which have been verified in Auckland, during the time I resided there.

Periods of lasting drought in New Zealand are unknown. Only in two instances during the last twenty years do the meteorological records at any one station show that a whole month passed without rain—a fact very encouraging to the farmer—who is thus assured of water for his crops. The region north of Auckland comes within the limits of the winter sub-tropical rainfall, but in the Middle and South Islands the rain is distributed more equally over all the months of the year. On the west coast rain is more prevalent in spring and on the east coast in summer. The table on p. 17 shows remarkable differences between the rainfalls at different places on or about the same parallel of latitude; for instance, Napier on the east has only half the rain of New Plymouth (Taranaki) on the west, while Hokitika on the west of the Middle Island has four and a half times the amount that falls at Christchurch on the east.

The proximity of Mount Egmont (8260 feet) to New Plymouth, and of the Southern Alps to Hokitika account for this fact, and so, in like manner, for other examples. It should be noted that the mountains of the North Island are still mostly covered with forest—"bush" it is called by colonists—but those of the Middle Island are open, well grassed with "tussock," and can be used for pasture. But so quickly are the forests of the Auckland district being cut down for the valuable Kauri pine (*Dammara Australis*) that a distinct decrease in the average annual rainfall there has been noticed already, and is still going on. As a slight means of comparison as to rainfall, I may mention that during 1882 rain fell on 191 days in Auckland, on 166 in Wellington, and on 187 in Dunedin.

The winds most prevalent round the coasts of the colony are from the west, south-west, and south. When a storm centre passes to the south of New Zealand, westerly winds prevail, and they are always cold. But when the centre of barometric depression goes round the North Cape (see map No. 1) the result is that north-east winds strike the east coast, bringing with them clouds, rain, and warm mist. This forms the weather called "muggy" by the Aucklanders and others, which is disagreeably enervating as long as it lasts. After three or four days it is followed by its exact opposite, a cold bracing south-west wind with dry weather and a clear blue sky. In winter this south-west wind in the Middle and South Islands is accompanied with heavy storms of rain and snow.

It is really astonishing how cheerfully one fresh from the gloom of wet days in London, Liverpool, Manchester, Glasgow, or other huge smoky cities, can wait indoors in New Zealand for the cessation of a rain-storm. There is almost always a glimpse of blue sky somewhere—and what a blue! Read Froude's eloquent description in "Oceana." And there is an exhilaration in the air, only temporarily veiled by the transient "muggy" weather.

As most health-seekers leave England for the prevention, alleviation, or cure of some pulmonary disease, my classification of the various belts of climate in this colony—now for the first time attempted—is based upon their adaptiveness, suitability, or unsuitability for invalids coming under this head, as well as for those whose nerve-centres require a change of climate and scenery.

The foregoing facts concerning the general climate of New Zealand will already afford some useful hints to the reader as to choice of *locale*.

While it would not be quite accurate to establish isothermal lines dividing these four Zones of Climate, yet the fact is that a similar average temperature during any particular month of the year is found to exist at any part of the zone, except indeed when a cold breeze or rain is lowering the heat of the air in summer at one spot and not at another. "Windy Wellington," for example, is a nick-name familiar to all New Zealanders, based on its meteorology, and therefore that city feels heat less than Wanganui, Woodville, or Napier in summer.

These divisions of climate are as follows:—

1st. A zone of latitude extending from the North Cape, S. lat. 34° 20′, southwards to Napier, and across the North Island to Hawera, S. lat. 39° 30′—Zone No. 1.

2nd. A zone stretching from this line southwards to the Hurunui River and Hokitika, both in the Middle Island—Zone No. 2.

3rd. A zone reaching from the Hurunui River to the southern coast line of the Middle Island, and including the South or Stewart's Island—Zone No. 3.

4th. An Alpine plateau, comprising a large portion of the middle of the North Island, extending upwards from an elevation of 1000 feet above sea level—this we may designate Zone No. 4. This zone is cut out of No. 1, being a distinctly different climate as regards its effects upon visitors, and must be regarded as an atmospheric rather than a terrestrial zone, a highland zone as compared with the lowlands. This zone includes the whole "Taupo Volcanic Zone" of map No. 3.

Zone I.

This climate is the warmest and mildest in the whole colony. The North Cape being nearly on the same parallel of south latitude as Sydney, Adelaide, Cape Town, and Buenos Ayres, we should expect this extreme north district to be very warm. And it is found by experiment that bananas, guavas, oranges, lemons, citrons, and other tropical and sub-tropical fruits can be grown there. But the constant sea breezes and saline moisture arising from the narrowness of the "toes of the boot" (see map No. 1), as we may call the north end of the North Island, and from the numerous estuaries running up far into the land, together with the exhalations from the forests which clothe most of the hills and valleys, all these features soften the dryness of the heated atmosphere, and produce, without malaria (such as exists in Florida and Jamaica), a wholesome warm climate, equable in its range of temperature, where men can work hard at manual labour all summer without a siesta at mid-day. By common consent this climate is considered the most delicious in New Zealand.

The mean average of the yearly temperature is 59° in the shade for the northern part of the zone. At Mongonui (S. lat. 35° 1′), the northernmost meteorological station in New Zealand, the *maximum* shade temperature in summer was 89°, and the *minimum* in winter 31°, for a period of ten years; while the mean summer temperature was only 66°·56, showing how much the solar rays were tempered by the proximity of the sea.

Fertile valleys, rich in virgin soil, intersect the country from N.E. to S.W., and N. to S., where fruits of every kind, both sub-tropical and those of cold climates, tobacco, sorghum, sugar-beet, coffee, tea, and the white mulberry (for the silk-culture) may be profitably cultivated. The average rainfall over the district extending from the North Cape, Cape Reinga (the Maori *Hades*), and Cape Maria van Diemen to Whangarei on the east coast and Port Albert on the west, is 51·7 inches, of which the greater part falls during the months of May, June, July, August, and September. There is no frost in winter near the coast, and but slight and transient phases of it in valleys shaded from both sun and sea breeze in the interior. The bold and picturesque volcanic scenery of the harbours of Whangaroa and Parua Bay; the cascades that are found in the valleys; the wild ferns, many of them esteemed as rare by European connoisseurs, and all of them wonderfully well grown; and the luxuriance of all vegetation, make this part of Zone I. most attractive to the visitor. Near Whangarei, 75 miles north of Auckland by sea, where the alluvial drift rests upon limestone rock, there are both extensive orangeries, citron, lime, and lemon groves, and the most prolific vineries in New Zealand. The "dessert grapes" usually carry off the prizes at the Auckland annual show. The worthy station-master here (Mr. Dobie) has cultivated oranges for fifteen years past so successfully that no visitor passes through without a sight of them, and his success has stimulated others to start the same culture elsewhere.

Mr. Geo. E. Alderton, in his useful treatise "Orange Culture in New Zealand," has shown that North Auckland has several places where the soil, with proper culture, the climate, and the rainfall are excellently adapted for raising this fruit to a profit. At an outlay of £750, in three years, 1000 orange trees planted on ten acres of suitable land will from the fourth year realise a profit, and by the end of the sixth year not only repay the £750, but leave a large balance for the proprietor.

The School of Forestry and Experimental Fruit-growing Farm, established by the Government, is situated near this pleasant and healthful town. For the visitor there are lovely walks, drives, and excursions to the falls, to the limestone caves of Waipu and of Whangarei, and to the mineral springs of Kamo. In winter Whangarei is a safer place for consumptives than even Auckland, because of its sheltered position, and of its limestone subsoil. The chalybeate spring at Kamo, seven miles by rail from Whangarei, is a valuable tonic. Though not far from the sea, this town has some of the advantages of an inland place. For instance, I have known asthmatic invalids who could spend the winter in Whangarei in comfort, while they suffered in Auckland.

There is less chance of contracting rheumatism in this district—the same may be said of Napier also—than in other towns near the sea in this Zone.

Throughout the whole area of this Zone, the climate is beneficial to cases of scrofula, of strumous glands, of enlarged joints and rickety bones in children, and of skin diseases of a strumous origin. The abundance and excellent quality of both meat, milk, butter, and eggs, vastly improve the pale unhealthy children born and reared in the large cities of England, where they can neither have this nourishing diet, nor breathe the pure oxygen of the New Zealand air.

The tourist of botanical tastes may be interested to learn that the *flora* of the Auckland provincial district comprises 675 species of flowering plants, and 123 of ferns and fern allies, including nearly every native plant, shrub, or tree of known economic value. The very valuable Kauri pine (*Dammara Australis*, Coniferæ) grows nowhere out of this district. The naturalist will find great interest in searching for the native birds and insects, yearly becoming scarcer, because driven out before the more vigorous or rapacious *fauna* of Europe. The Little Barrier island, N.E. of the Kawau, lying off the coast near Rodney Point, is one of the few remaining haunts of the rarer *avifauna* of New Zealand. The sportsman can enjoy shooting pheasants, wild duck, and partridges, or the tui, korimako, kaka, kakapo, and a variety of small birds of the parrot tribe, which relieve the silence of the dense woods. Taking the whole colony, there is no country in the world more rich in ferns than New Zealand, and none as wealthy in native woods, which take a fine polish for ornamental purposes. The kiwi, a wingless bird the size of a Cochin-China hen, is found in this district, the small representative of the extinct Moa (*Dinornis elephantipes*), a gigantic ostrich-like bird, whose bones are still found in caves and drift in this province, but rarely, owing to the careful searching of scientists during the last twenty years. It was *from one imperfect bone* of this bird that Professor Owen made his famous prognostication of the form, description, and habits of the Dinornis, which was so exactly verified.

Local Climate of Auckland.

While the general features of the climate of the city of Auckland and its suburbs correspond with those of the northern zone above described, there are some local peculiarities which must now be pointed out. In chapter iv. the situation of the city upon clay hills and scoriæ slopes is portrayed in detail. The clay subsoil retains the moisture when the ground does not slope sharply, so that some inhabitants contract rheumatism, bronchitis, or sore throats, and towards the end of the summer typhoid fever. Ill-health arising from this cause is soon removed by sending the family to reside on the slopes of Mount Eden, Mount Hobson, Mount Albert, or Mount Victoria on the Devonport side (see illustration, frontispiece). To live, however, on the slopes facing the north-east, close to the cemetery of Devonport, is unhealthy, though it would be safe to say, speaking in general terms, that despite a rather limited water supply Devonport offers a healthier site for a residence all the year round than Auckland city. The winter in the city of Auckland is extremely mild. A few miles out in the country there may be four to five degrees of frost, but none whatever in the city limits. The constant humidity tempers the heat of summer delightfully, but has an enervating effect upon highly nervous persons, who feel a restlessness possessing them. The peculiar "muggy weather" coming from the north-east, generally with warm showers of steamy rain, causes in such temperaments an irritability, combined with languor and debility, which is easier imagined than described. Fortunately this phase of weather is not of long duration (p. 18). This is about the only drawback to the climate of the city.

To lounge on an elegant and spacious verandah on a holiday afternoon, and gaze upon an Italian bit of scenery with a silent Vesuvius in the background; to listen to the familiar song of the skylark, the twitter of the swallow, the chirp of the sparrow, the humming of the bee, while at your feet in the garden bloom roses, heliotropes, fuchsias, geraniums, bougainvilleas, and countless other flowers—this is enjoyment! And these charms exist within the limits of the city.

The summer temperature ranges from 66° to 90°. But 80° is considered "very warm." In January, 1886, we had exceptionally hot weather, the thermometer in shade registering $72\frac{1}{2}°$ as the lowest, and 80° as the highest temperature. But, with properly ventilated head-covering, and avoidance of needless exposure to the sun, no inconvenience need be suffered. Labourers here seem to work as hard as in England and sunstroke is very rare. Insomnia is experienced by some in Auckland during the summer, and for such, sleeping a few nights out in some country place, such as Waikomiti, Henderson, or Bombay, is the only cure. While there are

VIEW OF AUCKLAND HARBOUR AND NORTH SHORE.

1. Mt. Eden.
2. North Head.
3. Mt. Victoria.
4. Devonport.
5. Government House.
6. Supreme Court.
7. Mechanics' Bay.
8. Parnell.
9. Waiheke Island.
10. Albert Park.

many spots near Auckland suited for a country hotel and sanatorium, no one has been found bold enough as yet to speculate in the matter. Howick offers an excellent situation for such a building, combining both country and marine views, a drying soil, and accessibility by road or water.

While Auckland is a very appropriate place for invalids suffering from bronchitis of a recurrent nature, and from throat diseases, it is a singular fact that tenor and soprano voices soon lose their pitch and intonation if much used. Bass and alto voices stand very well. For genuine tubercular phthisis Auckland is seldom suitable, yet I know at least three definite cases of apparent "cure" by the change from England. In chapter xii. I shall further describe these cases. In each the real improvement had begun *at sea*, and the patients had carefully timed their voyage as to arrive in Auckland during the southern hemisphere's *summer*. A consumptive invalid should arrive *not earlier* in the year than October 15th or 20th, *nor later* in the year than March 31st. Some doubtful cases of pneumonic phthisis I have seen cured entirely. The invalid may reckon upon obtaining in Auckland and its suburbs any quality of accommodation he may choose to have; an abundance of good food, facilities for riding, driving, &c.; and plenty of kindly friends, who will do as much as they can for his comfort. There are a large number and variety of good boarding-houses in Auckland.

Climate of Taranaki.

New Plymouth, 135 miles south of Onehunga, the port on the Manukau Harbour by which Auckland controls the traffic of the west coast, has a more bracing and healthier climate, but one which tries the *poitrinaire* too severely. South-west winds and storms prevail there. The sky is almost always clear, and the rain showers but brief. The snow-covered cone of Mount Egmont is the charm of the scenery. The mean annual temperature (fourteen years' observation) is 57°·5; the difference between the coldest and warmest months being 5°·66. The mean annual rainfall is 58 inches. Abundance of pure water is one of the comforts of the Taranaki district, derived from the streams that flow from Egmont into the sea. The dairy produce of the farms here is also a great element in the diet of invalids, being of such a high quality. The population of the district was, in 1886, 18,000, chiefly devoted to pastoral pursuits. New Plymouth, Hawera, and the other chief towns in Taranaki are now connected with Wellington by railway: by sea (twelve hours to Onehunga) frequent steamers connect it with Auckland. The ascent of Mount Egmont takes two days, and is not attended with danger or any special difficulty, ladies often mounting to the top.

Local Climate of Napier.

Crossing now to the east coast (see map) we come to Napier, the capital of Hawke's Bay Province. It is a lively and rising seaport, with a population of 9000, built upon limestone hills and upon a long neck of land called the Spit. The subsoil of the hilly part being drier than that of the other towns in this Zone, the well water is somewhat hard; but these peculiarities are rather beneficial than otherwise to consumptive invalids, for a winter residence. Much less rain falls here than at Auckland or Taranaki, the average for the whole year being 37·26 inches. The mean annual temperature is 57°·56, the difference between the coldest and warmest months being 19°·26. Most English trees, birds, and fishes seem to acclimatize well in Hawke's Bay district. The grass is more succulent and the cereals yield more bushels to the acre than in other parts of the colony. Many asthmatic invalids do better at Napier than at Auckland. All the conveniences of advanced civilization are to be found in this thriving town. It was rather curious to find, as I once found, the very newest books from home in a bookseller's shop in Napier, when these books had not yet reached Auckland.

The port of Napier is being improved by a large breakwater designed by Sir John Coode, whereby the heavy swell from the sea will be prevented from entering the harbour. Gas and water works, public, primary, and secondary schools, a hospital, a club, hotels, banks, and the usual Government offices and numerous warehouses, give Napier the completeness of a small capital. Its importance is enhanced by the agricultural and pastoral shows held there every year. The best judges of sheep and horses I know in New Zealand live in Napier. The people are a hearty, friendly, hospitable set.

Several interesting excursions can be made from Napier. For instance, along the railway line connecting it with Wellington, to Hastings, to Havelock, to Te Aute, where there is a theological training college for natives, and to Woodville, in the Seventy Mile Bush Or, in the opposite direction, to Lake Taupo; to Gisborne, where the wealthy Maori may be seen to perfection; or to the well-arranged mountain hotel at Kuripapanga, fifty miles inland, north-west, where the sub-Alpine climate of Zone No. 4 can be fully enjoyed without the booming of geysers, steamy mist from hot springs, or the odour of sulphuretted hydrogen.

Zone II.

This climatic belt includes part of the North Island, Cook's Straits, and part of the Middle Island as far south as the Hurunui River on the east, and Hokitika on the west. The general climate of this Zone resembles that of the south of England, but with keener winds, and a far more bracing atmosphere. Within its North Island division we find some lovely inland valleys, such as the famous Manawatu Gorge, and the valley of the Upper Wanganui River. The beautiful and varied " King Country " comes within this Zone, but is not as yet conveniently accessible to the tourist.

Palmerston North, at the western end of the Manawatu Gorge, is as healthy, bracing, and yet equable a place as I know. In the midst of summer the nights there are cool. This town has a strictly inland climate. It is furnished with a good water supply, very fair hotels, wide streets, good roads in all directions, and a lake for boating—quite an unusual luxury for a New Zealand inland town. The view of the "monarch of the north," snow-clad Ruapehu (8878 feet), from Palmerston in the early morning is a sight not soon to be forgotten. Wanganui, on the fine river of that name, is a healthy town having a mean annual temperature of 55°, but is not very interesting to the traveller.

At Woodville, only lately redeemed from the forest, the invalid can have the shelter afforded by the primæval vegetation of the island. The winter there is mild, and the summer not too hot. But *ennui* will sooner or later drive him to a larger town, and he will probably make for Wellington, the capital of New Zealand.

The Local Climate of Wellington.

When the Home Government, in its wisdom, in 1865, moved the capital of the colony from Auckland, the Naples of New Zealand, to a settlement reputed to be the most breezy and earthquaky place in the colony, it is evident that climate did not enter into its consideration. What the Yankee said of England is applicable to Wellington: "I guess you have plenty of weather here, but no climate that I can see." Its central position in the colony, its good harbour, and its easy defensibility, constituted the reasons, as Sir Frederick Weld informed me, when I visited him in Hobart in 1879, for the choice. The annual rainfall at Wellington is nearly fifty-one inches, and the mean annual temperature $55\frac{1}{2}°$. The city is much more bracing than Auckland, Wanganui, or Napier, and about as bracing as New Plymouth; but I have seldom met with any one who preferred to live in Wellington from unbiassed choice. Civil servants, insurance and bank clerks, steamship companies' officials, and retired ex-officials constitute the bulk of the resident population, which in 1886 was 25,945. The harbour is a grand expanse of deep water surrounded by hills intersected with ravines, and singularly resembling the Sea of Galilee in size, shape, and liability to sudden storms. The wharves are well constructed, and accommodate the largest number of ocean steamers simultaneously of any port in New Zealand. But even the direct mail steamers are storm-bound sometimes in the harbour. In the city, much of which has been reclaimed from the sea, the museum, the post-office, Government House, and other buildings, including what is supposed to be the largest wooden building in the world, are worthy of the colony. Cabs and tram-cars run at cheaper fares than in the other large towns. The North Island railways will in time all centre in Wellington. The great geological convulsion that formed Cook's Straits, dividing New Zealand into two islands, permanently altered the climates of both the adjacent extremities of the North and Middle Islands, by the in-draught of the west and south-west winds through the straits, and their collision with the east and north-east winds at the eastern outlet. The influx of the sea also has its effect. It will thus be understood that while Wellington has no terrors for vigorous healthy men, it is scarcely a desirable place for pulmonary invalids.

Local Climates of Nelson and Picton.

Nelson, at the head of Tasman Bay, on the north coast of the Middle Island, distant 106 miles from Wellington, is called "the garden of New Zealand" for all the fruits of the temperate and sub-tropical regions grow there in luxuriance. Large quantities of preserved fruit and jam of excellent quality are made there. Surrounded by mountains on all sides, the scenery of Nelson is very grand. To invalids suffering from slow chronic consumption, chronic bronchitis, rheumatism, and from senile decay, Nelson offers a delicious and restful climate. If the summer is found inconveniently warm, a visitor may resort to Top House on the mountains, 3000 feet above the sea. Nelson possesses the very best educational advantages, a comfortable club, cultured society, and an excellent local scientific association. The mean annual temperature of Nelson is 54°· 86; the difference between the coldest and warmest months being 17°. The average rainfall for the year is 61½ inches. Hops are extensively cultivated at Nelson, and both coal-mines and gold-mines are worked in the district. During 1887 the value of the gold exported from Nelson was £13,711. Its population in 1886 was 7315. While the climate of Nelson is tranquillizing to nervous invalids, it has been found by experience too sedative to women who are at all subject to menorrhagia, and who are burdened with the cares of a rapidly increasing family. Children born in Nelson during the summer are never robust. The winter, however, is more bracing than that of Auckland or Napier.

Picton is a small town of about 800 inhabitants, at the head of a beautiful arm of the sea, called Queen Charlotte Sound. The short distance, forty miles (fifteen miles across Cook's Strait and twenty-five miles of smooth water up the Sound), between Wellington and Picton enables the Wellingtonians to use Picton as a summer resort. For boating, yachting, and fishing, Queen Charlotte Sound is unsurpassed in New Zealand. The flavour of the Picton herring is, in my opinion, equal to that of the Yarmouth 'bloater.' When I visited the place in 1886, lodgings were cheap; the simplicity of the Pictonians, who flocked down in crowds to see the *Moraroa*, the largest Union steamer that had ever ventured up to their little wharf; and the exquisite situation of the sleepy-looking town, all indicated that Picton was not appreciated as it might be by the New Zealanders in general, or by that time it would have become a Llandudno or Scarborough on a small scale. But its time will come. From Nelson to Picton we steam through the "French Pass," a romantic channel, formed between the mainland and D'Urville Island, at one place only 117 yards broad, the tide running with tremendous force through it, between steep cliffs 500 feet high. Picton is the port of Blenheim, the capital of the provincial district of Marlborough, and is connected with it by railway. The mean annual temperature of this district (five years' observation) is 53°·4, the highest mean being 64°·3, and the lowest 42°·8. The average rainfall is nearly the same as that of Nelson. The country is mountainous, and covered with thick forests, chiefly of various kinds of pine and birch, of which a large quantity is annually exported. In Blenheim, I noticed a prosperity and complete absence of poverty, and a general contentment with each one's lot not too common in New Zealand at that time of depression, the summer of 1886. The summer is distinctly hotter in Blenheim than in Picton. It is not easy to find temporary accommodation there, except at the hotels, for every householder owns and occupies his own house. There are not the same social advantages as at Nelson, but as Picton is drier and colder than the latter city, it suits some cases of asthma better, and of hyperæsthetic nerve-irritability. Delicate strumous children thrive well here, being able to take plenty of open air exercise in boating, fishing, climbing the hills, riding ponies, and walking. When Picton and Blenheim are connected by rail with the Canterbury system, and with Nelson, I venture to predict that it will become the favourite sea-side resort of the Middle Island. Neither Sumner (Christchurch) nor Ocean Beach (Dunedin) have such attractions.

Zone III.

Extending from the Hurunui River and Hokitika, S. lat. 42° 50' to the south of the South or Stewart's Island, S. lat. 47° 20'. The general features of this climate have been sketched out on pp. 16, 17, and 19, but the peculiar local climates of Christchurch, Dunedin, Queenstown on Lake Wakatipu and Invercargill require individual description.

Local Climate of Christchurch.

"The Cathedral City," as it is called, is the most handsomely laid out of the four chief cities of New Zealand. Its Cathedral (Anglican) is at present the only one in the colony. In churches, schools, colleges, museum, and handsome private residences, it is the most English-looking city in New Zealand. Its population (32,000) includes the largest number of wealthy citizens and of cultured people of any of the four cities. But its climate is not conducive to the health of sickly people or of young children, from its extreme variations in the same week, or even in the same day. It is the only New Zealand city where a hot wind blows occasionally in the summer. This wind is from the west, and, though cool at its origin, becomes heated up by the hot, dry, fertile, wheat-growing Canterbury Plains about 100 miles before it reaches the city. It is at this season, (December to February) that cases of sunstroke occur.

The pallor, languor, and frequent illnesses among children in Christchurch in summer impress the stranger unfavourably. In winter, again, the prevalent winds, west and south-west, are very cold, blowing as they do across the Southern Alps, and thence over the Canterbury Plains at that season bearing frost on their surface. The greatest heat of summer (derived from the mean average of twelve years' observation) is 88°, and the greatest cold of winter is 25°. Yet the mean annual temperature is only 52°·88. At the change of season, corresponding to our spring and autumn, Christchurch weather is delightful. At all times a run down to the port, namely, Lyttelton, from which a range of hills, pierced by a tunnel 2838 yards long, is a cooling change. So also is a stay at Sumner, the sea bathing-place of Christchurch. The healthy person who dislikes long, cold, and damp winter will live more comfortably in Christchurch than in Dunedin; and a few cases of pure asthma do better in Christchurch than elsewhere. But invalids with weak chests, or those whose liver and kidneys are affected, should not go there to reside. When debilitated by Christchurch summer weather, a visitor should go west to Bealey, on the Southern Alps, 2104 feet above sea level, a station on the coach road from the east to the west coasts. Here, amid glaciers and snow peaks as grand as that of Switzerland, he can become braced up thoroughly. Good fishing and shooting may be had. Bealey is the coldest of all the Government weather-stations. The minimum temperature for the year is 12°, the maximum is 78°, and the annual mean average is 46°·7. The average rainfall here is 105 inches.

Crossing the well-made road, past terrific precipices, crossing roaring torrents, and skirting fields of snow—the grandest drive in New Zealand—from Bealey to Hokitika, we find ourselves in the wettest town in New Zealand, 112 inches being the average annual rainfall. The district called Westland is sparsely populated by an orderly people, although mining for gold and for coal are the chief industries. Forests are plentiful. The prevailing wind is westerly. The mean annual temperature is 52°·34; the difference between the coldest and warmest months being 14°·76. Westland cannot be recommended for invalids. Mount Cook, or *Aorangi*, the monarch of New Zealand, 12,349 feet high, first ascended by the Rev. W. S. Green in 1883, is in this district. The Midland Railway Company of New Zealand is now engaged in connecting Springfield and Hokitika by rail.

Akaroa is a pleasant little town on a beautiful harbour situated on Bank's Peninsula, forty-four miles south-east from Lyttelton, famous for its fruits. It has a milder climate than Christchurch, and romantic scenery.

Neither Timaru (pop. estimated at 5000), 100 miles south of Christchurch, nor Oamaru, seventy-eight miles north of Dunedin, both important seaports, need be described in a chapter devoted to climatic considerations. Healthy persons, able to withstand much stormy weather, can enjoy life there thoroughly.

Local Climate of Dunedin.

Dunedin, named after Edinburgh, is its representative in climate also. Built on steep hills surrounding a bay open at both ends to the north-east and south-west winds, it requires great care to select a lodging for an invalid which shall be sufficiently sheltered. The result of seventeen years' observations at Dunedin, 550 feet above the sea, gives the mean temperature of the whole year as $50°\cdot72$; the maximum is $84°\cdot74$, and the minimum $29°\cdot84$. The average temperature for winter is $43\frac{1}{2}°$; for summer $57°$; for spring $50\frac{1}{2}°$; and for autumn $51°\cdot8$.

In my own experience I found the change from Auckland, with its $85°$ to $90°$ in the shade in the summer, to Dunedin, where my thermometer stood at $47°$ every night, very delightful. An invalid with chronic liver trouble, or liable to congestive head attacks, would do well to spend the summer in Dunedin. It is a handsome city, with 45,000 inhabitants, and furnished with all the educational, ecclesiastical, social, and commercial facilities that one can possibly desire. The scenery around Dunedin is as beautiful as that of Auckland, but of a different character. Majestic, stern, bare, cloud-capped mountains, intersected by boulder-strewn valleys, rise all around. The drives round the peninsula to Larnach's Castle, across the bay from Dunedin, and to Blueskin (visitors miss the scenery by rail) are simply magnificent. And the walk up the Water of Leith Valley to the Reservoir is the prettiest I have ever seen in the suburbs of a large town. In the architecture of its churches, banks, city hall, and monuments, and in the possession of the Grand Hotel, Dunedin excels its three rivals. The severe climate stimulates the faculties of business men, and their bustling ways are a contrast to the languor of Auckland and the gentlemanly deliberation of Christchurch. There is a real winter here, of uncertain duration, July being perhaps the most severe month of the year, when sleet, snow, and hail descend with a charming variety! The youngsters of Dunedin, Queenstown, and Invercargill can sometimes enjoy the luxury of snow-balling fights. But for invalids Dunedin is to be avoided in winter and spring. Among the residents **cases of phthisis pulmonalis, pneumonia, pleurisy, bronchitis, and other** lung diseases, along with quinsy, **diphtheria, and** catarrhal sore throats, are common. Statistics show, however, that Dunedin **is a healthy city** compared with any **large city or town in England, and** that its birth-rate is high.

The children one sees are rosy, plump, and hardy. Two lines of cable tramcars render access to the upper parts of the city easy, and the Town Belt, a park extending round Upper Dunedin in a semicircle, affords a pleasant walk at any time of the year. After seeing the rain come down in summer one finds it difficult to believe that the average annual rainfall is only 32 inches; but this **is the official** record. It is the **only** New Zealand **city where I** found it necessary to carry an umbrella every day **in** the summer. The Dunedin Club, occupying Fernhill House is an excellent one. On inquiry I found the prices of hosiery, drapery, &c., to be as low as in England, and I am inclined to think that living there is rather cheaper, though house-rent is dearer than in Auckland.

Local Climate of Queenstown.

The Alpine resort in summer of the Middle Island families and of those tourists who "do" the Southern Lakes is Queenstown, on Lake Wakatipu, about 200 miles west from Dunedin by the rail, which takes a circuitous route. From three years' observation taken at this weather station, 1070 feet above sea level, we find that the mean annual temperature is 51°; the difference between the coldest and the warmest months is 21°; the maximum being $84\frac{1}{2}°$, and the minimum 23°.

The scenery is perfectly glorious. At the back of Queenstown is Ben Lomond, which a lady can ascend easily. Opposite the town are the 'Remarkables,' a serrated range of mountains 3000 feet high, where the lights of sunset and sunrise are transcendently lovely. The lake (pronounced "*Waw-ka-tip*," the final "u" being silent) is 70 miles long, 112 square miles in area, and bounded on the north by the grandest double-peaked mountain in the Middle Island, Mount Earnslaw. At its foot nestle the hamlets of Kinloch and Glenorchy, where perfect quiet, primitive but wholesome fare, and boating, fishing, riding *ad libitum* can be enjoyed if the visitor tires of the bustle of Queenstown. "No lake in Europe can at all equal Lake Wakatipu except Lucerne," says the Hon. J. C. Richmond, an experienced traveller and clever amateur artist. At this elevation many asthmatic sufferers enjoy peaceful nights. Invalids suffering from eczema, which is worse near the sea, from bronchitis coupled with asthma, from glandular swellings and from gout, will recover health at Queenstown, if the brief summer allows them to stay long enough. In six weeks my delicate wife and little son regained perfect health by a sojourn at Kinloch. Visitors must provide against the cold of the evenings and during the nights. Those coming from the North Island, Australia, the Cape, India, or the Pacific Islands, will find this whole district cold, even though the sun's direct rays are hot. The last night I was at Queenstown there was an earthquake shock, which was distinctly perceptible, but did no damage. I could not help comparing it in this peculiarity with Crieff in Scotland, close to Loch Earn, where shocks occasionally occur.

Local Climate of Invercargill.

Invercargill is the capital of the province of Southland, 139 miles south of Dunedin, and seventeen from the Bluff Harbour, the southernmost post of call for all steamers approaching New Zealand from the south. It has now over 10,000 inhabitants, and is an important pastoral centre. Invercargill is laid out on the American rectangular plan, with wide streets, handsome shops, tramcars, and lofty public buildings. The climate of the town, like that of Wellington, principally consists of "changes of weather." Along its wide streets the icy breezes, fresh from the Antarctic Pole, blow, according to the season, dust, sand, sleet, rain, or snow. A greater contrast to Auckland could not possibly be imagined. A bank clerk who was suddenly moved by the head office from Auckland to Invercargill had his memory so benumbed by cold that he forgot his overdue little bills! Thunderstorms are more common in Southland than elsewhere in the colony, being as 29·5 to 18 in Auckland and Mangonui; 16 in Taranaki; 14 in Hokitika; 7 in Dunedin; and 3 in Christchurch. The average annual temperature of Invercargill is 50°, the maximum temperature in summer being 83°, and the minimum of winter 20°. The average annual rainfall is 43·67 inches. It is a pity that this winter temperature is not low enough to freeze the rabbits which constitute the great pest of Southland, destroying the pasturage, and thus starving out the sheep. While it is only a Scotchman who can live comfortably in Southland, I must acknowledge that the children I met in the streets of Invercargill are rosy-cheeked, healthy, and active.

ZONE IV.

forms an irregular ovoid figure on the map, having Lake Taupo (1250 feet above the sea) as its centre. Upon this sub-Alpine plateau, the lowest part of which is 1000 feet above sea level, we have a dry, pumiceous, and scoria soil and a capital mountain air, which is particularly suited for asthmatic and emphysematous sufferers, and for those whose shaken nervous system requires a light stimulating atmosphere and cool nights. The average winter temperature on this plateau does not exceed 50° during the day, and 30° to 32° during the night. The light dry soil soaks up rain quickly, and on sunny days (the usual, not as in England, the unusual thing) reflects the sun's rays so strongly as to thoroughly dessicate the air near to the surface of the ground. At the sulphur baths (to be described in chapter v.), which abound in this region, the rapid cures of rheumatism and of skin diseases are accelerated by these characteristics. But the storminess of the weather at all seasons makes it dangerous for consumptive patients to visit or stay at Rotorua or Taupo. Ordinary tourists will, however, much enjoy the scenery, and find it not only comfortable but pleasant to travel through this Zone between December 1st and the end of February. Tourists who are not taking the thermal treatment, will find the location of this sanatorium at Rotorua (Ohinemutu) and the hotel at "Joshua's," Taupo, too near the hot steaming pools and too highly flavoured with sulphuretted hydrogen fumes to be enjoyable. The convenience of the invalids has rightly been studied first before all. Means of easy communication between Taupo and the wild and romantic "King Country" are still wanting, but the North Island Trunk Railway will effect this in due time, and then the grand tour sketched out on p. 135 may be made. For details of the climate and prevalent weather at Rotorua, I refer to chapters v. and vi.

CHAPTER III.

THE MAORIS AND THEIR CUSTOMS.

The name, origin, and appearance of the Maori—Tattooing—Language, with specimens—Rhyme for pronunciation—Grammar—History of Old New Zealand—Causes of their decline—Customs of *tapu*, *muru*, *utu* explained—*Korero*, *haka*, *tangi*, *mana* explained—Bishop Selwyn's defence of Maori character—Generous deeds—Old Mohi—Conversions—Future of **the race.**

ALTHOUGH this little book does not aim at including the history and ethnology of New Zealand, yet a few pages may be wisely devoted to the subject of the aborigines, seeing that the race is slowly but surely passing away, and that the Maori has proved himself to be the bravest and most intelligent of all the Pacific Islanders hitherto encountered by English soldiers.

The "Maori," from a word meaning "native" or "indigenous," seems to belong to the brown-skinned, that is, to the lighter-coloured races of Polynesia. Many books have been written and essays contributed to the Transactions of the New Zealand Institute upon the "Whence of the Maoris," and so little is known of their remote origin that various *savants* have held that they came (1) from Central America; (2) from Peru; (3) from Hawaii or Samoa; (4) from Sabea in the south of Arabia; while (5) a learned Hebrew believes them to be descendants of the Gibeonites who were made slaves by Joshua (see Joshua ix.) as a punishment for their deception of him, and who eventually were driven out of the Holy Land at the dispersion of Judah. He bases this strange theory on some undeniably Semitic customs and observances among the Maoris. For instance, the consecration ceremony at puberty, the mourning ceremonial, and the close resemblance of the *tapu* custom in relation to the dead to that of the law of uncleanness as delivered through Moses.

It is remarkable that the Maoris neither manufacture a native intoxicant like *kava*, nor any cloth resembling *tapa*, both productions being universal among their reputed ancestors of the South Pacific.

Whatever may be the correct theory, it is generally admitted that the present Maori race came to New Zealand about the year 1100 A.D. in canoes, the names of the largest of which are still borne by the various tribes, or *hapus*, such as the Arawa, Waikato, Ngapuhi, &c.

It is clear also that they found in these islands an aboriginal of a Papuan type, of whom they made slaves, as we see by some of their ancient carved temples, *whare-kura*, and as we trace here and there among themselves by observing men of short stature, darker complexion, brachycephalic skull, full lips, and curly and coarse but not woolly hair.

The pure Maori may be thus sketched. The men are tall, muscular, and well formed, the feet and hands being well proportioned, though the legs are shorter than in the average European. Their average height is 5 feet $6\frac{1}{4}$ inches. The shades of colour of their brown skin vary from a tint fairer than that of the Basque or South Italian to that of a modified Papuan. The hair is usually black, but sometimes dark brown. As a rule, there is little or no beard. The features of the chiefs are regular and symmetrical, the nose being large and often aquiline, in spite of the detestable custom of flattening the Maori babies' noses in infancy; the mouth is large, and the lips not as full as in the negro; the eyes are dark, vivacious, and expressive; the teeth are white and regular, lasting to old age. The face is greatly under self-command; for the Maori, while keenly observant, and possessing a most tenacious memory, can effectually conceal his thoughts and feelings. Yet his fount of tears is always ready; he can weep at a moment's notice. "A Maori may be in a violent rage," says the Rev. J. Buller, "or bitterly weeping, or as sulky (*pouri*) as a mule from the same identical cause." The women are handsome, powerful, and muscular, with large, dark, lustrous eyes, and long hair of a less coarse fibre than that of the men. But they reach maturity early in life, and from very heavy work become prematurely aged and ugly, while the tattooing of the lips in blue is to our notions a deformity in every woman of whatever age.

In connection with the custom of tattoo—which when on the face is called *moko*, on the body *whakaairo*—every adult Maori who could afford the high fee exacted by the professional tattoo artist, and every adult woman had a right to it, contrary to what visitors are generally told, namely, that these marks are distinctive of the chief or his family (Buller).

The language of the Maoris is a dialect nearest akin to the Rarotongan, Hawaiian, and Samoan. So close a family likeness exists between Maori, Samoan, and Hawaiian that a Maori can follow the debates in the House of Representatives in Honolulu without the aid of an interpreter, while a *kanaka* or Samoan who happens to be cast ashore in New Zealand can make himself understood by the Maoris. One fundamental resemblance in these four Polynesian dialects consists in their being composed of monosyllabic root-words, by the duplication and combination of which new words more complex in their meaning are made. This feature also proves that these languages belong to the primæval ages of human speech. Their lingual affinities are also very marked. For example, the Maori and Hawaiian dialects substitute the aspirated "h" for the sibilant "s" and "sh" existing in Samoan. I never heard a Maori pronounce our sibilants, and I was informed by Judge Maning that only one tribe could be taught to utter it. "You give me one herring," said a Maori to me at the Hot Lakes. For a time I was nonplussed, but a colonial bystander interpreted it to me, "You give me one shilling," the "1" being also lacking in Maori. In the Hawaiian and Samoan dialects the "l" and "k" take the place of "r" and "t" in the Maori respectively.

As in all the Christian islands of the Pacific, the missionaries have reduced the native language to writing for the purpose of translating the Holy Scriptures. The first part of this task was not difficult for the ordinary purposes of intercourse, because of the simplicity of the structure of the language and the uniformity of the vowel pronunciation; but owing to the non-existence of words conveying abstract ideas the work of translation was very hard.

The Maori alphabet consists of five vowels: a, e, i, o, u; nine consonants: h, k, m, n, p, r, t, w, and ng; and five diphthongs: ae, ai, ao, au, ou, all of which are pronounced as in Italian. The palatal sound "ng" is very soft, the "g" being inaudible at the beginning of a word such as *nga-rua-wahia,* the two rivers, pronounced "Nah-ruah-wahya," whereas in Onehunga the "g" is distinct, though not nearly as hard as in the English word "hunger." Each consonant must be followed by a vowel, and every word in Maori ends in a vowel, though elision is practised in rapid utterance, for the English visitor hears Lake Wakatipu called "Wakatip," &c.

The following *jeu d'esprit* in rhyme gives a fair idea of the sound of the native names of seven places in the colony, I underline the seven Maori words:—

> "*Ohau* shall I cross this swift river, Ohau?
>   *Waikanae* not swim to the shore?
> *Otaki* a boat now and merrily row
>   In the *Manawatu* did before.
> *Oroua*-way gently, for you must beware
>   Of the *Horowhenua* afloat.
> *Waikawa*-rdly stand I and shiver on shore
>   Till the ferryman brings me the boat?"

It is to the credit of the colonial governments of New Zealand that they have officially perpetuated the Maori names of both mountains, lakes, rivers, valleys, bays, and settlements in the colony, for they are most appropriate, sometimes poetical and connoting an interesting legend; always mellifluous; and the Maori language will one day be extinct. But at the same time it must be admitted that some names are untranslatable so as to be in accordance with decency.

A few of the more common words I will now translate as a help to those who study the map of our colony for the first time. The Maori language is copious, consisting of at least six thousand words. They gave descriptive names to everything visible in earth, sky, or sea, and they have no less than twelve names for different shades of colour. Observe that in Maori the adjective follows the noun.

1. The chief numerals are: *tahi*, 1; *rua*, 2; *toru*, 3; *wha*, 4; *rima*, 5; *ono*, 6; *whitu*, 7; *waru*, 8; *iwa*, 9; *tekau*, 10.

2. Perhaps the commonest root-word at the beginning of a name is *wai*, which means "water." We thus have: **wai-wera**, hot spring; **wai-kato**, high river; **wai-heke**, flowing water; **wai-makiriri**, cold river; **wai-roa**, tall water (a waterfall); **wai-uku**, clay water, &c.

3. Other common words are *roto*, lake; *motu*, island; *whare*, hut or house; *whanga*, harbour; *pah* or *pa*, fort; *puke*, hill; *kai*, food; *rangi*, sky, heaven; *wako*, canoe; *mana*, power; *maunga*, hill.

4. Among the adjectives useful to know are *pai*, good; *kino*, bad; *mate*, dead; *pouri*, sad or sulky; *poto*, short; *roa*, tall or long; *tapu*, sacred; *nui*, great.

In conversation *ae* (sounded like the Scottish "aye") means "yes;" *kahore*, "no."

The ordinary salutation is "*Tena ra ko koe?*" literally "Hold; there you are!" usually shortened into "*Tena koe?*" which is colloquially equivalent to our "How do you do?" and the correct reply is, "*Tena koutou*," "How are we both?"

The colonists do not trouble to learn Maori, except the commonest words and phrases, for he who would converse fluently with the natives must live among them and study the manner, inflection of voice, the gestures, emphasis, and pronunciation of their best speakers (and they have many very good orators) because the same word may have its meaning altered by all or any of these arts of oratory.

A monthly newspaper in Maori, called the "Korimako" (the name of the Bell bird of New Zealand, now nearly extinct), was established and endowed by a philo-Maori American gentleman, the late W. P. Snow, of Massachusetts, for distribution among the reading natives. It has proved of good service in the Gospel and temperance work among them, and also as a means of diffusing information about Europe and America.

From it I extract the first verse of the translation of Sankey's well-known hymn:—

HOLD THE FORT.
"E te iwi! haere ake
Ki te nui mau
Haere ake ki te ora
I te ara hou,
Puritia mai te Taonga
Kia piki ai
Whaia ko te ture tika
Whaia ko te pai."

These lines pronounced as I have indicated on p. 42 will be found quite euphonious and well adapted to the original stirring music. The Maori children have thin voices, but not unpleasing, and they sing in admirable time.

When we come to the substantives and verbs, we find that Maori possesses not only a singular and plural number but also a dual. There are also two pronouns denoting the first person plural, "we," namely, *matou*, meaning "we" *excluding* the person spoken to, and *tatou* "we" *including* the person addressed. But I must not pursue the subject further, lest I should discourage any readers who may emigrate to New Zealand from learning the native "lingo."

The first missionaries sent out to convert the Maoris had, as I have stated, much difficulty in translating the Bible for the want of abstract terms in the Maori. But after years of self-devotion, prayerful study, reflection, and judicious collaboration the task was completed about the year 1845, the Old Testament having been translated by my friend Dr. Maunsell, Archdeacon of Auckland, who still lives, honoured by all who know him, and the New Testament by Bishop Williams, who has gone to his rest. The first Maori convert, named Rangi, was baptized September 14, 1825, after ten years' missionary work. The Maoris eagerly learnt to read, and showed great shrewdness in questioning their teachers on Biblical subjects. And now the whole nation are actually or nominally Christian. A lady could now traverse even the wild "King country" in personal safety. In this day of severe criticism of missions and missionaries my readers should notice this fact in connection with what I shall describe later on. In conveying to the native mind European ideas, several words have been introduced by the missionaries from the English into the Maori, by splitting up as it were our numerous double consonants, *e.g.* newspaper becomes *nupepa*; book, *puka-puka*; England, *Ingaranga*; Auckland, *Akarana*; Graham, *Kéréhama*; John, *Honé*; William, *Wiremu*; Featherston, *Petatoné*, &c.

When the first white men settled in New Zealand, the aboriginal Maori was a brave but cruel and bloodthirsty athletic savage, reckless of human life, selfish to the backbone, revengeful, treacherous according to our ideas, yet in time of peace courteous and hospitable to the white man—*pakeha*, "foreigner," he was called. Mr. F. E. Maning, who wrote two graphic and witty books, entitled "Old New Zealand" and "The War in the North," under the *nom de plume* of "Pakeha-Maori," describes the country when he landed as a Pandemonium, from the constant and furious wars of extermination waged by the various tribes (*hapus*) upon each other. There was, he states, ample evidence to show that, centuries before, the native population had been much more numerous than it was found to be when he first settled there. The diseases induced by famine and malaria, besides the slaughter in the wars, had caused a rapid decrease in the numbers of the natives. A continuous state of warfare had become so much the natural condition of life with the Maori that all his customs, sentiments, and maxims had been formed accordingly. Nothing was so esteemed as courage and strength, and to acquire property by war and plunder was more honourable and more desirable than by honest labour. To kill the wounded and captive and to eat your dead enemy was noble and glorious. You assimilated by cannibalism all the courage and strength as well as the *atua*, or soul, of the man you devoured, besides striking terror into all his tribe. The knowledge of this horrible custom was the chief cause of the panic that sometimes seized our own soldiers in the Maori wars. Our wounded men have been known to implore their comrades to kill them rather than let them fall into the hands of the cannibal Maoris.

No aboriginal nation, except perhaps the Zulus, has been more difficult to conquer than the Maoris; and at last they obtained an honourable peace from our commanders. The bravery, the skill in fortification, in attack and defence, and the knowledge of strategy of the Maori have extorted admiration from all military men who have served in New Zealand. For some years after the settlements grew in the colony, the intertribal wars became still more sanguinary because of the use of firearms. But the spread of Christianity, the practice of trade and barter, and the influence of the *pakeha* checked the depopulation by gradually substituting the peaceful arts of agriculture and the manufacture of articles from the native flax shrub (*Phormium tenax*) for bloody and fruitless war.

The low morality of the Maori in his heathen state conduced to the decrease of the race. His ideas and expressions were full of obscenity in ordinary conversation. Polygamy, infanticide, the abandonment of the sick, infirm, and aged; the suicide of widows, the slaughter of all a chief's slaves at his death, and the ruthless retaliation of murder upon the innocent were universally practised in Maoridom. Latterly, from the adoption of European clothes and blankets, from intoxicating drinks, from contagious diseases introduced by the white man, and from the swampy, unhealthy places often selected by the native for his hut, called *whare* (built of *raupo*, a kind of rush, and the leaves of the *nikau*, or cabbage palm) their numbers have been declining. But since the New Zealand Government have provided free education, free medical advice, and medicines, and in some cases free quarters and rations, and since intermarriage with the *pakeha* has become common, the annual decrease has been but small. In analysing the census returns of 1886, and comparing them with those of 1881, the Registrar-general of New Zealand comes to the following conclusions concerning the vitality of the Maori race:—

1. That there is a much smaller birth-rate among the Maoris than among the rest of the population.

2. That there is a higher death-rate at all the younger ages of life.

3. That there is, in addition, a much higher death-rate among the adult Maori females than among the adult males.

I shall allude to the diseases prevalent among the Maoris in chapter xii.

There are, it is estimated, though not with exactness, about 40,000 natives in the North and about 2000 in the Middle and South Islands; just about the number of Lapps remaining in Scandinavia. Thousands of these are Christians, many quite consistent in their behaviour, and hundreds own horses, oxen, waggons, geese, fowls, and bees. In 1881 the Maoris owned besides horses no less than 112,850 sheep, 42,103 cattle, and 92,091 pigs. What with pigs *ad libitum*, potatoes, *kumara, taro*, peach and apple trees, and fish everywhere in plenty, it is his own fault if the Maori starves. Each adult Maori has a vote for one of the four native members of the House of Representatives, according to his district. There are also two Maoris in the Legislative Council. There is a native department, with a Cabinet minister at its head, and a Native Lands Court system specially devoted to Maori interests. More than 2600 native children attend the 79 free schools, where, I am glad to state, the English language alone is *now* taught. Some natives, notably those of Hawke's Bay and Poverty Bay, have become quite wealthy from the sale or lease of their lands to settlers. The ancient customs of the Maori are, as might be expected, falling into disuse from the spread of civilization and Christianity, and from the death of the old warriors (*ariki*) and the *tohungas*, or priest-magicians, whose arts failed them against the superior knowledge, weapons, and apparatus of the *pakeha*. The last of these *tohungas*, old Tuhoto, said to be a centenarian, perished from the effects of the Tarawera volcanic eruption in 1886. The present generation of adults have less of the brutality and ignorance of their ancestors, but have acquired some of the white man's vices—drunkenness, lying, extortion, thieving, and bullying. However, there are many exceptions, as I shall presently note.

For an exact and profound study of the Polynesian customs of *tapu, muru, utu*, and others, I would refer readers to Dr. Fornander's book, and to Dr. E. K. Tylor's "Manual of Anthropology;" but a brief description of these, of the past meaning of the word "*mana*," and of the ceremonies called *korero, tangi*, and *haka*, must be permitted.

1st. The custom of making anything *tapu*, or sacred, or unclean, still survives in some of the remote villages or *kaingas*. But whereas in ancient times there were many kinds and degrees of *tapu*, everything worn or used by a chief being *tapu*, for instance, everything worn or used by a stranger who was *tapu* by the chief also, the place of a birth, death, or burial being ditto; and the *tohunga* being able to *tapu* any land, hut, person, or thing, and likewise by a certain *karakia* (incantation) to release it from *tapu*, the breach of any of these being punishable by death. Nowadays even the burying-place, the *wahi-tapu*, is barely respected by the quarter-civilized Maori, and not at all by the colonist.

2nd. By *muru* was meant an organised and legal confiscation of goods inflicted upon one who killed another by accident, or stole any property belonging to another. This *muru* generally included personal chastisement of the offender, who however was allowed to protect himself. The pillaging party was called a *taua-muru*, or 'battalion for punishment.' Such was the perverted moral sense of the Maori that if a child in a family got burned or drowned the rest of the *hapu* would come and inflict *muru* upon the parents!

3rd. The *utu* or satisfaction for murder (*lex talionis*), theft, or any other crime, identical with the Mosaic "eye for an eye," "tooth for a tooth," &c., law, a law common to all primitive nations, was rigorously carried out among the Maoris. Most of the massacres of the boats' crews on the coast of New Zealand in early days, and those that take place now in some of the uncivilised islands of the Pacific, have been enforcements of *utu*, or blood for blood. For, as the islanders make no distinction between Europeans, the crimes of the French, German, or Dutch sailors are visited upon the more humane Englishman.

The Maoris always regarded it as just and right to kill any members of the *hapu* or clan to which the slayer of their own clansman belonged. Nor had they any sacred fane, or city of refuge, as in Israel, where the manslayer could find asylum. Many years elapsed before they could understand or would submit to the English law on the subject of murder. So great has been the consideration shown by the successive colonial governments for this custom of *utu* that if a Maori murdered a settler for *utu* and then escaped to his *hapu*, the authorities used merely to demand that he should be given up to justice, and if the *hapu* refused, took no steps to enforce the law. Thus was the law of England defied; but this is not now the case. The Government of New Zealand would have gone to great lengths then rather than provoke a Maori rebellion. But indeed there is not much fear of that now, ever since the plucky arrest of Te Whiti, the false prophet of the Maoris, at Parihaka, by the Hon. John Bryce in 1881, and the impressive effect on the native mind of King Tawhiao's visit in 1884 to England. Those natives who directly trade with the settlers, and have tasted the luxuries of civilization in the form of money, tobacco, liquors, furniture, clothes, silk dresses, watches, jewellery, &c., have more common sense than to provoke a rupture which would deprive them of these things for a time. By a wise provision of the law, it is a punishable offence for a white man to sell liquor, arms, or ammunition to a Maori. Though frequently evaded, this law has done much to put down intertribal massacres and murderous quarrels, the result of drunken sprees. For it must be borne in mind that the Maori drinks liquor in order to get drunk, and knows no such thing as moderate drinking. The natives are now amenable to New Zealand law, exactly the same as the whites. There is very little crime among the Maoris, and what there is decreases year by year.

4th. The *korero*, or tribal assembly for the public discussion of war, peace, or other matters, was always held in the *whare-puni*, or council-room, the largest building in the *kainga*, adorned usually with elaborate carvings, and painted. The head of each family squatted on the ground in a circle round the chief of highest rank among them. There was no want of ready speakers. One generally finds this to be the case in aboriginals of comparatively high cranial development who are not possessed of a written language. This circumstance so trains the memory that the old chiefs and priests could not only recite to the visitor all the old legends—many of them weird and poetic, some grotesque and indecent —but could reckon up at least twenty-seven generations back with perfect correctness. Furthermore, every white man was known by a certain native nick-name, derived from some personal peculiarity, and by this name was known throughout the Maori nation. Nor did any Maori forget a face he had once seen. The meetings I have witnessed between Judge Maning and Maori friends who had not seen him for twenty, thirty, or even forty years were quite affecting—so fond were they all of him—and were interesting corroborations of the possession of this gift of quick and tenacious observation and memory. To return to the *korero*, however, one orator after another would spring to their feet and with *mere*, a sharp-edged club of greenstone (very valuable), or spear in hand, and mat or cloak waving from the shoulder, would move up and down with stately step, which would quicken to a run when the speaker became excited. His length of walk (or run) being timed exactly to the length and point of the sentences gave a rhythmical cadence which almost converted the speech into an operatic recitative. Graceful action, impassioned appeal, the chanting of a song of love, war, or death, the apt quotation of proverbs, legends, and epigrams, and the clever choice of natural similitudes—all this evinced oratorical power of a high order. At the end of the *korero* the tribal policy resolved upon was announced by the chief, and a feast terminated the proceedings.

For the preservation of the best Maori legends and poetry, Sir George Grey, who has had such a marked success in his diplomacy with the natives, has done more than any other living man. For the story of the good "Maui," who is fabled to have brought up New Zealand from the depths of the ocean—hence its name "*Te Ika o Maui*," "the fish of Maui;" for the pretty story of Hinemoa and Tutanekai and other legends, readers are referred to the collection made by Sir George Grey, to Domett's "Ranolf and Amohia," and to works by J. White, T. W. Gudgeon, E. Tregear, and others.

5th. The celebrated *haka*, or national dance, similar to the *hula-hula* of the Hawaiians, seems to have gone out of fashion, and the tame and "got up" imitations of it by travelling Maori troupes, or by native loafers to amuse visitors at the Hot Lakes are not like what the old settlers saw. It was a dance of an indecorous nature, accompanied by the chanting of amorous songs, and was usually performed by the women only. As I have never had the opportunity of seeing one, I cannot describe it, and it is the unanimous wish of the philo-Maori that it should be allowed to disappear.

6th. The *tangi*, or weeping, meant originally the ceremonial mourning for the death of a chief or great man, but the weeping was also practised on the occasion of meeting a long-absent relative or friend. The entire *tangi* ceremony, of which I was fortunate enough to be a spectator at Ohinemutu, in December, 1880, in company with Judge Maning, Mr. S. Jackson, sen., and Mr. R. Proude, is an interesting relic of the elaborate and demonstrative mournings for the dead common to most primitive nations, of which we read in Genesis l., Numbers xx., Samuel xxxi., Zechariah xii., and other parts of the Old Testament.

I will briefly describe what we saw at Ohinemutu. The chief who had died was of high rank, and the visitors were expected to consider it an honour to be invited to this *tangi*. The leader of our party of four, Judge F. E. Maning, being a great favourite with the Maoris, was specially urged to attend, and was good enough to translate to us much of what was "said or sung."

Many natives walking in to Te Ngae, the name of the mission station where the *tangi* was being held, were overtaken by our carriage, and everyone greeted the worthy judge with enthusiasm. Most had come long distances to do honour to the deceased.

The body of the dead chief had been laid on a bier, wrapped in flax mats, but leaving the head exposed, which was decorated with feathers; the sons and nearest relatives of the deceased were seated on the ground near the corpse. As each visitor arrived he or she went straight up to the body, and was greeted by each relative by the *hongi*, or rubbing of noses, the Maori substitute for kissing, followed by each embracing the other and weeping upon the neck, in true Eastern fashion. Round the inner circle of relatives were the professional mourners, women who continued all day a wailing chant without words, like the "keening" at an Irish wake. Some of these women also kept up another ancient custom, that of cutting their faces, arms, and breasts with pieces of obsidian and sharp-edged shells, making the blood flow—mildly, however, not as profusely as described so graphically in "Old New Zealand" by my departed friend, Judge Maning, who remarked the contrast of the old-time *tangi* and the modern affair. Each native visitor joined in the wailing for a few minutes and then mixed in the crowd that sat around. Some of the women kept lifting their hands to heaven, quivering in that strange way one sees Maoris do when under real or assumed excitement. All this went on until sundown, when the funeral feast was spread, the *pakehas* being cordially invited. Huge piles of pork, cooked in the Maori ovens, of potatoes, sweet potatoes, bread, and *koura* (a very palatable fresh-water crayfish), were vigorously attacked by the company. The only incongruous and injurious element in the repast was the whisky passed round by a white man, who wished to ingratiate himself with the natives, and perhaps once again become **Minister of the Native Department**. I was glad to see many Maoris refuse it, being total abstainers. Up to the time (9 P.M.) our party left there was no intoxication.

In old times the corpse of the chief was wrapped in his best garment and buried in the ground in a sitting posture, his face turned towards the north, where is Te Reinga, the Maori Hades (somewhere about Cape Maria van Diemen); or placed in a tree in the darkest recesses of an adjacent forest. Then, after about two years, the body was exhumed, the bones were scraped clean, painted red, and, with another *tangi*, placed either (1) in a small house resting on a pole, or (2) on the top of a sacred (*tapu*) tree, or (3) in a cave difficult of access. Nowadays Christian burial is the rule, and the bone-scraping with its attendant and subsequent ceremonies is a thing of the past.

7th. The word "*mana*," so freely used in Maori traditions, and in all literature descriptive of the Maoris, deserves a passing explanation. Its meaning, according to the way in which it is used by the speaker, comprises prestige, power, influence, and a certain magical property which we call "luck," the Germans "glück," the Romans "virtus."

There was the *mana* of a *tohunga*, or priest, which was proved by the truth of his predictions. Some of these gentry were skilled in ventriloquism (*vide* "Old New Zealand"), which gave them great *mana*. The success of a chief or warrior gave him *mana*, which he might lose by subsequent defeat. A spear, club, or *mere* may have a *mana* which by tradition had become regarded, like King Arthur's sword Excalibur, as something supernatural.

Among the leading men of the colony who have had the greatest *mana* with the Maoris have been the first Bishop Selwyn, Sir George Grey, Dr. Featherston, and Robert Graham, Esq.

Some colonists have complained that while the Maori has a sense, though limited, of justice and of honesty, he has no gratitude, and is selfish and covetous. To this charge a noble answer was made by the great Bishop Selwyn, the founder of the Church of England in New Zealand. "When I hear of the covetousness and ingratitude and selfishness of the Maoris," said he, "I have only to look into the faces of Henry and Lot [his two native lay helpers], the most helpful, the least self-seeking, and the best tempered of all companions, and forget all the accusations brought against their race by Englishmen who see their own failings reflected in the native mirror, without recognizing them as their own. The charges of ingratitude made against the natives are generally made by those who have given them the least reason to be grateful. For myself I must say that I have met with so much disinterested kindness from the Maoris that I should be as ungrateful as they are supposed to be if I did not acknowledge my obligations." I can corroborate from personal experience the testimony of this great and good man. Even though the Maori language does not contain words directly meaning gratitude, hope, faith, and other abstract ideas, yet the Maori can express these sentiments in his simple and terse way. We must not take our ideas of the typical Maori, as so many transient visitors do, from the loafing, shilling-hunting, grog-drinking Maori of the Rotorua and Taupo districts —a man who has lost all the virtues of the savage and gained the vices of the European. Should we, as Englishmen, like to be judged as a race from many of our fellow-countrymen who haunt our show places and attend our horse-races? The history of the colony shows the Maori in a far from unfavourable light on the whole. Even during their wars of independence the natives showed generosity to their foes. At Kororareka they captured Lieutenant Philpotts, a son of the celebrated Bishop of Exeter, and in admiration of his bravery not only released him, but returned him his pistols and sword. In the war of 1863, the hostile chief, hearing that General Cameron's forces were short of provisions, sent down the river Waikato canoes carrying a large supply of food for our soldiers. A chief's daughter, baptized as Julia, and her husband saved the entire crew of the ship *Delaware*, which was wrecked on the coast at Wakapuaka, near Nelson (Middle Island), by bravely swimming out in the breakers with a rope to a rock from which they threw it on board the ship. Space fails to mention many other pleasing facts of a like kind. An eminent young Baptist Christian, Graham Tawhai, whose early death, a few years since, was widely deplored, showed what a grand character natural talent, deep conscientiousness, early conversion to the faith, and a good education could evolve from a pure-blooded Maori, the descendant of thirty generations of cannibal ancestors. An interesting little book, entitled "Our Maoris," by Lady Martin, narrates many touching incidents of genuine conversions to Christianity and of adherence to the faith, in the face of ridicule (to which all Maoris are keenly susceptible), boycotting, persecutions, and war. Old "Mohi," as he is called, Moses being his baptismal name, one of the converts mentioned in this book, is personally known to me. For more than thirty years he has been an honest and faithful servant, first to the Hon. William Swainson until his death, and latterly to Sir George Grey, and a consistent Christian. He speaks very little English, but travellers would, by the aid of an interpreter, find a talk with him very interesting, as he is one of the few remaining living links with the past ages of Maori heathendom.

No Polynesian race has shown a greater aptitude for civilization than the Maori. The wonderful vigour and tenacity of life of the Maori race induce me to believe that in time they will blend into the mixed nation called "young New Zealand," just as the Celts have blended into our Anglo-Saxon-Danish-Norman nation, and that the ranks of this young nation will furnish to the world orators, politicians, poets, merchants, and warriors equal in bravery, ability, and energy to any of those born of a purely white race.

CHAPTER IV.

AUCKLAND, THE NAPLES OF NEW ZEALAND.

Its position — Geographical and commercial importance — The Corinth of the South — The third city in Australasia by population — Sheltered harbour — Graving docks — Picturesque approach to the city — Public buildings — Grey collection of MSS. — City government — Newspapers — Developments of Art, Music, Science and Literature — Queen Street shopping — Telephones — Halls and theatres — Y. M. C. A. building — Ostrich farming — Acclimatized farmers — Wonderful growth of the city during past nine years.

As the limited space of this volume will not permit a detailed description of all the four chief cities of the colony, I have selected the place of my residence for nine years, many features of which find their counterparts in the other New Zealand towns.

The city of Auckland, situated in south latitude 36° 50′, and east longitude 174° 50′, is the metropolis of the Auckland Provincial District, the climatic characters of which have been described in chapter ii. This district extends from the North Cape southwards to Gisborne, and thence westwards along the 39th parallel of latitude to the Tuhua and Mokau rivers, and contains an area of seventeen million acres, or about one-fourth of the whole area of the colony. The population of this area has increased from 85,773 in 1878 to 135,627 in the year 1887. In the latter year there were 4286 births (including one case of triplets and 47 twin births), 833 marriages — the largest number in any province during 1887 — and 1501 deaths. The population of the City of Auckland has increased even more rapidly than that of the district. For by the last official census (1886), if we place Auckland in the same plane with the cities of Wellington, Christchurch, and Dunedin, by including her suburbs, "we are struck by the fact," says the *Evening Star*, "that her population amounts to 62,000, thus placing her in the position of the premier city of New Zealand, and the third city in Australasia." That is to say, Auckland comes after Sydney and before Adelaide in population. The order of the New Zealand chief cities then, according to the *Evening Star*, is—

Auckland	62,000
Dunedin	46,205
Christchurch	39,000
Wellington	27,000

A glance at our map of New Zealand will show that Auckland, situated on the inlet of the Hauraki Gulf, called Waitemata, is the northernmost, and therefore nearest to Australia (Sydney), to the Pacific Islands, and to America, of the four provincial capitals. This geographical advantage makes it the Liverpool of the colony, for it will become the great distributing port when once the North Island Trunk railway connects it with Wellington; and this advantage will be enhanced by the opening of the Panama Canal at some not too distant day, let us hope. The opening of the Canal would bring Auckland within twenty-eight days of Liverpool. It has been called the "Corinth of the South," because of its site on an isthmus between the east and west coast. By Onehunga, distant only six miles by rail, on the Manukau harbour, it commands the traffic to New Plymouth, Wellington, and Nelson southwards, and that to the Kaipara district northwards (see map No. 1). Froude so aptly terms it the Naples of Maoriland, and the "City of Delightful Views," that I have borrowed part of his first epithet for my chapter heading. Nowhere in the whole of New Zealand is the *dolce far niente* so alluring as in Auckland, where the *lazzaroni* are faintly represented by the Maoris, and Vesuvius by Rangitoto or Mount Eden—both, however, dead apologues of their living prototype. There is not in the

Southern Hemisphere a more extensive or lovely scene than the panorama of Auckland, its suburbs, its harbour, its islands, the coasts on both sides of the North Island, and the hill ranges on the south viewed on a clear sunny day from the summit of Mount Eden. Nor is there a more enjoyable drive anywhere in the colony than from Queen Street to St. John's College through Remuera, and back by Ellerslie and the Great South Road.

The founding of the settlement of Auckland took place in 1840, when Queen Street was a marshy valley, down which a sluggish stream found its way to the sea. It became the seat of government on the 19th of September, 1840, and retained that proud position until the Imperial authorities moved the capital to Wellington, as being more central, in 1865, during the premiership of my friend, Sir Frederick Aloysius Weld, K.C.M.G. The blow to Auckland was great for a time, but it rapidly emerged into prosperity again, the Thames goldfields bringing in population, capital and machinery. The clay hills abutting on the harbour were cut down, scarped, and terraced for residences. Queen Street developed into the main business artery of the city, and streets were cut out of the hills, at right angles to it, up to the foot of Upper Queen Street, where several side streets debouch in a fan-shape at the present day. The rapid growth of the population may be judged of when I state that in the period between the two last censuses—those of 1881 and 1886—Auckland increased by 62 per cent., while in the ten years between 1871 and 1881 Melbourne had only increased by 37 per cent., and Sydney by 64 per cent. Our photograph in the frontispiece is the only one obtainable on a small scale, showing the prettiest part of the view looking northeast from Mount Eden, the houses in the foreground being those in Symonds Street and Grafton Road. Besides the numerous islands (Great and Little Barrier, Tiri-tiri, Waiheke, Motutapu, Motuihi) that shelter the Waitemata harbour we have, in this view, the extinct crater island of Rangitoto (1), built up by

Nature from the bottom of the sea, whose summit is 902 feet above high-water mark, and the long, narrow peninsula called the North Shore, with its two extinct craters of the North Head (2) and Mount Victoria (3), 344 feet in height, which guard still more surely the tranquillity of the waters from the storms which rage outside. The breadth of the harbour, at its entrance, opposite the North Head (2) is two miles. The borough of Devonport (4) is about three miles from Queen Street Wharf. In the illustration, the small portion of the adjacent eastern suburb of Parnell (8) is visible, also Mechanics' Bay (7), the Supreme Court (6), where the assizes are held; the Government House (5), where the Governor lives when he visits Auckland, and a glimpse of the Albert Park (10) of fifteen acres, beautifully laid out, where a band plays in summer, and whence charming views are obtained of the harbour and islands. To the right of the foreground of our photograph, but only marked by the tops of two trees is the Domain, a lovely but "unkempt" park of 196 acres in area, dividing Auckland from the borough of Parnell, and containing the finest cricket ground in the colony, so large that fifteen matches have been played simultaneously upon it. Besides hundreds of acclimatized trees and shrubs from every part of the world, the Domain displays the native *flora* of this part of New Zealand. Otherwise the visitor will not find the native shrubs growing anywhere until he reaches Remuera, where there is a patch of the *Manuka* bush, the Ti-tree (*Leptospermum ericoides*). The *Kauri* is not to be found nearer than Waikomiti, eleven miles to the north-west. Queen Street lies to the left of our picture, outside its limits.

The boast of Auckland being its facilities and advantages as a port, let us state a few facts which amply justify this. Queen Street terminates at its harbour end in a fine wharf 1680 feet long, having a depth of 24 feet at low spring tides. Thus any of the largest steamers (5000 tons) that visit Auckland can lie, load, and unload at the city, instead of being eight miles away at a separate seaport, as in the case of

Christchurch (Lyttelton) and Dunedin (Port Chalmers). There are two other wharves, the railway wharf, 1000 feet long, and Hobson Street wharf, 500 feet. The old graving dock is near the latter. The new graving dock, called "Calliope Dock," after having been opened by the ironclad of that name in 1887, is the largest south of the line, being 550 feet long, 83 feet wide, and 33 feet deep on the sill. It cost the Auckland Harbour Board £150,000, and has greatly enhanced the value of the port as a place for the repair of the large vessels of her Majesty's navy and of large steamers. The "fairway" of the channel is so capacious that even at low water several large steamers, ships, and war ships can ride together at anchor without fear of colliding or of grounding. Sir W. F. D. Jervois, the late Governor, whose departure is still regretted, stated in his "Report on the Defences of New Zealand" that there is no harbour in Australasia more suitable for naval defence. In accordance, therefore, with his advice powerful batteries have been erected on Stark's Point, North Head, and Mount Victoria (North Shore), and at Parnell, on Point Resolution. "It is worthy of note," says Brett's Almanac, "that for the last fifty years not a single shipping accident of any great importance has occurred in this harbour." The port of Auckland is the last place of departure and the first of arrival of the American steamers which at present carry the monthly mail between New South Wales, New Zealand, and the United States, delivering them in eighteen to twenty days from Auckland to San Francisco, whence they are forwarded across to New York, reaching London generally in thirty-four or thirty-five days from New Zealand. The Direct Mail steamers of both lines visit Auckland as cargo requires; the Colonial Line run regularly; the Union Steamship Company of New Zealand have much traffic there; the Northern Steamship Company have their headquarters there; and, besides large ocean ships, there is a very large fleet of smaller ships trading to the Pacific Islands. During the year 1887 there entered the port 4085 vessels, of the aggregate tonnage of 355,608 tons; and 3850 vessels of 393,342 tons total cleared the port. The crews of inward and outward vessels numbered no less than 56,067 men. In tonnage Auckland exceeds that of any other New Zealand port.

Let us now imagine ourselves entering the harbour from the ocean. Having passed the island of Tiri-tiri, marked by its lighthouse, we obtain, as we coast along the north or ocean side of the North Shore peninsula, our first glimpse of the picturesque city across the low-lying land near Lake Takapuna. It reminds some travellers of the first distant sight of Constantinople and the Golden Horn, and gives the impression of a greater area than the city covers in reality. Two groups of hills with a valley between them are covered with houses, churches, public buildings, and gardens, as far as the eye can reach. In a few minutes we lose sight of Auckland, and do not regain it till we pass round the North Head on our right hand, leaving the curious round island-volcano, Rangitoto (the meaning of which is "bloody sky") on our left. We pass another island, Waiheke, away upon our left, before turning round the Head. The Bean Rock lighthouse now guides us to the channel. On the left we now have the wealthiest and most highly ornate suburb of Auckland, called Remuera (pronounced "Rem-u-air-a"), where the hospitable commercial magnates mostly live. Steaming further on, Parnell, with some lovely residences and gardens sloping to the water's edge, is passed on the left, Devonport and the big dock on the right, and then Auckland, "the Queen City of the Pacific," as my friend Mr. Consul Griffin enthusiastically styles her, is reached. The existence of the batteries, torpedoes, and submarine mines, which defend the harbour, is so carefully concealed, that an air of perfect peacefulness and security pervades the scene. On the Devonport side the broken-up irregular outline of the rocky beach, resembling that of Biarritz, and the luxuriant verdure of the hills and trees, serve to heighten the picturesqueness of the brightly painted and verandah-shaded houses. On the city side the handsome Hospital, standing on an eminence in its own capacious reserve, the church of the Holy Sepulchre, the red-and-white Supreme Court, and Government House arrest attention. Auckland, we see, is built on groups of clay and scoria hills, intersected by valleys all trending to the sea, and is backed up by volcanic peaks, like Honolulu, one of which, Mount Eden, is 644 feet high, and is now utilized as a reservoir. A lively district must this have been in ancient times, for Dr. Hochstetter counted no less than sixty-three distinct craters within a ten-mile radius! However, no fear is felt now of any revival of volcanic action, especially since the outburst of Tarawera, chronicled in chapter vii., has relieved the pent-up forces in that district, 120 miles distant. Looking up Queen Street, the main thoroughfare, we notice the Baptist Tabernacle, built for the son of Mr. C. H. Spurgeon, which holds the largest congregation in the city.

Farther up the harbour, on the Auckland side, the charming residences and gardens of Ponsonby extend along the cliffs. A singular-looking island, called the Watchman, stands in mid-channel, while to the right, on high ground, stand the North Shore suburbs, Northcote, Birkenhead, and Chelsea. If we wish, we can steam fifteen miles farther up the Waitemata, meeting delightful views at every turn. The abundant sunshine, illuminating an atmosphere absolutely free from smoke and fog, reflected from the sparkling blue waters of the harbour, and from the gaily painted houses, the numbers of pleasure-boats darting here and there, and the absence of all appearance of squalor and poverty—all combine to make one love Auckland at first sight.

Though not yet quite half a century old, Auckland is very well provided by the Government, by the city council, and by the munificence of its citizens, with public buildings. Sir George Grey, J. T. Mackelvie, Edward Costley, Dr. Campbell, and others, have literally bestowed the accumulations of their lifetimes in art, literature, science, and money upon their fellow-townsmen. The special pride of the educated Aucklanders is the Free Library and Art Gallery recently built in

Wellesley Street East, at the cost of £40,000, by the city, because it is enriched by the noble gift of Sir George Grey's priceless collection of old MSS., rare books, autographs, antiquities, and ethnological curiosities. Sir George Grey presented it to the city in 1887 as a free gift for ever. Having inspected these treasures myself at his beautiful home in the Kawau Island, seven years before the generous donor presented them to Auckland (where he now resides), I may be permitted to make an extract from my note on that occasion. "Some of the gems of the collection are the following: The MS. of the Four Gospels, tenth century, with a picture of St. Matthew; the MS. from which the first Bible was printed by Gutenberg in 1450; a copy of the first Dutch Bible, and of the first book printed at Delft in 1477; a *Missal ad usum* (2 vols.) written on vellum, fifteenth century, in Gothic hand, with music of the chants and sixty-three miniatures, each six inches square; a Petrarch on vellum, with miniature portraits of the finest kind; a rare copy of the first Malagasy Bible; a New Testament in the aboriginal language, now extinct, of New South Wales, and a dictionary of another extinct language, the Cree Indian; the original MS. of the secret treaty Cromwell made with the Low Countries; the signatures of Marie Antoinette and Louis XVI.; autograph letters of Cromwell, Queen Victoria, Prince Albert, Livingstone, Moffat, Florence Nightingale, Carlyle, Thiers, and of many other famous men and women."

If even the services rendered to New Zealand by her most distinguished statesman are in time forgotten, the Grey Library, unless destroyed by fire (which Heaven forefend!), will immortalize his name and fame.

The various philanthropic and religious institutions aided or constructed out of the magnificent legacy of nearly £100,000 left by Edward Costley, an Irish mechanic who amassed money in the early days of Auckland, and lived so frugally as to be called a miser, are seven in number—The Sailors' Rest and Home, the Kohimarama Training School, the Costley Industrial Home, the Parnell Orphan Asylum, the District Hospital, the Old People's Refuge, and the Free Library. The Sailors' Home, including the Sailors' Rest, founded by Bishop Cowie in 1881 " for the physical, moral, and spiritual benefit of the seafaring community," was built out of the Costley legacy of £12,150, and opened in 1887. An excellent site was given *gratis* by the Harbour Board, near the graving-dock at the foot of Albert Street. The cost, including furniture, was £4500, and an endowment income of £500 a year was still left. The building is a credit to the city, and harmonises well with the adjacent handsome Harbour Board offices. The Home accommodates fifty inmates, and is largely used by sailors, especially when ships of her Majesty's navy are in port. The mission work among sailors, oyster-men, fisher-boys, and longshoremen, in which ladies take a part, goes on earnestly and successfully. In no other New Zealand seaport is so much done as in Auckland to give them a hearty welcome and to keep them out of temptation and danger.

The Costley Industrial Home, under the wise management of Colonel Haultain and Captain Daldy, gives free board and education to poor boys of good character until they are of an age to be apprenticed to trades. After that it still supports them until they are able to earn their living. The endowment income from the Costley legacy accruing to the Free Library is set apart for the annual purchase of books. The other institutions enriched by Costley need no special description, except that of all the blessings showered upon his tomb none can be more fervent than that of the poor old men and women of the Refuges who are about to change their damp and unhealthy abode for a spacious and salubrious country residence.

The large and imposing building of the Young Men's Christian Association in Wellesley Street West is the centre of much aggressive Christian work. I believe the building cost £7500. The Rev. J. S. Hill was when I left its energetic president. On the top floor of this building is to be found the best-equipped gymnasium in the colony. The lecture-room will seat 700, and has the best acoustic properties of any room I ever spoke in. Under the auspices of the Young Men's Christian Association, Major Dane, Joseph Cook, the Earl of Aberdeen, and other distinguished visitors have addressed large audiences in the City Hall, which is the transformed Theatre Royal of old. In 1888 the aged but vigorous Pastor George Müller addressed crowded audiences here for several weeks. In 1887 the Countess of Aberdeen delivered an address to above 500 ladies of Auckland, including the large Young Women's Christian Association, which for love, pathos, and wisdom was almost the best I ever read. Should these pages ever meet the eye of the gracious lady who thus cheered the hearts of the toilers of her own sex in that distant city, let me assure her that there were hundreds who benefitted by its perusal in the papers who could not even get near the door of the building.

The Auckland Savings Bank is a handsome building in Queen Street, built out of the profits of the first twenty years of its existence. The architecture of the other banks is not equal to that of similar buildings in Christchurch or Dunedin. The Post and Telegraph Office in Shortland Street is scarcely large enough for the rapidly increasing mail business of the city. The Choral Hall in Symonds Street seats 900 persons, and is owned by the Choral Society, who enjoy the distinction of being the only society of the kind in Australasia who own their hall. The orchestra and chorus number about 150, and at least five subscription concerts of high-class music, conducted by Herr Schmitt, are given every season. Distinguished visitors are sometimes honoured by a special concert, and leave Auckland highly pleased with the excellence of the performances. The latest development, I learn by the newspapers, is a Ladies' Orchestra. It is in contemplation to build a town hall and also a Mackelvie Art Gallery. I have no space to mention all the other public buildings.

Auckland is governed by a mayor, elected annually by the whole body of ratepayers, as in the United

States, and by eighteen councillors, two for each of the nine wards into which the city is divided. The municipal debt is £424,000; the rateable value of real estate in 1887 was £367,822; and the rates amounted to two shillings in the pound. The endowments of the city from leaseholds amount to £10,000 per annum. A recent loan, negotiated in London, realized the highest price ever obtained for a colonial security in the London market. The city is fairly well drained and lighted; has an excellent water supply; fresh and salt water baths; is well paved; and well supplied with trams, omnibuses, and cabs. The electric lighting of a part of the city and of the wharves is being arranged for. The telephone system is a great success in Auckland, there being over 500 subscribers already to the Exchange. Telephones are a Government monopoly, but are very moderate in cost, namely, £10 for the first year and £8 a year afterwards; consequently doctors and chemists invariably use them, and business men have their residences and offices connected by telephone.

The newspapers of Auckland are well conducted and widely read. The *New Zealand Herald* is the only daily morning paper (2*d*.), and the *Auckland Evening Star* (1*d*.) is now the only evening paper; its certified circulation is 11,500 daily. By means of cablegrams and enterprising English and American correspondents the Auckland public are kept well informed of what is passing in the world. The great questions of policy, imperial or colonial, are often ably treated in the leading articles. I have often been thankful that there is no Whig or Tory in New Zealand, for there is no "Government by party;" nor is there that acerbity in the discussion of burning questions in the newspapers of New Zealand that one finds at home. The two parties in New Zealand consist of the "Ins" and the "Outs," and it is curious to see the same newspaper advocating the "Ins" at one time and the "Outs" at another.

In Art, Music, Science, and Literature Auckland is quite in the front rank of New Zealand cities. The annual Art Exhibition held by the Society of Arts is a most successful one, and elicits from visitors a large mead of praise. In chapter xi. I shall allude more particularly to the development of Art in Auckland. In Music, Auckland may, without conceit, claim to be the premier city in New Zealand, for it has now a Chair of Music in its University College, the first occupant of which, Professor Carl von Schmitt, Knight of two foreign orders, is a distinguished musician and most enthusiastic in his work. It is his intention to establish a Conservatoire of Music in Auckland which shall give a complete musical education to the student. His numerous compositions are of high merit, and should be known in England as well as in Germany. Except in that country there is no town of the size of Auckland that has so many students of promising talent in all branches of music. The genial climate, the colouring of the sky and sea, the surrounding scenery, and perhaps a certain dreamy languor belonging to the air creates artistic longings which find their expression in poetry, music, or painting.

Science is represented by the Auckland branch of the New Zealand Institute, by the small but well-arranged Museum, and by the Science Department of the University College. The membership of the Auckland Scientific Institute is about 300, and its meetings are held in the winter in the lecture-room of the Museum, to the painstaking, learned, and courteous Director of which, Mr. Cheeseman, I must here express my obligations for much kind assistance in scientific matters. A Field Naturalists' club and a Microscopical club have arisen from among the members of the Institute.

In literature the Athenæum Society takes the lead and is doing good work. Its meetings are held in the winter in the Arcade building, and the subjects discussed range over a wide area. There are numerous literary societies in connection with the various denominations, and frequent popular scientific and literary lectures are delivered in the rainy season.

There is only one theatre at present in Auckland, Abbott's Opera House, in which operas, dramas, and other entertainments are given with very little intermission all the year round. The city is well off for amusements both outdoor and indoor. The grounds of Government House are open for lawn tennis, and there are several other clubs for that amusement (see chapter xi.).

Cycling, rinking, bowling, yachting, canoeing, boating and fishing are the chief outdoor amusements. No maritime city is better off for excursions by sea than Auckland. The delightful health resort called Waiwera, twenty-six miles north-east of Auckland, the Kawau Island (until lately Sir George Grey's home) Motutapu, where red deer may be shot by invited guests, Coromandel, the Thames, and other places within easy reach are greatly resorted to on holidays. Three miles out from the city, southwards, are the Athletic Clubs' Recreation Grounds, where the international, intercolonial, and other football matches are contested, always attended by thousands of spectators.

Apropos of matches, hundreds of boys manage somehow by acrobatic feats on trees and posts to get a free sight of some of these, to the disgust of the managers of the Athletic Recreation Grounds. But an incident which was an exception to the proverbial love of Aucklanders for a "free show" is narrated of the visit of "Professor" Baldwin, the aeronaut and parachutist, who performed his ascent and descent in Auckland in the summer of 1889. Thousands of sightseers assembled on Mounts Eden and Hobson, where they had an excellent view of the performance without payment. But during the following week, Baldwin's agent was inundated with letters containing stamps for the amount of the gate-money—a circumstance which deserves chronicling, as being honourable to Auckland citizens. It has become the usual thing for the mayor to order a public half-holiday when a football or cricket match comes off.

A new attraction has been lately added to Auckland, in the shape of an ostrich farm. At Welford Park, about twenty-two miles ride from the city, Mr. Laurence Nathan has started this affair at a great expense, which I hope he will recoup. It is one of the most interesting sights in the world to see the young ostriches, hatched by an incubator, issue from the egg as large as Cochin China fowls, and immediately start devouring voraciously the chopped lucerne which is provided for them. Each male bird has two hen birds in his enclosure and has to be approached with great caution. I am reminded of an amusing exercise a Balclutha schoolboy wrote upon the ostrich, while object lessons on cork and on water were floating in his mind.

"Dear Sir, I take up my pen to let you know what I know about an ostrich. An ostrich is the biggest bird in the world. It is opaque and boyant, and lives in the desert of araba and africa, it is of the camel class because it has a long neck. An ostrich has three feathers, which the Prince of Wales says is 'I serve.' It has three states sold liquid and gas. They have two toes on each foot. An ostrich lays ten eggs at a time, and the mail bird helps the hot sand to catch them. They are very fast runners and they would never manage to catch them if the horses did not run very fast in a zig-zag style like a Z. It pays well if you can catch a good lot of birds, and the Hawklanders are trying to rear ostriches in that province, because they can't grow oats there, and the Maories eat their sheep."

Sunday is decorously observed, now that Sunday closure of the hotels, except to *bonâ-fide* travellers, is strictly enforced by the licensing committees. Not being a total abstainer I am the more free to say that a great change for the better in the state of the streets at night and on Sundays has resulted from the week-day closing at 10 P.M. and the Sunday closing. Taking the colony as a whole, the cause of teetotalism is gaining ground. This is largely owing to the eloquence, energy, and organising power of my friend Sir William Fox, K.C.M.G., who is president of the United Kingdom Alliance for New Zealand.

Auckland is the centre of the educational system of the Province, comprising free Primary Schools, at which

21,000 children were attending in 1887, secondary schools, the High Schools, Auckland College and Grammar School, and others, and the Auckland University College, founded in 1883, which has proved very successful. An account of these institutions is reserved for the section Education in chapter ix.

The city of Auckland is well provided with table luxuries at moderate prices. Not only are there thirty-three kinds of edible native fishes in the sea, the principal of which in the North are schnapper, kahawai, mullet, flounder, garfish, and cod; also small oysters of delicious flavour, crabs, lobsters, and crayfish, but California salmon comes in, preserved in ice, by the mail steamers; turbot and sole from England, and turtle from the South Pacific.

The Acclimatization Society of Auckland has done noble work in importing game and song-birds, but all its preserving efforts to naturalise the trout and salmon-trout in the province have failed. The warmth of the climate, the absence of both ground-food and flies similar to those of Britain, and the voracity of the eels and crayfish (*Koura*), which devour the young fry, are thought to be the causes of this failure. In the Wellington district, along the Wairarapa valley, however, I understand that the trout are thriving. The license fees exacted by the Government for the privilege of shooting during the "open season" are wisely transferred to the exchequer of these Societies—of which there is one in each Province—who are thus enabled (being also assisted by subscriptions) to carry on their good work. In the country districts, hares, pheasants, the partridge, quail, snipe, plover, teal, and red grouse afford excellent sport, a fact which should be noted by my sporting readers. Whitebait is found in profusion in the Waikato river. In the lakes, rivers, and streams of the Middle Island acclimatization has been so successful that the angler can now catch trout of 15 or 20 lbs., and salmon of 30 lbs. weight in the Lakes of Otago, while perch, tench and carp, are also thriving in suitable places. When first colonized the lakes and rivers of New Zealand only produced eels, crayfish, and a few salmonoid fishes of little value. Unfortunately for the country, however, the sparrows, blackbirds, (Australian) minahs, rats, and rabbits have acclimatized only too well! Stoats and weasels are now being imported to keep down the rabbits, but it is feared that the former will vary their rabbits' blood diet with the vital fluid of fowls and ducks.

Much more—in fact, an interesting little book—might be written about Auckland, but I must refrain. Enough has been described to convey to the English reader the great vigour, activity, resources, and advanced position of this flourishing city. I will conclude by simply enumerating some of the improvements and additions to the city made since the beginning of 1880, and included within the nine years of my residence. In some of these I was privileged to take a share:—The harbour greatly improved by the lengthening of Queen's Wharf; the construction of two new wharves; the importation of a powerful steam dredge, and the addition of several new "tees;" a complete system of harbour defences constructed; a submarine cable laid to Tiri-tiri; the immense Calliope Dock opened; the New Zealand Sugar Company's great refinery, wharf, and workmen's village built at Chelsea; near the water-front the Sailors' Home, Harbour Offices, Palmerston Buildings, railway station, and Firth's Eight Hours' Mill, lit up by electricity; in the city the Free Library and Art Gallery, Abbott's Opera House; Young Men's Christian Association Building, Baptist Tabernacle, St. Sepulchre's and St. Benedict's churches, eight large hotels, the Victoria Arcade, Australian Mutual Provident Building; New Savings Bank Building; Turkish baths, Auckland College and Grammar School, Boys' Training Home; new wing to Lunatic Asylum, two new reservoirs, *Star* printing-offices, many large warehouses, shops, and private residences. Tram-cars have been introduced; the side walks have been asphalted under the reign of Mayor Waddel, and the following societies and clubs established: the Benevolent Society,

Christian Evidence Society, Sailors' Rest, Boys' Rest, Athenæum, Field Naturalists' Club, Sketching Club, Amateur Photographic Club, Amateur Opera Club, and others. " If a more general knowledge," says Mr. Consul Griffin, of the United States, " prevailed abroad in regard to the genial climate of Auckland, I am sure that a large migration hitherward would be the result; and I have not the slightest hesitation in saying that, as a site for extensive commerce, she stands the Peerless Queen of the Pacific."

CHAPTER V.

THE MINERAL SPRINGS OF NEW ZEALAND.

New Zealand first, Continent second, California third as to importance of their mineral springs—Seventy-three already analyzed—Arranged in five classes—Three well-established spas: Waiwera, Te Aroha, Rotorua—The new town of Rotorua—Arrangements for visitors—Mineral springs and baths described—Priest's Bath—Madame Rachel—Blue Bath—Pain-killer—Lake House baths—Oil bath—Wonders of Tikitere—Te Kute—Hot waterfall—Diseases successfully treated by these baths—Leprosy probably curable by them—The season for Rotorua—Advice to invalids—"Business first, pleasure afterwards"—Diet, &c.

No inhabited country in the world possesses mineral waters in greater number, variety, and medicinal value than New Zealand. Writing with a pretty extensive experience of such springs in three quarters of the globe, I am of opinion that New Zealand ranks first as regards these advantages; next in value comes the central part of the continent of Europe; and thirdly, California. In some places in New Zealand thermal springs are the sole remains of past subterranean energy, while in others, as at White Island (Bay of Plenty), they exist side by side with tremendously active volcanic forces. With a few exceptions, the hot springs are confined to those districts of the North Island where volcanic forces have been active during the latest Tertiary period; but some are found to issue from the Upper Mesozoic rocks in localities such as the East Cape, where the source of heat can only be attributed to the chemical decomposition of bitumen and bituminous shales, and of sulphides. Three warm springs (90° to 104°) have been found also in Palæozoic rock formation in the Middle Island.

During the last few years travellers and invalids from different parts of the world have been attracted to these springs in increasing numbers, so that recently the New Zealand Government have officially recognized their benefit to the colony by establishing in the centre of the Hot Lake district a sanitorium with a competent medical officer at the head of it. Rotorua having been thus favoured, Te Aroha is claiming a similar recognition, and will no doubt soon obtain it. This chapter is the first attempt yet made by a medical man to group together *all* the well-proved mineral springs of New Zealand, and *to contrast or compare* them with those of Europe, in such a way as to inform the general reader, without confusing him by chemical technicalities, and the medical reader without useless vagueness of statement as to their nature and value. As no less than seventy-three of these springs have been already analyzed, it is important that English medical men who recommend invalids to go to New Zealand should have some definite information of this kind. The excellent pamphlets of Drs. T. Hope Lewis and Ginders are not circulated at Home, nor are they sufficiently elaborate to base many recommendations upon.

Before giving a detailed account of the most important groups of these springs in the order of medicinal value, I must remind readers that, first, the constituents of a thermal spring do *not remain constantly uniform,* but *vary within slight limits;* and, second, that the temperatures of all thermal springs vary considerably at times, according to the direction of the wind, and are influenced by certain subterranean changes. Both these facts show the absolute necessity for frequent as well as accurate observations and analyses of each mineral water.

New Zealand contains hot sulphur springs of a kind not found elsewhere, except in the Yellowstone Park in Wyoming, U.S., and silicious geysers not equalled anywhere in the world. It also has mineral waters of equal strength and of similar constituents to those of Vichy, Ems, Fachingen, Bilin, Aix-la-Chapelle, Pyrmont in Waldeck, Eaux Chaudes (Basses Pyrénées), Royat (Auvergne), Harrogate, and Strathpeffer in

Scotland. This fact alone should be an inducement to many sufferers from chronic ailments (gout, rheumatism, gravel, skin diseases, syphilis, &c.), who remain still uncured after trial of the spas in Europe to visit the colony and try what its springs will do for them. For I am sure that in this grand exhilarating climate the mineral waters best suited to his case will be found to do him more good than they would on the continent of Europe.

Commencing with the feebler spring most resembling that European spa which had best suited him, the invalid will go on to one more powerful until he completes the course of treatment, about which he will find valuable suggestions in this chapter. He will, of course, consult the resident medical man wherever there is one, at these thermal resorts. There are fewer potable mineral waters in New Zealand than in Europe, because of the widely pervading sulphides in their composition, and the more recent character of the strata through which they emerge. From the analyses made in the colonial laboratory at Wellington by Mr. Skey and Sir James Hector, the mineral waters of New Zealand have been classified into the following five groups:—

1. Saline, containing chiefly chloride of sodium (common salt), for example, the Crow's Nest spring, Taupo; the Onetapu spring, Mount Ruapehu.

2. Alkaline, containing carbonates and bi-carbonates of soda and potash, such as Waiwera, Puriri, Whangape.

3. Alkaline-silicious, containing much silicic acid, but changing rapidly on exposure to the air, and becoming alkaline, such as the geysers at Whakarewarewa, Kuirau, Whangapipiro (Rotorua).

4. Hepatic or sulphurous, the prominent character of which is the presence of sulphuretted hydrogen and sulphurous acid, such as Te Kute (Rotorua), and Otumahike (Taupo).

5. Acidic, in which there is an excess of mineral acids, such as hydrochloric and sulphuric acids. Examples of these are found at Ohaeawai (Bay of Islands) and Sulphur Bay, Lake Rotorua.

Iodine springs. It seems that out of the seventy-three mineral springs analysed up to 1886, only three contain iodine in appreciable quantities. In the Taupo district Tarawera Spring contains 0·7 of a grain per gallon, and Parkes's Spring contains one grain per gallon; in the province of Wellington the cold spring of Pahua contains a little more than two grains per gallon. The Maoris distinguish the various forms of the hot springs as they appear on the surface by the terms *puia*, applied to all geysers; *nyawha* to a hot steaming spring; and *waiariki* to any pool of hot water or mud suitable for bathing.

The principal chalybeate springs are those of Kamo, Akiteo No. 2 (Wellington), Amberley (Canterbury), and Chain Hills near Dunedin (Otago).

Before describing the composition and uses of the mineral waters at our three principal spas—Waiwera, Te Aroha, and Rotorua—I will briefly describe a few isolated springs of peculiar properties which deserve notice.

1. At Ohaeawai, near a small lake seventeen miles inland from the Bay of Islands (see map), is a group of springs which deposit sulphur, alum, and silica on cooling. The temperatures vary from 60° to 116° F., and there is along with the hot water a remarkable escape of mercurial vapours, which deposit cinnabar and metallic mercury. These springs are used as baths by the Maoris, and by a few Europeans, for diseases of the skin, and chronic rheumatism of syphilitic origin. I believe that Ohaeawai is unique in these characteristics.

2. Puriri, ten miles from Grahamstown (Thames), near Auckland, is a cold effervescent spring, having valuable properties from the presence of a large percentage of alkaline carbonates. It is bottled both as still and aërated soda-water, and has a reputation as an aperient and a preventive of gravel and gout. It would prove useful in "acid" dyspepsia. The famous Napa soda-water of California resembles this Puriri water when bottled. Its chief constituents, estimated in grains per gallon, are: chloride of sodium 22, sulphate of potash 5, bi-carbonates of lime 28·5, of magnesia 25·6, of soda 452·3 grains.

3. Onetapu Desert Spring, situated at the sources of the Waikato and Wangaehu rivers, in the vicinity of the still active volcano Ngauruhoe (7481 feet), and issuing from the base of the Monarch of the North Island, Ruapehu (8878 feet), is so strongly charged with sulphates of iron and alumina (58 grains per pint) as to taint the water of the river Wangaehu along its whole course to the sea, a distance of seventy miles.

4. The cold spring of Pahua, in the province of Wellington, deserves mention on account of its iodine and of the large amount of its solid constituents, amounting to 1474 grains in the gallon. The waters of this spring, though excessively salt in taste, will, in moderate doses, prove curative in chronic abscesses, swollen lymphatic glands, and other strumous or scrofulous affections. The aperient action will be limited and controlled by the lime salts (126 grains), while children suffering from rickets and deformities of the joints will here find supplied to their blood plasma the elements in which it is deficient.

5. The Hanmer Plain Springs at Amuri, in the Canterbury district of the Middle Island, are alkaline, having temperatures ranging from 90° to 104°, with a strong escape of sulphuretted hydrogen. They are suitable baths for cases of rheumatism and diseases of the skin. Being the only hot springs in the Middle Island, they deserve the special attention of those sufferers in the south of New Zealand to whom the journey to the Hot Lakes of the North Island would be too painful or too costly.

The established spas of New Zealand, where proper hotel and bathing accommodation is provided for visitors, consist of three, which I will now describe in some detail: Waiwera, Te Aroha, and Rotorua.

1. Waiwera. This charming health resort, situated twenty-six miles north of Auckland, on the east coast, opposite the Kawau Island, consists of a large hotel built by Mr. Robert Graham about twenty years since at the mouth of the Waiwera river, and of an ever-flowing hot alkaline spring known to the natives from the

earliest times. Mr. Graham laid out the estate on which the hotel is built with a taste, liberality of expenditure, and foresight always characteristic of him. All visitors from abroad are delighted with the scenery, the baths, the various recreations, and the *table d'hôte* at Waiwera. To visit Auckland and leave it without seeing Waiwera, as many travellers do, is as great an omission as to visit Naples without seeing Capri, or Lisbon without spending a day at Cintra. A steamer leaves Auckland twice a week for Waiwera (four hours), and three times a week a coach leaves Devonport on the North Shore for the same place, doing the trip in about six hours. Until the jetty is built at Waiwera an invalid should go there by coach, but all who can endure a little inconvenience in the primitive mode of disembarkation should go by steamer. For the exquisite view of the little bay of Waiwera as the steamer *Rose Casey* rounds the last promontory and approaches the shore cannot be surpassed, particularly at sunset, for beautiful colouring, charm of contour, and rich foliage. The visitors receive on landing a cordial welcome from Miss Graham, the buxom hostess, who has the Queen's faculty of never forgetting the faces of those she has once met. A stranger is made to feel quickly at home, and I can say from experience that there is no resort anywhere near Auckland so refreshing and so restful to the jaded nerves of the overwrought merchant or professional man as this popular sanitorium. Boating, fishing, sea bathing, fern and flower gathering, picnics up the river, rides, walks, and lawn tennis, besides the amusement of bathing several times a day in the springs, enable a week or two to be passed most agreeably at Waiwera. In summer the richly stocked gardens yield the largest and longest supplies of strawberries that are supplied to any hotel in the colony. The curious plants, trees, and shrubs naturalized there by Mr. Graham are evidences of the mildness of the climate and richness of the soil. Every evening some social entertainment is promoted by Miss Graham, so that even in wet weather one can amuse oneself at Waiwera. Of all the visitors whom I met on my frequent visits there, the Australians were the most enthusiastic in their praises of this lovely spot, probably because they lack any such cool summer resort in their own country, for even the delicious air of the Blue Mountains, near Sydney, and the Alpine atmosphere of Mount Macedon in Victoria, are permeated all day by the rays of a burning sun, which compel invalids to keep indoors during the noonday hours. But at Waiwera, fanned by the never-failing sea breezes, the most delicate visitor on the hottest day in summer may sit in comfort under the trees on the hillside, or in one of the numerous arbours which line the long walk to the baths in perfectly "cool, translucent shade." So inspiring are the lovely scenes around Waiwera that even prosaic people rush into rhyme—people who never committed poetry before! Need I say that this is the favourite place for newly married Aucklanders to spend their honeymoon? Yet, though "far from the busy hum of men," the telegraph and the daily mail keep Waiwera in touch of the outside world. Though the summer is considered *the* season, Waiwera affords a mild and well-sheltered winter residence.

I must now describe the mineral waters. The temperature of the spring as it issues from the sand near high-water mark is 110°, and that of the enclosed swimming bath is generally 100°. At the end of a fagging day in town or of a very active day at Waiwera, a swim in this bath is a most luxurious sensation. In rheumatism, bronchitis, and bronchial catarrh these baths are useful, aided by the soothing effect of the sea air and the sheltered warmth of the place. Used as a drinking spring the Waiwera water is not disagreeable, resembling diluted Wiesbaden water. Being a light saline aperient and excitant of the kidneys, it may be used as a preventive of calculus, and to relieve acidity of the stomach. The principal mineral salts, in grains per gallon, are as follows: Chloride of sodium 116, bi-carbonate of soda

87, carbonate of lime 10, silica 2, bi-carbonates of magnesia 0·95, and of iron 0·68, sulphate of soda 0·383. The water also contains small amounts of free carbonic acid and sulphuretted hydrogen gases. On the whole the waters are less energetic than those of Te Aroha. But even if the spring were to cease flowing the manifold attractions of Waiwera would be but imperceptibly diminished.

2. Te Aroha, 126 miles south-east from Auckland, and now the terminus of a railway which strikes off from the main Waikato line at Frankton junction, is rising into importance as a thermal resort. Nestling at the side of a spur from the great Te Aroha mountain (3000 feet), one of the highest of the Upper Thames range, and having the river Waihou meandering at its foot, Te Aroha presents some of the picturesque features of a Swiss Alpine town. There are two routes from Auckland, one by steamer to Grahamstown, Thames river, eight hours; thence by coach the following day to Te Aroha, six hours; the other by rail in eight hours. Approaching Te Aroha by rail from the town of Morrinsville, and crossing the plains so well drained and cultivated by the Patetere Land Company, the scene reminded me of the view of Santa Barbara, California, as it lies at the base of the Coast Range. Te Aroha has now a resident population, inclusive of the mining township, three miles south, of 1000. Hundreds of visitors in the summer season (November to March) find capital accommodation, suited to slender as well as large means, in the four hotels and three boarding houses of the town. There are three places of worship (all such are called "churches" in the colonies); a Public Hall, Free Library, boating establishment, the usual postal, telegraph, and banking offices; and, now, well-fitted bathing arrangements. Horses for riding and driving are good, moderate in hire, and abundant. A favourite excursion, to the lovely glen of Waiorongomai, where the exquisite ferns, tree-ferns, creepers, forest trees, and the waterfalls are a never-failing joy to the visitor, and are not spoiled by the working of the mines

above the hills. Another trip, very enjoyable to the active man or woman with sound lungs, is up to the summit of the Te Aroha mountain, by an easy track, whence a grand panorama, extending for 100 miles in every direction, is obtained. Besides all the islands in the Bay of Plenty (see map), including White Island, the Sulphur Volcano, one can see on a clear day the giant volcanoes Mount Ruapehu, and Mount Tongariro, described in chapter vii. To those unable to make the complete ascent, a lower spur of the mountain, called "Bald Hill," affords a plateau whence the invalid may enjoy both a bracing air and a pleasing view. As a change from Waiwera, Te Aroha, while more bracing, is still calmative and tranquillizing to highly nervous persons.

Eighteen springs, of which fifteen are hot, issue from the hillside overshadowing the town. All except two, Nos. 16 and 17 in the official list, published in Dr. Alfred Wright's "Medical Guide to Te Aroha," are alkaline, being heavily charged with bi-carbonate of soda; and all the eighteen contain free carbonic acid gas in large quantities. Sir James Hector compares these springs to the waters of Vichy (France), Bilin (Bohemia), and Ems (Nassau).

The analyses of the three principal springs, the temperatures of which, at their sources, range from 105° to 119° F., are given by Mr. J. A. Pond (1885), Colonial Analyst for Auckland district, as follows, expressed in grains per gallon.

	No. I. Bath.	No. II. Bath.	Cold Drinking Spring.	
Bi-carbonate of soda	728·73	698·513	682·123	
Carbonate of ammonia	3·55	·112	·980	
Carbonate of iron	·04	·063	·042	In addition to these constituents, there were "heavy traces" of carbonate of lithia, and of sulphuretted hydrogen. "The free carbonic acid gas was not estimated."
Chloride of sodium	73·514	72·072	77·748	
Phosphate of soda	2·063	2·203	1·696	
Phosphate of alumina	·143	·023	·476	
Sulphate of soda	27·546	28·056	25·438	
,, potash	10·293	9·800	10·794	
,, lime	2·989	2·228	2·989	
,, magnesia	·378	·336	·662	
Silica	8·568	8·778	8·778	
Total solid matter	857·814	822·184	801·702	

A later analysis, given by Sir James Hector on the 4th of January, 1887, which is too long and elaborate to quote here, exhibits a decrease in the amount of mineral constituents, but no decrease in the gases nor in the temperatures, thus illustrating the truth of the remark made (p. 75) upon the variations of thermal springs.

Since 1884, an area of twenty acres, including all the eighteen springs, has been enclosed, and laid out as a garden, with walks, trees, lawns, seats, and bath-houses, (public and private), by the newly constituted Domain Board, but at the expense of the Government. The rapidly increasing popularity of the baths is shown by the fact that during 1886 thirty thousand bath tickets were issued. The baths have cured many cases of rheumatism, sciatica, lumbago, paralysis of a rheumatic or syphilitic nature, eczema, insomnia, Bright's disease, amenorrhœa, ophthalmia tarsi, and rheumatic-gouty contraction of the joints. Certain cases of asthma and chronic bronchitis have been benefitted by those baths that are richest in the evolution of sulphuretted hydrogen. Still further clinical experience of these springs will doubtless bring more diseases under their control. The cold drinking spring (No. 3) is excellent as a diuretic for gouty and obese persons with inactive livers. In healthy persons, as I found experimentally, it produces a vigorous action of the kidneys, and slight diarrhœa. This spring is so much in demand as a natural soda-water that a company has been formed to buy the right of bottling it at its source, and it is now largely used in the colony.

3. Rotorua. A thoroughly inland alpine resort, at an elevation of a thousand feet above sea level, forms a striking contrast to seaside places like Waiwera, and to the inland health resorts such as Te Aroha, which is only 130 feet above the sea. Rotorua is the highest place in New Zealand possessing thermal springs, and can boast of the most powerful hot sulphur baths in the southern hemisphere. Lake Rotorua (see map 3), situated on a mountainous plateau about forty miles from the Bay of Plenty, is the largest lake but one

(Taupo) in the North Island, being six miles across, and about twenty miles in circumference. The lake is shallow, having an average depth of between twenty and thirty feet, and is considered by Dr. Hochstetter to have been formed by the subsidence of part of the ground forming the plateau, not to have been a volcanic crater. A conical hill 400 feet high, in the centre of the lake, forms the island called Mokoia. Of the mountains encircling the lake, Mount Ngongotaha (see chapter iii. for the pronunciation) towers up to a height of 2554 feet. I am thus particular in giving the elevation of this the highest mountain in the neighbourhood because the whole Rotorua district is liable to changes by upheaval and subsidence. Earthquakes are frequent; and new hot springs gush out from the ground now and then, making great holes, and altering the water level in the lake, the height of which above the sea is usually 961 feet. The Government of New Zealand, following the wise example of the United States, have preserved the Rotorua district from land speculators by a special Act of Parliament, entitled "The Thermal Springs District Act, 1881." By this Act a large area of the Hot Lake country, containing all the important springs, is reserved for the Government to deal with. The Rotorua township of 600 acres was laid out on the southern shore of Rotorua close by the ancient Maori village of Ohinemutu, in square blocks. After making liberal provision for the hospital, bath-pavilion, church, school, cemetery, post-office, &c., all the allotments were put up to auction for lease of ninety-nine years for the Crown. All the "mineral waters, hot springs, and streams" are by this Act "vested in the Crown." The allotments were promptly bought up, and the town of Rotorua has steadily grown ever since, in spite of financial depression, and the large falling-off of visitors since the destruction of the terraces of Rotomahana in 1886. The real and permanent merit of the hot sulphur springs will always keep Rotorua going. There are already three excellent hotels and two or three boarding houses. An able medical man has been appointed as resident officer of the "Sanatorium," as the hospital and bath-pavilion together are termed. A pure supply of drinking water is obtained from the Puarenga stream.

The new town of Rotorua is reached by two routes from Auckland. The most direct route is by rail to Oxford, 133 miles; next morning by coach from Oxford to Rotorua, thirty-four miles. In less than two years the railway will be continued right through to Rotorua. The other route is by sea from Auckland to Tauranga on the Bay of Plenty, 135 miles, and thence by coach early next morning *viâ* the Gorge Road, through a magnificent forest, for eighteen miles, and open country for twenty-four miles, to the township. Visitors from Wellington and the south generally take rail or steamer to Napier, whence they take coach to Taupo, ninety-six miles, spending one night on the way; from Taupo they proceed to Rotorua, fifty-six miles, arriving on the evening of the third day. This is a romantic and varied journey, but only healthy and robust persons should take this route. The present arrangements of the journey *viâ* Oxford make it as easy for invalids as the nature of the country traversed can admit of.

In this chapter I shall confine myself to the mineral springs and the climate, reserving for chapter vi. the description of the Geysers, Terraces, and other wonders as I saw them before the eruption of Tarawera. The information given in the "Medical Guide to Rotorua," by T. Hope Lewis, Esq., M.R.C.S., the first resident medical superintendent, and in the pamphlet by his successor, Dr. A. Ginders, supplemented by my own personal knowledge, and the accounts of numerous patients "at first hand," has enabled me to set before my readers the first succinct, complete, and systematized account of these famous sulphur springs that has yet appeared. The medical profession throughout Australasia hope that each resident medical officer will keep careful records of all cases under thermal treatment, so as to *precisionize*, as years roll on, our knowledge of the specific qualities of each spring. Invalids " of weak chest "—that is, those suffering from consumption, phthisical pneumonia, or pleurisy—patients, in a word, who ought never to take a hot mineral bath—should not visit Rotorua, even in "the season"—from October till April. For they will not be able to breathe such rarefied air as one has at Davos or St. Moritz, the elevation not being great enough, and the summer weather being showery and stormy. From May till September, comprising "autumn" and winter, the rain keeps delicate people indoors, except during an "Indian summer" of about four weeks usually, when the clear sunny days and fine frosty nights form agreeable weather. On these nights the sight of the Southern Cross, the Argonaut, and the other southern constellations, and occasionally, though rarely, the Aurora Australis, is a grand spectacle. The elevation of the plateau is sufficiently great to relieve cases of pure asthma, bronchitic asthma, and a few cases of bronchitis contracted in smoky cities or at seaports. At Rotorua a south-west wind in the morning, and a north-east breeze in the afternoon (just what the tourist desires for a sail to Mokoia and back) indicate settled weather. Sometimes a north-easter blows for three days, with squalls of rain, but is followed by the south-west wind, with its characteristically clear sunshiny weather. It would be correct to say that, all over the North Island, a south wind brings with it clear weather and sensation of reinvigoration; and the same is true of that part of Climatic Zone No. II. which lies in the Middle Island.

There are in Rotorua township and its outlying settlements of Whakarewarewa, Te Koutu, Arikikapakapa, and Tikitere, examples of four out of the five classes into which New Zealand waters are divided (p. 76). I shall give the full analyses of the eight most important springs out of twenty that have been made by Mr. F. C. Skey, *partly on the spot* (this is important) and partly in Wellington. In the estimation of the volume of gases contained in the springs at their source, it is necessary to analyze them, at least roughly, near their sources. A careful though brief description, without analysis, of nine less important springs is added, and their special qualities in the treatment of disease. For still more precise directions to the invalids than I here give, readers are referred to the two useful works, by Drs. T. H. Lewis and **Ginders**, mentioned above, p. 75. The numbering of the springs described is that of Dr. Lewis's book, and not that of Sir James Hector's "Handbook of New Zealand" (Edinburgh, 1886).

In Rotorua Township.

1. The Priest's Bath (Class V., Acidic) so called from Father Mahony, of Tauranga, a Roman Catholic priest, who was the first white man to discover and be cured by its healing virtues. Its native name is Te Pupunitanga. It is aluminous and strongly acid. Temperature 98° to 106°, averaging 99° in the swimming bath.

ANALYSIS OF THE PRIEST'S BATH.
(In grains per gallon.)

Sulphate of soda	19·24	
,, ,, alumina	21·67	
,, ,, lime	7·41	Traces of sulphate of
,, ,, magnesia	3·03	potash were observed.
,, ,, iron	1·24	
Sulphuric acid	22·12	
Hydrochloric acid	3·65	
Silica	18·41	
Total solids	96·77 grains per gallon.	
Sulphuretted hydrogen	2·98	
Carbonic acid gas	2·16	

The first visible effect of a swim in this bath is a reddening of the skin, which, in sensitive persons, is followed by itching. Next ensues a stimulation of the liver, as shown by the flow of the bile, making an improvement in the *excreta* in patients suffering from sluggish liver and chronic jaundice. No very plethoric person, nor one suffering from organic disease of the heart or of the great arteries (such as aneurism), should bathe in this spring. The following complaints and diseases have been successfully treated by the Priest's Bath:—gout, dyspepsia, sciatica, chronic rheumatism, eczema (as a change from the baths), parasitic skin diseases, such as scabies and chloasma, obesity, inactive liver, abdominal congestion (piles, &c.), cold feet, anæmia, chlorosis, and sexual impotence. As a rule the patient is cured by a course of thirty-six baths taken during a period of three weeks, intervals to be prescribed by the medical superintendent. In cases of obesity combined with piles, the course should begin with the Priest's Bath for three days, followed by three days of some alkaline bath; then two days' rest, again the Priest's Bath for three days, and so on, for a period of four to six weeks, by the end of which the patient is completely restored to health.

In some of its effects this spring resembles those of **Eaux Bonnes** and of Eaux Chaudes in the **Basses Pyrenees**. But the Priest's Bath excels these famous springs by the superior heat of its source, and by its richness in mineral constituents, containing three times the amount of those in Eaux Bonnes, and five times the quantity of those in Eaux Chaudes.

2. Madame Rachel's Spring, or **Whangapipiro**, (Class III., Alkaline-silicious). Temperature 174° F. at its source. Reaction alkaline.

ANALYSIS OF MADAME RACHEL'S BATH.
(In grains per gallon.)

Chloride of sodium	69·43
,, ,, potassium	3·41
,, ,, lithium, traces	
Sulphate of soda	11·80
Silicate of soda	18·21
,, lime	4·24
,, magnesia	1·09
Iron and alumina oxides	2·41
Silica	5·87
	116·46
Carbonic acid gas	3·79

The exquisite softness of this water and the characteristic power which all the alkaline-silicious waters of Rotorua possess of imparting a gloss to the skin have led to its fanciful name. A swim in this bath gives the most luxurious sensation to the bather, and certainly improves the complexion, by some unexplained solvent action upon the epidermis. In gout, psoriasis, and ecthyma, and in the carbunculous tendency, this bath is most useful. Internally the water is drunk in cases of rheumatism, gout, and dyspepsia, with the beneficial effect of increasing the elimination of urea and uric acid. Silica and the silicates in combination probably exercise a similar action to that of lithia, an ingredient which gives Royat Spa in Auvergne the value it possesses in curing gout. The Maoris have for many years known the virtues of silicious mud used as a dressing in chronic and indolent ulcers.

3. The Blue Bath, or Chamæleon Spring—Oruawhata (Class I., Saline), resembles "Madame Rachel," but is more saline than silicious, and is used in rheumatic cases as a change from other springs. Its temperature is 140°. The Government have constructed a capital swimming bath of concrete, 62 by 23 feet, with dressing-rooms on three sides; the tank holding 32,000 gallons of the water. A peculiar feature here is the natural sulphurous vapour bath, supplied by the gas issuing from a cavity broken into during the excavations. The composition of the gas is ($2 HS + SO_2$). Both these springs have the property of encrusting with silica articles immersed in the water for a few weeks. Ferns, branches of trees, feathers, and birds' nests form beautiful specimens of incrustation. The water of Oruawhata cooled to 130° is an admirable means of destroying slugs, snails, and other enemies of plant life.

4. The Laughing Gas or Cameron's Bath—Kauwhanga (a).

5. The Pain Killer—Kauwhanga (b).

6. The Coffee Pot—Kauwhanga (c).

These three springs are of similar constitution, and belong to Class IV., 'Hepatic' or sulphurous waters. Each spring evolves a large amount of mixed gases, chiefly sulphuretted hydrogen and carbonic acid. The effect of the gas arising from the surface of No. 4 bath is so exciting and exhilarating as to give it the name it bears. The temperature is 108°. Bathing in the spring itself is to be avoided, as fainting has been often caused by the gases breathed.

The Pain Killer is safer and more useful than No. 4. It is one of the most valuable hepatic springs in Rotorua. It is fed by an intermittent geyser, which spouts up at a temperature of 214°, and is cooled down by being led into a hole in the ground near the lake-margin. In this hole there is a large quantity of silicious mud, which is impregnated with the mineral constituents of the geyser. The name of this bath is given it from its success in relieving gouty and rheumatic joints. It forms the best alternative with the Priest's Bath for cases of chronic gout.

ANALYSIS OF THE PAIN-KILLER.
(In grains per gallon.)

Chloride of sodium	46·42
,, ,, potassium	1·71
,, ,, calcium	2·66
,, ,, magnesium	1·47
,, ,, iron and aluminium	4·22
Sulphate of soda	29·14
Hydrochloric acid	6·84
Silica	18·02
	110·48
Sulphuretted hydrogen	4·84

7. Stonewall Jackson or McHugh's Bath—Hinemaru (Class III., Alkaline-siliceous), has a temperature of from 98° to 118° F. It is saline with silicates and has an alkaline reaction. As a bath it is efficient in removing skin diseases such as eczema, and as a drinking spring, when filtered, it is beneficial in cases of atonic dyspepsia, and in the uric acid diathesis.

ANALYSIS OF STONEWALL JACKSON.
(In grains per gallon.)

Chloride of sodium	93·46
,, ,, potassium	4·69
,, ,, lithium, traces	
Sulphate of soda	2·76

Mono-silicate of soda	6·41
Silicate of lime	2·89
,, magnesia	1·02
Iron and aluminium oxides	2·10
Silica	8·29
	121·62

In Ohinemutu.

Nos. 8 and 9. The Lake House Hotel Baths. These two baths, of which (*a*) is clear and (*b*) is muddy, are called by the natives Waihunuhunukuri, the meaning of which is "water for scalding a dog." They belong to Class V., Acidic Waters, and have properties somewhat similar to those of the Priest's Bath. As the muddy Waihunuhunukuri is ferruginous with excess of silica and without alum, and as it has proved especially useful in anæmia and chlorosis, I here give the chemical analysis.

ANALYSIS OF LAKE HOUSE MUDDY BATH.
(In grains per gallon.)

Sulphate of soda	22·44
,, ,, potash	0·62
,, ,, lime	9·81
,, ,, magnesia	1·82
,, ,, iron	12·66
Sulphuric acid	18·49
Hydrochloric acid	7·66
Silica	18·06
	91·56

The existence of so large a quantity of sulphate of iron and of the mineral acids necessitate the very careful and sparing use of this water when taken internally.

Nos. 10 and 11—Waikite (*a*) and (*b*), belonging to Class II., Alkaline, resemble in a general way Madame Rachel, being feebly saline, with silicates, and their reaction being alkaline when cool. The former is the bath reserved for Mrs. Morrison's hotel and the latter, known as Scott's bath, is in use at Kelly's hotel. These baths are useful for the same diseases in which Madame Rachel's bath is beneficial.

No. 12, Te Tapui, in the Te Koutu settlement, is an alkaline, highly silicated hot spring, usually 90° to 100° F. in temperature, but rising to 180° when the wind is north or east. It is beneficial in psoriasis.

In Whakarewarewa.

No. 13. The Spout Bath—Turikore (Class II. Alkaline), is a warm waterfall, a natural and powerful douche, which is admirable in muscular rheumatism, lumbar myalgia, and local palsy. There being no hotel, Maoris hire out their *whares* to invalids and engage themselves as nurses for those who need them. After using the hot douche of the waterfall one can swim in the warm pool below, and then finish up by a swim in the cold stream "Puarenga," into which the Turikore spring pours itself. But as active exercise in hot water is apt to make even a robust man feel faint, no invalid or tourist should attempt this programme without having a friend or attendant near him.

ANALYSIS OF THE SPOUT BATH.
(In grains per gallon.)

Silicate of soda	16·32
„ lime	1·61
„ magnesia	1·14
„ iron	0·39
Sulphate of soda	13·47
Chloride of potassium	1·24
„ sodium	53·61
Phosphate of alumina, traces	
	87·78

No. 14. The Oil Bath—Korotiotio (Class II., Alkaline), is so strongly alkaline as to have a slightly caustic effect on the skin. Hence its name from the peculiar smooth, soapy feeling it gives to a sensitive skin. The Maoris use it in washing clothes. Of course in any case their washing bill would not be very extensive! Bathing in this spring is very sedative to the nerves. The geyser which feeds Korotiotio, having a tempera-

ture of 214° F., has formed a curious mound of silicious rock, which is covered with beautiful sulphur crystals. It is particularly well adapted for treating skin diseases accompanied with nervous irritation.

ANALYSIS OF THE OIL BATH.
(In grains per gallon.)

Mono-silicate of soda	2·08
,, ,, lime	3·16
,, ,, magnesia	0·76
,, ,, iron	0·85
Sulphate of soda	7·49
Chloride of potassium	1·46
,, ,, sodium	66·34
Silica, free	22·40
Chloride of lithium and phosphate of alumina—traces	
	104·54

At Tikitere.

Nos. 18 and 19. The hot waterfall called "Te Mimi o te Kakahi," having a temperature of 90° to 112°, and the Great Spring "Te Kute" are powerful hepatic waters belonging to Class IV.

ANALYSIS OF TE KUTE.
(In grains per gallon.)

Sulphate of soda	12·66
,, ,, alumina	11·22
,, ,, potash	0·59
,, ,, lime	1·01
,, ,, magnesia	0·69
,, ,, iron	1·73
Phosphoric acid—traces	
Sulphuric acid, free	0·77
Hydrochloric acid, free	1·63
Sulphuretted hydrogen	5·74
Silica	12·40
	48·44

In appearance Te Kute is a large furiously boiling pool, dull brown in colour, strongly odorous of sulphuretted hydrogen, from which dense volumes of steam arise. The water is conducted by a small channel into a very primitive bath situated inside a small native *whare of raupo*, and is there reduced to a temperature which is safe and pleasant. Many remarkable cures of chronic muscular and articular rheumatism of many years' standing have been effected by this bath. Some parasitic diseases of the skin have been cured here in a short time. Dr. Ginders tells us of two cases of cure by this bath which it is desirable to note. First, a man from Tauranga, who had been reduced to a state of extreme prostration by a severe cervico-brachial neuralgia, which had for many months resisted all kinds of treatment, was cured here in a fortnight. Second, a man aged thirty-two, who had suffered for more than a year from paraplegia involving the bladder (of syphilitic origin), was cured completely in fourteen days by spending three hours a day in the bath.

The scenery of Tikitere, which is on the shores of the lake, twelve miles from Rotorua, is gloomy in the extreme; it is compared by most writers to Dante's Inferno. It is this characteristic, and the lack of all comfortable accommodation that keep the greater number of rheumatic sufferers away. But the tourist should visit Tikitere for its curious sights, sounds, and odours; and, as a relief to his eye, afterwards explore the lovely Lake Rotokawau, on the plateau close by.

To sum up, then, the diseases that experience has taught us thus far to have been unmistakably benefitted or cured by the thermal treatment at Rotorua are the following, though I cannot undertake to say that the list is a complete one:—chronic rheumatism, muscular and articular; rheumatic gout or rheumatoid arthritis; sciatica; lumbar myalgia; various neuralgiæ; dyspepsia; obesity and piles; all the scaly, vesicular, and parasitic diseases of the skin; some cases of chronic sore throat; amenorrhœa, dysmenorrhœa, anæmia, ovaritis, and sterility in women. As our exact knowledge of these potent springs increases I have no doubt that many other derangements of health will in time be brought into their curative sphere. I even conceive it probable, from what I have seen of its early manifestations in Hawaii and in Norway (Trondhjem) that the most loathsome of all chronic diseases, LEPROSY, might be *arrested* in its fatal course by the strongest of the acidic baths.

A word or two may be addressed to my *confrères* in New Zealand or Australia as to the kinds of cases that should *not* be sent to Rotorua. Patients suffering from consumption (second or third stages); from chronic Bright's disease; from spinal caries; from myelitis; from cerebral softening; and from organic heart disease, especially mitral obstruction, should never be sent there by their medical attendants. A few useful specific directions to invalids concerning the use of the baths may now be given, but not to interfere in the slightest degree with the more minute instruction that they are sure to get from the skilled balneologists at Rotorua and Te Aroha who conduct the courses of treatment.

1st. For chronic rheumatism a course of from two to three months is usually sufficient to cure. Take two or three baths daily, beginning with the Priest's Bath. Once take a swim in the Blue Bath, and drink a tumblerful of Madame Rachel's Spring after each dip. After three weeks of the foregoing, resort to Whakarewarewa or Tikitere for the douches.

2nd. Gout is admirably treated by the Rotorua Baths. Every day bathe twice in the Priest's Bath, and follow each bath by a pail douche of water 10° lower than that of the bath. After two weeks or so use the Pain Killer Spring. For cases of gout, where there is a marked tendency to complication of internal organs, such as the heart, brain, stomach, or lungs, the thermal treatment is not suitable.

3rd. If acute attacks of either rheumatism or gout occur during the course the baths must be at once suspended until they are quite gone.

4th. For very obstinate cases of psoriasis or lepra a course of four and a half months' treatment is required, taking the following baths in succession:—Turikore, Korotiotio, Te Tapui te Koutu, Hinemaru, and Whangapipiro. In the middle of this course a break-off of a fortnight is often an advantage, the waters acting with greater vigour upon a renewal of the systematic bathing. It is often found in cases of chronic sciatica that though the pain has not completely left the patient at the conclusion of his prescribed course of baths, it leaves off entirely and permanently within a month after he reaches home. If an invalid's malady is not cured by the end of the month of April, and he finds himself overtaken at Rotorua by the winter rains, it is best for him to leave for Auckland, Tauranga, or Napier, where he may spend the winter in sheltered quarters and enjoy both town society and varied amusements.

Dr. Lewis lays it down as an absolute rule that patients undergoing systematic thermal treatment must abstain from alcohol. Regular exercise must be taken daily, but never to the extent of fatigue; and the clothing must be carefully adjusted to the state of the weather. Dr. Ginders so pithily expresses one of the difficulties of the medical superintendent in turning out "neat cures" that I take the liberty of quoting it from his pamphlet. "Our visitors to Rotorua may be divided into three classes: the tourist, the invalid tourist, and the invalid. With the invalid we know what we have to do; with the tourist we have nothing to do; but the invalid tourist is a decidedly unsatisfactory person. He expects to be able to exhaust his energies to any extent in sight-seeing, and yet to be cured of his ailment by taking a bath here and a bath there, as it happens to suit his convenience. He is generally disappointed, of course, and goes away to tell the world that the Hot Lake district of New Zealand is a much over-rated place. 'I have tried it, sir, and I came away rather worse than better.' No doubt of it. My medical brethren should advise the invalid tourist to attend to business first and to take his pleasure afterwards."

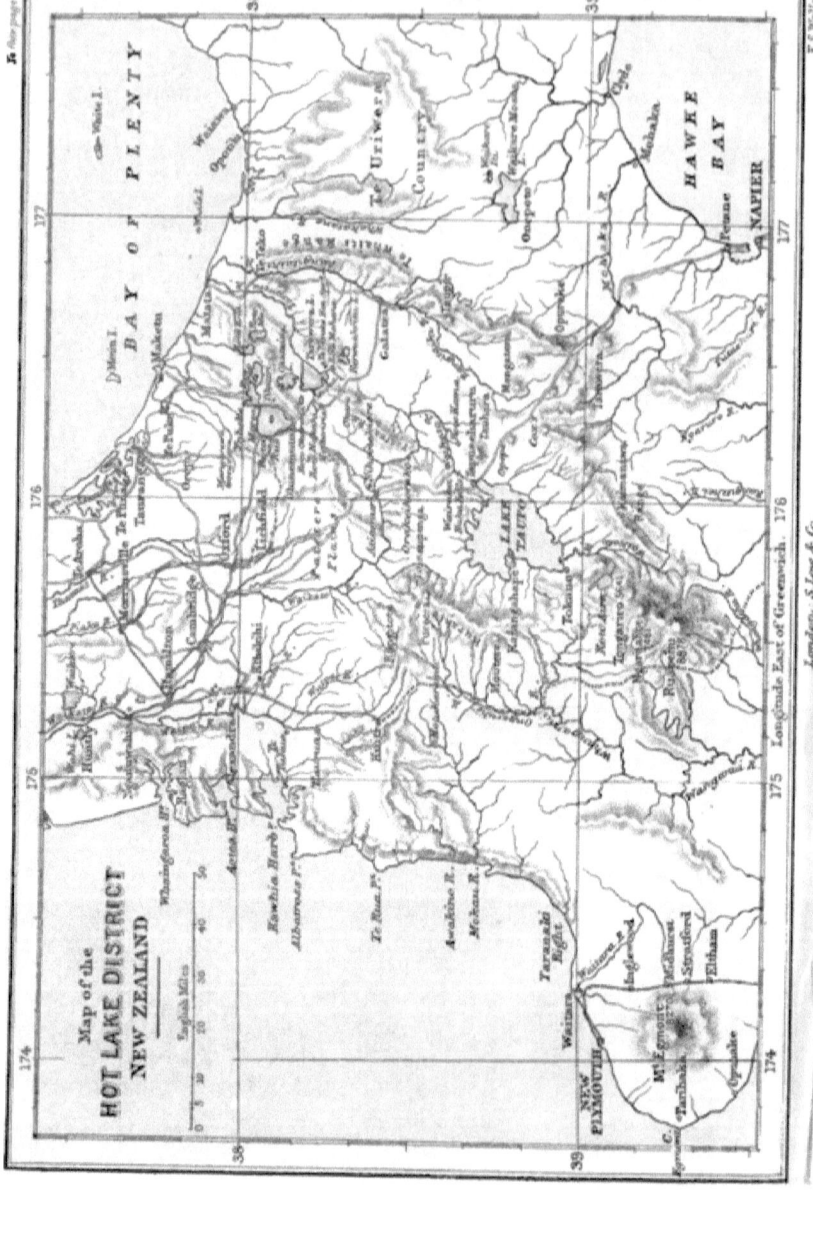

CHAPTER VI.

THE WONDERLANDS OF NEW ZEALAND: EXCURSIONS TO THE HOT LAKES AND TO THE WEST COAST SOUNDS.

Excursions to Rotorua, *viâ* Tauranga in the summer of 1880-1—Tauranga—Oropi—Gorge Road—Beauty of the forest—Ohinemutu—Loafing natives—Baths *al fresco*—Wairoa—Tikitapu bush—Lake Tarawera—White Terrace—Geysers and mud fumaroles—Pink Terrace—Luxurious bathing—Return down the swift hot creek of the Kaiwaka—Fate of the extortionate Tuhourangi Maoris—Scenic attractions of the Middle Island—Lakes, mountains, glaciers, fjords—Lakes Wakatipu, Te Anau and Manapouri—West Coast Sounds, thirteen in number—Annual excursion by Union Company's s.s. *Tarawera*, Captain Sinclair—My visit in January, 1884—Excellent arrangements—Port Chalmers—Preservation Inlet—Cuttle Cove—**Dusky** Sound and Mr. Doherty—Spinach discovered by Cook in **Dusky** Sound—Vancouver—Entertainment by crew—Wet Jacket Arm—Hector's theory of the formation of these fjords—Caswell Bay marble—Milford Sound : its Narrows, Upper Bay ; Mitre Peak, the glory of Milford Sound—Bowen Falls—Ascent of Mitre Peak—Sutherland Fall, 1900 feet—Reischek and his dog—Return.

HAVING in the previous chapter confined my description of the Hot Lake district to the mineral springs and their distinctive characteristics, I now propose, by the aid of **my** journal, to give my readers an idea of the original appearance of what has been aptly called "The Wonderland of New Zealand," namely, the White Terraces of Rotomahana, and the Plutonic manifestations in their neighbourhood—now, alas! no longer visible, having been destroyed **by** the catastrophe of June 10th, 1886, chronicled **in chapter vii.** Just as the paintings of the lamented **Terraces are** enhanced in value now that they have ceased **to exist, so** I trust that a truthful and unexaggerated account **of them** by an eye-witness may not be without interest or a certain historical value. The reader will bear in mind that in 1880, when my visit was made, there was no railway to Oxford; the sea route from Auckland *viâ* Tauranga was the only way of reaching Rotorua; the natives in that region were mostly demoralized loafers; and the Government had not yet organized the township of Rotorua, the Sanatorium, the tenure of land, &c., which have now so civilized the Maoris, and improved the whole arrangements for the tourist and invalid.

My friends Judge Maning (author of " Old New Zealand"), Mr. S. Jackson, sen., of Auckland, and Mr. Robert Proude, of Razorback, Waikato, and I, started from Auckland in the steamer *Waitaki* on a fine summer evening, December 20th, 1880, and reached Tauranga in time for breakfast the next day, December 21st, the longest day in those latitudes. In this sleepy little town, with its very pretty surroundings, we rested for a day, and engaged a coach and four horses, with relays provided, for the eight or ten days of our excursion. The expense amounted to only five shillings apiece per day, and we had much comfort and enjoyment in not being tied to particular routes, stages, or times. One of Kelly's *employés*, a merry, lively fellow, drove us skilfully and amused us with local gossip. Starting, then, early on the morning of the 22nd December, we ascended to Oropi, ten miles from Tauranga, and 900 feet above the sea, which was at that time the extreme limit of cultivation in the direction of the Hot Lakes. "Oropi" is the Maori name for Europe. The views of the beautiful harbour of Tauranga, terminated seawards by the extinct crater-hill of Mangonui, made this, the first stage of our coach-journey, very interesting. Next we plunged into the Gorge Road, made after the fashion of a "corduroy road" in the United States, *ti*-tree fascines, tree-fern stems, and wooden stakes being laid across the road on all the soft places. The bumps, thumps, and dislocatory jolts to which the traveller has to submit made this part of the journey "a terror." Since 1880 another road, *viâ* Te Puke, has been cut, having fewer soft muddy places, so that there is less inconvenience. We joked each other about the roughness of the way, and the Judge especially chaffed me about the *lomi-lomi* of the Sandwich Islanders which I had been describing down in tranquil Tauranga. Eighteen miles of this became rather wearisome, but I was enchanted with the beauty of the rich and varied New Zealand "bush," as the forest is always called in the colonies, and thus my attention was diverted from the soreness of my bones! I had been lately in Australia, where the forest is monotonous, consisting principally of tree-ferns, blue-gum trees, wattles (*acacia*), with few shrubs and no creepers. The New Zealand trees are mostly evergreen; so are the shrubs which picturesquely fill in the lower spaces between the trunks; and multitudinous graceful vines, plants, creepers, and parasitic vegetation delight the eye in luxuriant profusion. The "bush" in this colony is intermediate in variety, density, and brilliancy between those of Australia and the tropics. I should not rank it as equal to those I saw on the Isthmus of Panama or in Brazil. My friends, being all old settlers, named the various trees for me—the *nikau* palm, with its edible pith, the cabbage tree, from which hats are made; the *totara, rimu, rata,* birch, *maitai,* lance wood, *rewa-rewa, pohutakawa*—all valuable building and furniture woods—and the *karaka, puka-puka, tupakihi,* and many other pretty shrubs. But no *kauri* was visible, for this, the most valuable tree in the colony, does not grow south of Mercury Bay. The only sounds in the forest were the occasional clear note of the *tui,* the chatter of the *kaka,* and the cry of the *kakapo,* otherwise it struck me that the woods were singularly silent. A river ran along the gorge, but almost noiselessly, being contracted to its summer dimensions. In the evening we emerged on to the mountain plateau, at a point about fourteen miles distant from Ohinemutu, and we soon sighted Lake Rotorua and the clouds of steam from the geysers at Sulphur Point. The mountains round the lake, and the hilly island of Mokoia, diversified and filled in the scene. On arriving at Ohinemutu we were greeted by the crowds of natives, men, women, and children, with begging requests in a manner reminding one of Killarney, only with more "cheek." Finding the hotels very full, we divided, two going to Lake House Hotel and two to Morrison's, where we found the Maoris less noisy. It appeared, on inquiry, that, owing to the great difficulty of complying with the provisions of the Native Lands Courts, in order to obtain the signatures of every male member of a tribe or *hapu* (which is necessary for the ownership of any plot of land held as communal property), the man who builds or leases an hotel feels bound to give free liquor and tobacco to the natives when they demand it. If one refused, the court might turn him out of his holding. Violent scenes used to take place. In 1880 the Maori loafer of Ohinemutu was indeed a low and degraded creature—a baser and coloured imitation of the low white man—of whom there were dozens living there. A bad state of things: rather improved, however, when Mr. Froude visited Rotorua, and still more mitigated now, since the Thermal Springs Act of 1881 has been in working operation, and since there has been a modification in the Lands Courts' procedure. We, as visitors, were inundated with these beggar-Maoris, many of whom claimed the Judge as an old acquaintance. He was in the old times a powerful *rangatira*, or chief, among the natives, and we found him everywhere received with acclamation. I believe that this was Judge Maning's first visit to the Hot Lakes. What we saw on this trip interested him as much as myself—a "new chum." At Sulphur Point, where several hot springs are situated, it was an amusing sight to see native men, women, and children swimming about or standing up to the neck in hot water for hours, while close by Maori women were cooking their food in a spring (generally fish which they had caught close by in the lake), and at another spring other women were washing clothes. The stranger at first wonders how the Maoris stand both the heat and the acidity of the sulphur waters as they do; for I tested a rivulet that ran into their bathing place and found that it blackened silver intensely in ten seconds, and that it had a very acid reaction. Testing eleven springs by my own thermometer, I found the temperatures to range from 83° to 105° F. Our first excursion from Rotorua was to where the mud geysers and other hot springs are situated. The arrangements here for bathers are very primitive, the Maoris hiring out their grass and fern huts, called *whares*, to invalids, and assisting those who need it in getting into and out of the baths. I noticed one terrific looking natural hot douche (noticed in chapter v., p. 92) which seemed powerful and hot enough to melt the spinal cord! It seemed a favourite spot for rheumatic sufferers; all whom I interrogated said they were steadily improving in health. The natives themselves believe this hot waterfall will cure everything, even the scrofula, to which they are subject. An emaciated little Maori baby, suffering, I found, from *tabes mesenterica*, was brought to me for advice at this place. Having been thus detained and separated from the rest of the party, I sought a Maori guide, who uttered the strange phrase that I have quoted in chapter iii., p. 41, as a specimen of the native pronunciation of English. The enormous subterranean force in action at Whakarewarewa impressed our minds almost with terror, a feeling only relieved by the beauty of the coral-like fringes of silica and alum on the basins round the geysers, the quaintness of the cups, saucers, humps, and nests built up all around by the continual deposition of sediment, and by the mental satisfaction and gratitude we felt to the Almighty Power who had endowed those steaming waters with such beneficent qualities.

Next day we had planned an excursion to the "Ellen's Isle" of Lake Rotorua, Mokoia, the scene of the romantic story of Hinemoa and Tutanekai, so prettily worked up in the poem "Ranolf and Amohia," by Alfred Domett; but a storm on the lake prevented our starting. Judge Maning gave me his prose version of the Maori legend, just as he had heard it, hundreds of times, from the old men who make it their business to collect the traditions of the nation and store them in their memories. These Maori memories are truly wonderful, and have been recognised by the Native Lands Courts in the settlement of tribal and individual claims to property. I fear that the multiplication of books, newspapers, and periodical literature is destroying *our* memories in Western countries, by the phantasmagoria of mental objects flitting before them every day. " The daily perusal of a newspaper for three months," I heard Max Müller once say, " will destroy the strongest memory." Yet what should we do without the daily enlightener? There is no space here for this Hero and Leander-like tale, but should this little book ever see a second edition, I will add it to the Maori chapter, for it is a beautiful and characteristic story, and historically true.

We next 'girded up our loins' to *the* excursion of the tour—a visit to Wairoa, Tarawera Lake, and the Pink and White Terraces of Rotomahana. Leaving our hotels early on a lovely summer morning, our coach accommodating, besides our four selves, the two native women-guides, Kate and Sophia, we drove to Wairoa, eleven miles from Ohinemutu, full of health and spirits. The guides kept up a running fire of jokes in their own language with the Judge, who translated for us anything that was really spicy, and the scenery was most picturesque. Before arriving at Lake Tikitapu (see map 2) the water of which is of a deep blue colour, the road runs through the most exquisite piece of "bush" that I have seen in New Zealand. This, alas! is now gone, perished in the Tarawera eruption. After passing Lake Tikitapu, we reach Lake Rotokahi, the Green Lake, the colour of which, derived from copper and iron salts in solution, forms a most peculiar contrast to the former lake. At Wairoa we halted for the day at Macrae's Hotel, and explored the hills around. A very pretty cascade, the Wairoa Falls (a rather common name in the colony), is formed here by the stream that issues from Rotokakahi and falls into

Lake Tarawera. We visit the charming little ivy-covered mission chapel, from the trellised window of which one has the loveliest possible Alpine view of Tarawera, and the good Charles Albert Haszard, the devout teacher, minister, and friend of the natives, tells us all the traditions of the place, and gathers the children to sing some hymns. Could we have foreseen that in a few years this good man and more than half his amiable family would have been overwhelmed in the ruins of their own home, the chapel destroyed, and Wairoa blasted with sudden destruction, how sad would our parting have been! I found that Mr. Haszard, with his wife and daughter (who happily survived the terrible 10th of June, 1886), had thoroughly Christianized and teetotalized all the Maori children. The visits of tourists had demoralized the parents by treating to drink, but the children were safe.

At 7 A.M. on a hot Christmas morning, this being the only day available for the guides, our party of four, with the two guides, six native boatmen, and Apero, their captain, proceeded in Indian file down the glen leading from Macrae's to the banks of Lake Tarawera. The track descends 200 feet in one mile, passing over diluvial pumice and sand, abounding in lumps of dark green obsidian (volcanic glass), of which I secured excellent specimens for my mineral cabinet. Though much chaffed about "picking up stones," I always find that it adds much to the enjoyment and the enduring recollection of a trip through interesting places to bring away specimens illustrating some one of the natural sciences. My hobby is Mineralogy. Very soon we were comfortably seated in a large whaleboat, built by the Warbricks, who do a large business in this line on these lakes, and rowed along the southern shores of Lake Tarawera.

This lake is the largest of this district, next to Rotorua, and reminds one of Loch Awe in Scotland. It is ten miles long by two broad, indented by several bays, and enclosed by stern-looking mountains. On its south-eastern side the lake has for its background a grand table-mountain, Tarawera, whose three rounded peaks, Wahanga, Ruawahia, and Tarawera, of an average height of 3650 feet above the sea, formed the *foci* of the great eruption of 1886, described in chapter viii. Tarawera Lake has an elevation of 1037 feet above sea level, and receives the drainage of Lakes Rotomahana, Rotokakahi, and Rotomakiriri. Its waters are drained into the sea by the River Tarawera, which debouches on the east coast of the Bay of Plenty at the port of Matata (map 3). In our strong and capacious boat we are quickly rowed along the southern shore for nine miles, passing halfway the Rock of the Taipo or Devil, on which Maori voyagers never fail to place a present or coin, to secure themselves against a tempest. Somehow or other we forgot to pay this customary tribute, and I hope our dusky friends noticed that no harm followed. Arriving at the Kaiwaka Creek, in the Bay of Te Ariki, a narrow swift stream of warm water which flows down for two miles from Rotomahana (The Hot Lake, "*roto*" always meaning "lake"), we disembark, leaving our wraps, &c., in a native "dug-out" canoe, and walk the distance up to the Lake of the Terraces, the far-famed Rotomahana, through open country, covered with low scrub, consisting of *ti*-tree (*manuka*) and fern. At first sight Rotomahana appeared to be a small, tame and uninteresting mountain tarn of dull green water, fringed with sedges, rushes, and *ti*-tree, and abounding in wild duck. No sign of human habitation anywhere. We enter a canoe kept for the purpose, and are paddled across to the White Terrace, the Maori name of which is Te Tarata. Here begin the marvels of the unassuming lakelet; and our admiration goes on *crescendo* until, after a bath on the Pink Terrace, our vocabulary of wonder and delight is exhausted.

Standing on the lake shore, at the foot of the White Terrace, we look up and behold a crescentic mass of white, coral-like platforms, piled up one upon another to the height of what would be eighty feet vertical, but that they gradually shelve backward and upward to the summit, which is 300 yards from the water. The shelves thus formed are covered with basins and cups filled with warm water of a deep blue colour, perpetually rippling down from an unseen source above, over their edges, fringed with innumerable stalactites into the lake at our feet. Gazing upwards we see at the top of the Terrace nothing but clouds of steam, and we hear bubbling, roaring, and booming noises, as of a huge cauldron of boiling water. Ascending slowly and cautiously, some of us in rubber shoes, some without— because the water becomes hotter as we go higher—we climb forty of these shelves, the lowest having a frontage of 300 yards to the lake. Mineralogically speaking, each shelf or terrace is formed of white silicious sinter, deposited by the gradually cooling hot water that flows down from above, the latest layers showing themselves as exquisitely delicate fretwork upon the surface, which it seems almost sacrilegious to crush beneath our tread. Having reached the summit (one of us with a scalded foot), we are startled to find the source of all this hot water to be an immense geyser, which shoots up into the air from the unknown depths of a vast cauldron of rock, upon the rim of which we are now standing. Twenty, thirty, forty, or even sixty feet into the air, at uncertain intervals, the geyser fountain plays; its temperature of 210° to 214°, rendering all near approach dangerous, and making an abrupt retreat into the scrub necessary whenever the wind blows the steam towards the spectator. By chemical analysis this geyser water contains :—

Chloride of sodium	62 grs.	per gallon.
Silicate of soda	68 ,,	,,
Monosilicates of iron, lime, and magnesia	3 ,,	,,

Medicinally I thought this water would prove beneficial if taken internally in rickets and *mollities ossium*. Our party now turned and looked over the lake. With but a little knowledge of geology, a comprehensive glance around showed us the process of formation of this beautiful structure. Centuries ago a geyser of great force and volume, forced up by Plutonic fires below the earth's crust, burst out near the lake margin, through a hill formed of mixed clays and decomposed lava. After partly crumbling away the slope of the hill, it kept depositing on the ledges into which the ground was formed, by the water flowing over rock and soil of various resisting powers, the silicates which had been dissolved in its water under enormous subterranean pressure at a very high temperature—thus building up the wondrous terraces, basins, and stalactites before us. What remains of the harder strata of the original hill is a nearly vertical wall of rock surrounding the geyser, except at one side. The day was warm and bright, with a pleasant breeze. What, I thought, is the much-praised Taj Mahal of Agra, and what are the most elaborately carved cathedral sculptures of the old country, all the work of man, beautiful though they are, compared to this lovely tracery sculptured by the Creator! The sapphire blue of the water in the countless cups and pools sparkling in the brilliant sunshine, and contrasting beautifully with the alabaster fretwork done in semi-transparent yet permanent stone, inimitable by man; the awe-inspiring geyser roaring above; the dull green dismal lake below; the barren hills around, desolate, treeless, and uninhabited; the dusky aboriginals grouped around us; heaven's azure expanse above us—all these elements combined to produce a picture which even a skilful artist could but inadequately portray, and which my words can but feebly represent to those who have never been there. The scene impressed us all as something unique, not possible to be reproduced elsewhere in the world.

Our party then, carefully guided, for the ground is thickly honeycombed by volcanic fumaroles, solfataras, and hot springs, explored the neighbourhood at the back and side of the Terrace. Two other large geysers, Te Hutu and Kakarike, we observed close by. The Devil's Blow Hole, whence steam issues with a terrific noise exactly like that of the escape pipe of a large steamer; the green lake emitting an odour of rotten eggs; the mud spring which the natives take internally as a cure for certain diseases; the Alum Cave; and many other wonders, exhibit the prodigal and varied energy of the kingdom of Pluto.

After an excellent *al fresco* lunch, we embark in the canoe, and paddle across the lake to the Pink Terrace, called Otukapuarangi in Maori. Here a similar formation of sinter terraces has been going on for ages, but some coloration of a pink or coralline hue, due to iron in the soil it is thought, has modified the white in a very pretty manner. Some are of the opinion that the discoloration is the effect of a fire or series of fires among the *ti*-tree, but in my opinion this is an erroneous, because an insufficient explanation. The summit geyser of the Pink Terrace is neither so hot as that of the White Terrace nor so violent in its action. The water, running more slowly down over the slope and containing the large quantity of forty-three grains of free silica in the gallon, forms cups and basins more rapidly than in the case of the White Terrace, by depositing a transparent film, which soon hardens and turns white on exposure to the air. Objects placed in this or the other mineral water become very prettily encrusted with silica. Five of the upper steps of the Pink Terrace have deep basins filled with warm bluish water of a temperature varying from 80° to 100°, forming most luxurious natural baths, which we enjoyed most thoroughly. The subaqueous deposit feels smooth and gelatinous to the skin, and the traveller feels so happy in his bath that, like the Lotophagi, he cares not how time flies. But time does fly (a way time has); the sun is declining, and after a shuddering inspection of an awful "lake burning with fire and brimstone" near by, a look at two other terraces whose geysers have subsided; and at six other geysers that may form terraces, some day, we have reluctantly to leave this wonderland. The Kaiwaka Creek, bordered by boiling mud springs and steam jets, bears our narrow canoe swiftly down its warm stream to Lake Tarawera, where our trusty whale-boat awaits us. It is nearly dark when we leave the mouth of the creek for home. Captain Apero and his oarsmen pull us along lustily, with many a native song and chorus, keeping admirable time, Kate and Sophia smoking their pipes in much good-humour, for they look upon Judge Maning as the great *rangatira*, whom it was a distinguished honour to conduct. We arrive at the Wairoa boat-house about 10 P.M., tired, but none the worse for the dangers we had encountered, except our friend with the scalded foot, which speedily healed.

At the time of our visit the Maori tribe who owned the Lake Rotomahana, the Terraces, and the Inferno near them had the sole monopoly of guiding the tourists; hence it cost us £8 for the day's excursion. They also obliged any artist or photographer to pay at least £5 down for the privilege of obtaining any picture or sketch of the 'show places.' Loud and frequent were the complaints of visitors, artists especially, of these extortions. But the terrible eruption of Tarawera swept the tribe away as well as the objects they so jealously guarded.

Our subsequent adventures and experiences even at the *tangi* held at Te Ngae, on the western shore of Lake Kotorua, described in chapter iii., were tame compared with the excursion to the Terraces. There linger in my memory an exquisite rosy twilight and gorgeously coloured sunset one evening at Tauranga, and the witty conversation of Judge Maning, who was a perfect fountain of Maori lore, acute character-sketching, and amusing stories. In chapter vii. I shall point out to the reader the very numerous and striking curiosities of nature (especially the Wai-o-tapu Valley), that remain since the destruction of the Terraces.

The West Coast Sounds.

We now turn to the Middle Island in search of the picturesque and the wonderful. The tourist asks, "What is best worth seeing?" I reply, "Whatever you miss, *don't fail to visit* the West Coast Sounds." If the North Island has volcanic scenery excelling Italy, the

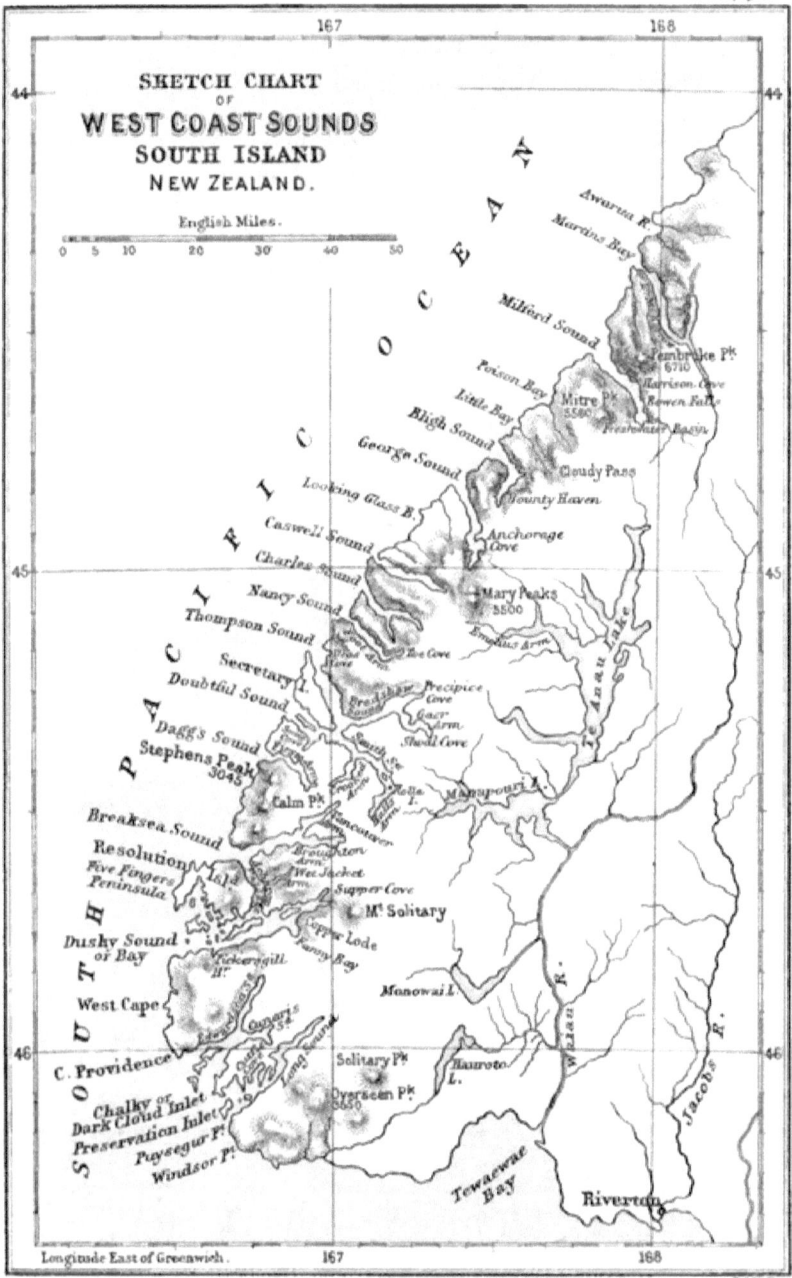

Middle Island has scenery surpassing in some features both Switzerland and Norway. Here we find magnificent gorges threaded by coach roads running along the edge of giddy precipices; grand forests, differing from those of the warmer North Island; roaring torrents and waterfalls; wide river beds, all but dry in summer, but well filled with rushing water in winter; lakes of great size, surrounded by snow-clad mountains as yet unscaled by man; vast glaciers, to which those of Norway are but small; and the most magnificent fjords in the world.

It is to these last that I wish to draw attention, as I visited them in January, 1884, and as the Union Steamship Company of New Zealand makes them accessible once a year in a most convenient and enjoyable manner. Here, then, is a sphere of exploration for the Alpine Club,—to ascend Mount Cook (12,379 feet), as was done by the Rev. W. S. Green in 1882; Mount Aspiring; Mount Earnslaw, and other " virgin " peaks; and to open up tracks overland to the heads of Milford, George, and Doubtful Sounds, from the heads of Lakes Wakatipu, Te Anau, and Manapouri respectively. What keep away the mass of tourists from these Sounds are the stormy seas outside them and the limitation of the two fixed excursions in summer (in January usually), when only it is possible to visit them in a large steamer, at leisure. Among passengers by sea in general, the writer, who has traversed 50,000 miles of ocean since 1869, has found only a small proportion able to preserve their equanimity in rough weather; and " the long wash of Australasian seas " that beats upon the hundred miles of rocky coast which is indented by the thirteen Sounds is always turbulent. The only chance, other than the annual excursion by the Union Company's Steamship *Tarawera*, of visiting them, is when the regular steamer from the Bluff to Melbourne, or *vice versâ*, calls in at Milford Sound. There is no natural harbour on the west coast from Milford Sound northwards to Nelson. The *Tarawera*, a steamer of 2000 tons, commanded by Captain Sinclair, is selected for this special cruise; and the tempting programme drawn up by the Union Steamship Company for the ten days' trip is strictly carried out, weather permitting. Now that the trip has become a regular institution, there are so many travellers anxious to go that not only does the *Tarawera* make two successive trips to the Sounds—the second one commencing the day after she reaches home from the first—but scores even are shut out of both trips for want of room. The fare for the round trip is £12 from Port Chalmers, or £10 in addition to the ordinary saloon fare to Port Chalmers from any other New Zealand port. I should advise travellers visiting New Zealand to secure their berths for this trip in November, for the exact date of starting is usually fixed by that time. The very courteous manager of the company, Mr. James Mills, will, if requested, give an organized party state-rooms all on one side of the vessel, so that they may all take their meals together. There are so many passengers that the meals have to be doubled, passengers on the port side taking the first breakfast, those on the starboard the second, and so on throughout the day. Every detail conducive to the comfort and happiness of the passengers is studied by the manager. The table (always good on the Union Company's line) is extra well supplied; a double number of stewards is provided; the crew are men selected for good conduct and musical or mimetic talent; there are plenty of boats taken for fishing, excursions, &c.; a photographer and professional pianist accompany the party, and even a carpenter is taken along to make boxes for the ferns and plants the ladies may collect. For my own part I never enjoyed a sea picnic more thoroughly, and the fellow-passengers whom I met in after years had the same feeling. Any New Zealander or Australian who has not "done the Sounds," should lose no time in securing a berth in the good ship *Tarawera* when next summer comes round. He will enjoy the most magnificent and stupendous marine scenery south of the line amongst pleasant and hearty company.

Leaving Port Chalmers on Wednesday, the 9th of

January, 1884, with 110 saloon passengers and Captain Cameron as general director of the excursion, the *Tarawera* made direct for the nearest sound, called "Preservation Inlet" by Captain Cook, who in 1773 discovered and named these fjords. We reached the inlet at 4 P.M. on Thursday, the 10th, so that we were not many hours on the ocean; but several unfortunates were forced to "seek the seclusion that a cabin grants." The weather was fine in this fjord, and the sea-sick passengers emerged on deck like rabbits from their burrows, or like the prisoners in the opera *Fidelio* glad indeed to breathe the fresh air, and to drink in with their eyes the exquisite beauty of this, the tamest of the sounds. Forest-clad-hills all round us; shrub-covered islets; snowy peaks in the distance; numerous waterfalls, the plash of whose waters alone broke the calm almost oppressive silence; these were the features that attracted and charmed us, so that all sea-sickness was forgotten. After steaming for some distance up the fjord, the *Tarawera* returned to Cuttle Cove to anchor for the night. Boats, of which there were eight provided, were got out, and fishing commenced. And what a variety we hauled up!—butterfish, blue-rock, and red-cod, barra-couta, gropers, sea perch, trumpeters, dog-fish, and sharks, besides others. The sharks were certainly a great nuisance, carrying away lines and bait, but when caught, killed, and cut open were interesting. In the shallower parts of the sounds we found cray-fish, which are caught by spearing, and proved to be capital eating. Throughout the trip it is the practice of Captain Sinclair to enter a sound by daylight, and anchor at night in the next sound further on. All the intricate navigation is done by daylight, there being only one lighthouse (Puysegur Point) for 400 miles along the coast. This course just harmonized with the comfort of the passengers. My fellow-passengers proved to be a thoroughly agreeable set, ready to display their musical and other talents for the benefit of all. Mr. A. J. Towsey, of Dunedin, a professor of music, skilfully evoked and regulated these talents at the piano and organ. And the first evening, usually dull on board ships, was spent as musically and socially as if we had organized an evening party. By 11 P.M. the order "lights out" was given. What a blessing that electric light is on board ship! No heat, no consumption of the air, a soft and clear light, and it can be turned on as well as turned off. At 6 A.M. next day "all hands" turned up on deck for fresh enjoyment. We made out the peaks round us by the map: Treble Mount, 3200 feet high; Forgotten Peak, 3682 feet; Needle Peak, 4120 feet, these being suitable introductions to the giant mountains we saw further north. It is interesting to note that as the traveller proceeds northward from Preservation Inlet and Long Sound, the character of each fjord becomes grander, and the surrounding mountains loftier, till the grandest of all is reached—Milford Sound. But to resume our voyage. The next day, Friday, January the 11th, we spent at Cuttle Cove, fishing, botanizing, exploring, and sketching, although the continuous rain was rather a damper on our energy. Those who landed found it hard work to penetrate the dense jungle of the forest, which reached from the tops of the mountains down to the water's edge, the feet sinking everywhere into decayed vegetation, trunks of trees which had decayed where they fell, and spongy moss which had water underneath it. Our botanists had a good field for collecting orchids, rare ferns, the crimson-blossomed *rata*, the blue *veronica*, the snow-berry of a pink colour, and many other species of the Middle Island *flora*. In several I added to my collection of native woods sections of well-grown young trees such as the *ti*-tree, *rata*, *rimu*, birch, cedar, spiderwood, and others. The shell collectors were disappointed, there being no real sea-beach anywhere in the sound. The industrious photographer, Burton of Dunedin, "took shots," as he called it, at the scenery whenever the rain permitted. He also took the passengers and crew in two groups, these forming very agreeable *souvenirs* of the trip. On Saturday, the 12th, the *Tarawera* weighed anchor at daylight and steamed out into the ocean, and round the lofty frowning cliffs —the north of Ireland magnified sixty-fold—into Dusky Sound, going slowly right up to the head of it. Here we left letters for Mr. Doherty, who with his mate lives in this solitary place. He is a good practical geologist and mineralogist, it being his business to examine the neighbourhood for valuable mineral deposits. He brought on board a large number of specimens of ore, chiefly copper, which he said were valuable. Though professing to like his isolated life amid Nature's wonders, he is not loth to visit Dunedin sometimes by our vessel.

It was in Dusky Sound that Captain Cook, searching for herbs to relieve his men's scurvy, discovered spinach, that dainty and nutritious vegetable. Dusky Sound is twenty-two miles in length, and through it are scattered many picturesque wooded islands: Anchor, Petrel, Parrot, Pigeon, Seal, Indian, Useless, and Noman's Islands. In the hills, which rise so abruptly from the water's edge that there is no landing-place for boats anywhere, lithographic stone and asbestos have been discovered by Mr. Doherty. The characteristic feature of this Sound, we all thought, was the abundance of waterfalls, (all very full in January,) because of the melting of the snow on the mountain tops. From one point of our course we counted no less than eleven falls on one side of a certain mountain, and eighteen on the other side. Each of these falls was large enough to have made the fortune of a village in our own Lake country. As we turned along Acheron Passage, so named after the Admiralty surveying ship, H.M.S. *Acheron*, we were [reminded by passing Vancouvertown,· that the great Dutch navigator ran in here for shelter in his ship *Discovery*. How much New Zealand and the Australasian colonies owe to these heroes of the sea, not one of whom either owned personally or annexed for his nation the lands he discovered and named! It may be some pleasure to their "shades" to know that their heroic names are stereotyped for ever on these islands and the island continent of Australia.

On the evening of this day, Saturday, a lively entertainment was given by the musical part of the crew and officers to the passengers. The orchestra consisted of bones, tambourine, tin-whistle, accordion, and flute. One of the seamen, Woods by name, possessed one of the most delicious tenor voices I ever heard; he was vociferously encored every time he sung, but was so nervous that he forgot the words of his songs on two occasions. One of the musical officers was appropriately named Nightingale. Our evenings were all occupied in some fun or other. Among the 110 tourists there were eight of my own profession, twelve teachers of both sexes, but not a single parson! We moved on during Saturday night to Breaksea Sound (see map 4), so as to spend the Sunday tranquilly in Wet Jacket Arm; another befitting name conferred by Captain Cook, for it rained incessantly while we were there. The vegetation here is most luxuriant, and even in rain the scenery most lovely, reminding me of Lago Garda, in the Italian Switzerland. We had the episcopal Morning Service very well read by Mr. H. Worthington, of Auckland, the chants and hymns being also well rendered by an amateur choir of passengers, drilled by Mr. Towsey. In the afternoon and evening the American organ was kept going by hymns and sacred music. Wet Jacket Arm should always be included in a choice of photographs of the sounds. Early on Monday morning we moved along Acheron Passage out into the open sea, retracing our route for a few miles; then, entering Doubtful Sound by its Bradshaw Arm about noon, we proceeded up Smith's Sound to Rolla Island; and returning by Thompson Sound to the open ocean, we entered Caswell Sound in the evening and anchored there for the night. Assuming Dr. Hector's theory to be correct, we can explain most of the appearances of these sounds, their shoreless margins, numerous islands all in deep water, luxuriant vegetation, &c. He is of opinion that all the sounds were formed by a *sudden sinking* of the *whole south-west coast* through some interior convulsion of nature. The adjacent hills had been much above their present apparent height, and the deep water of the sounds had then been represented only by small intervening valleys. After this convulsion the water from the ocean had rushed in, filling up the gaps between the hill slopes to their present sea level. Thus the shoreless islands now represent tops of submerged hills.

The evening spent here, the anchorage being in Shoal Cove, was agreeably filled in by a concert given by the passengers to the officers and crew. During the night a thunderstorm came on, and Captain Sinclair for a time experienced some anxiety lest the *Tarawera* should drag her anchor and drift on the rocks, but the anchor held firm. Caswell Bay Marble is famous throughout New Zealand, but the comparative inaccessibility of the quarry, and the limited extent of the market, make it at present a profitless product. Next we entered George Sound, where the bush is richer than in any sound. I joined an exploring party, who traced up to its source in a small lake the river whose handsome cascade is quite a prominent feature in this beautiful fjord. The rain was here so heavy that we had to abandon our proposed regatta, although £15 had already been collected for prizes. Mountains of 5000 feet now surround us, preparing us to some extent for the tremendous proportions of our next sound, the crown of them all,

Milford Sound.

We reached this, the final point of our excursion, at noon on the 16th of January, passing by Bligh Sound, and two other bays. In Bligh Sound Governor Bowen was once detained by an accident to H.M.S. *Clio* for a fortnight during an official tour, and was released by the daring and successful journey made across the trackless mountains by Dr. Hector from Martin's Bay to Queenstown on Lake Wakatipu. On entering Milford Sound we miss the forest-clad hills rising from the water's edge to which we have been accustomed in other fjords. We pass from the ocean into Anita Bay, a gateway of lofty frowning rocks, 4500 feet high and proceed up the Narrows, a deep channel only 300 yards wide, the sides of which tower up to 3000 or 4000 feet. It seems as if the Titans had hewn a canal through the mountains. The glacial theory of the formation of the West Coast Sounds would seem to explain this and other features of Milford Sound more satisfactorily than the other plausible theory framed by Sir James Hector, mentioned on a previous page. When the Sound opens out into the upper bay the grandeur of the scene is indescribable. In front you have the (then) largest and highest known waterfall in the colony, the Bowen Fall, 540 feet in actual height. Its peculiarity consists in the fact of the river forming the cascade falling into a rocky recess forty feet below the ledge of the river bed, which has become so hollowed out in the course of centuries that it now causes the fall to rebound in a great arch, and to leap clear over the rocks 500 feet into the sound below. This magnificent fall has been named after Lady Bowen, the wife of the popular Governor above mentioned. On approaching the fall in a boat the spray wetted our party while yet at a long distance from the fall. In 1888 the prestige of the Bowen Fall of being the highest in Australasia was eclipsed by the discovery by Mr. Sutherland, the resident of "Milford City," of a fall 1900 feet high, near Lake Ada, far up in the Southern Alps. It has been named Sutherland Fall after its discoverer, and is higher than the Great Yosemite Fall by 500 feet. It is the highest known in the world with the exception of that fall in Norway, which is estimated at 2000 feet from the mountain ledge to the bottom of the valley.

Let me now try to give the reader an idea of the panorama of this glorious upper bay. To the right, as one looks southward towers up Mount Kimberley, which has the shape of a lion *couchant*; and behind it rises the far-famed Mitre Peak, 6500 feet high, the subject of so much artistic attention. Resembling in shape a bishop's mitre, this mountain, when the sunlight or evening glow gilds its twin peaks, surpasses in wondrous beauty Monte Rosa, the Matterhorn, or Mont Blanc. In the early morning of a calm day the outline of the upper part of Mitre Peak, Mount Kimberley being in front sloping to the water's edge, is mirrored in the deep brown waters of the sound; and then is the time when the photographer's camera or the artist's brush can portray some of its beauty. But when a thunder-cloud settles on its head Mitre Peak is changed beyond recognition. An "instantaneous" photograph, representing a dense dark cloud settling on the mountain's brow, that I bought from Burton, makes the whole scene wonderfully like Vesuvius emitting its cloud of smoke. Friends, when looking over my album of views, invariably ask, "Which of the volcanoes is this?" Mitre Peak was ascended in February, 1883, by two intrepid mountaineers, D. Sutherland and S. H. Moreton. They report a good many difficulties, such as having to scale precipitous walls of granite, to cross glaciers, moraines, deep water-courses, and very rough rocky ground in general. The *flora* was of a distinctly Alpine character up to 5500 feet in altitude, and then vegetation ceased. From the summit there is the grandest possible view of the Southern Alps: Mount Cook, nearly 13,000 feet; Mount Aspiring, 9940 feet; Mount Pembroke, 8710 feet; Moreton Peak, Underwood Peak, and Mount Christina, each about 9000 feet; Mount Tetoku, nearly 10,000 feet; and snow-fields with a glacier underneath 100 miles in extent—all these form a panorama which the Bernese Oberland may rival but cannot surpass. Neither the Svartisen nor Folgefond glaciers of Norway (the former of which I visited in August, 1889) are more than half the size of the immense Pembroke Glacier. All the scenery in Milford Sound is on such a gigantic scale, excelling even the best Norwegian fjords, except perhaps Geiranger Fjord, that one visit of so short a duration is not sufficient to realise its grandeur. From the deck of the *Tarawera*, which kept slowly moving round the bay, because there was no anchorage anywhere, the spectator could see eighteen waterfalls at one time; and as far as the eye could reach it ranged over torrents, scarped rocks, forests, valleys, snow-peaks, and glaciers. The more adventurous of our party longed to land and explore some of these romantic gorges, one of which formed by the Arthur River leads up to Lake Ada. One interesting phenomenon I had never observed before in all my travels. An enormous quantity of fresh water from countless rivers and streamlets is continually poured into the head of the sound. The sea water, from its greater density, remains underneath this layer of fresh water, so that our screw propeller seemed to churn up the water into two colours, for it went deep enough to turn up the green sea water from below, which thus displaced and mixed with the dark-brown fresh water of the surface. The upper part of Milford Sound resembles the Yosemite Valley of California, as far as a fjord can resemble a valley. The little shanties, forming the pigmy village, which facetiously calls itself "Milford City," constitute a step from the sublime to the opposite. D. Sutherland, a native of Wick in Scotland, is a bit of a humourist, and trots out a Latin quotation now and then, as, for instance, on one hut we read, "Esperance Chalet, No. 1, Kennedy Street;" on a second hut, "D. Sutherland, No. 1, Rotorua Street, 4—11—78 *Semper Paratus.*" The double visit in summer of the *Tarawera* excursionists is the great event in the hermit's life. Both Doherty and Sutherland have the companionship of dogs endowed with an intelligence almost super-canine, reminding me of the accomplishments of "Cæsar," the hunting Newfoundland dog my friend A. Reischek takes with him in his rambles. During many months of hardship and solitude in these Sounds—"the world forgetting, by the world forgot"—this naturalist, aided by his four-footed friend, has contributed more than any other scientist to our knowledge of the *avifauna* of New Zealand. Our captain, after only eight hours' stay amid these wonders ruthlessly carried us off as the shades of evening gathered round; and truly even a summer's day is short in Milford Sound, from the manner in which it is closely shut in by lofty mountains. Steaming carefully back to the open sea, after firing a cannon and awaking a thousand echoes, we steered direct to the Bluff Harbour to land some passengers who wished to explore Lake Wakatipu (the Windermere and Ullswater in one of the colony), and some who preferred taking rail to Dunedin to another night at sea. Next morning we arrived safe at Port Chalmers as happy as possible, but loth to separate, as so many warm friendships had been formed on the voyage.

I find I have not mentioned one little drawback to the comfort of tourists who land anywhere in the sounds, I mean the sand flies, whose bite is more tedious in its consequences than that of a mosquito. Travellers of both sexes should wear gloves and a veil while on shore; if gloves cannot be obtained, the next best protection is to rub kerosene on the skin. For the bite itself the best remedy is the tincture of a plant called the *Ledum palustre.*

The wonderland of the Middle Island—in which we find the best features of Switzerland, Norway, and the Tyrol combined—is composed of these thirteen sounds, the Southern Alps, the Otago lakes, and the road from Bealey to Hokitika.

CHAPTER VII.

THE VOLCANIC ERUPTION OF MOUNT TARAWERA.

New Zealand a link in the chain of the Pacific Ocean volcanoes—Principal volcanic eruptions from 1883 to 1886—Upheaval of North Island—Great fissure in earth's crust, running north-east to south-west—Taupo volcano zone—Its craters and hot springs—Premonitory signs of the Tarawera outbreak—The eruption of June 10, 1886—Analysis of the ashes—Results of the eruption—Loss of life—Death of C. Haszard, Edwin A. Bainbridge, and Tuhoto—T. Minett's narrative—The Wonderland that remains—Waio-tapu Valley—New Sinter Terraces forming—Pink Cauldron and Crow's Nest Geyser of Wairakei—Mount Horo-Horo—Lake Taupo—The new grand tour: Te Aroha, Rotorua, Ruapehu National Park to the Upper Wanganui River.

A COMPREHENSIVE glance at a physical map of the whole Pacific Ocean will show, if the volcanic regions be marked, that within its enormous expanse of seventy-two millions of square miles, and around it on north, east, and west, are numerous active and extinct volcanoes. And the history of this district during the last ten years affords examples of eruptions breaking out in new places on a gigantic scale. Of these outbreaks not the least formidable was the eruption of Tarawera, a mountain 3650 feet high, situated in the Hot Lake region of the North Island of New Zealand in S. lat. 38° 15', and E. long. 176°, which took place on the 10th of June, 1886, with the disastrous results of the loss of 111 lives; the injury of the pasturage and agriculture over 500 square miles; and the destruction of the most lovely ornaments of the land of *Pounamou*, (a Maori name of New Zealand),—the White and Pink Terraces described in the previous chapter. Volcanologists assert that in the Pacific Ocean and the coasts

of the continents bordering it there is an immense amount of subterranean and sub-aërial volcanic action always going on, which demands vents of sufficient number and magnitude to liberate its forces, and that a distinct connection or sequence can be traced between eruptions, whether accompanied by seismic disturbances or not, at places far distant from one another. An ordinary amount of subterranean energy may be set free at an old vent, a crater previously active, as in Alaska, the Aleutian Islands, Hawaii, and the Andes. But an unusual amount often breaks out in a new place, upheaving an island from the immensely deep ocean bottom, as at Tonga and White Island; or changing completely the form and structure of a once active crater, as at Krakatoa, in the Straits of Sunda; or, lastly, blowing out the side of a mountain, not a previously existing crater, blazing out through each of its three peaks, and permanently elevating them by 170 feet vertically—as in the striking event, unique in both the history and tradition of the colony, which is the subject of this chapter.

White Island, or Whakari, is a sulphur volcano, in the Bay of Plenty, twenty-eight miles off the shore near Tauranga, and is always active. It forms the eastern visible limit of that extensive belt of subterranean agitation which extends from White, Mayor, and Whale Islands through Rotorua and Taupo Lakes, across Mounts Ruapehu (8878 feet), Ngauruhoe (7481 feet), still active, and Tongariro (6500 feet), to the Wairarapa Valley and the city of Wellington. The White Island crater is now in the solfatara state. It is important to note that the great eruption of Krakatoa—whereby whole towns were destroyed, a mountain lowered, the navigation of the Straits of Sunda seriously impeded, and such an enormous and unprecedented mass of volcanic *ejecta* were blown into the air as to modify (in the opinion of many eminent scientists) the colour of the sunsets for many months all over the globe—occurred August 27, 1883. On the next day, August 28th, the waters of Lake Taupo, fully 5000 miles distant, fell fully two feet in level, and rose again. Such a phenomenon had never occurred before, nor has it since. This recalls the fact that after the great Lisbon earthquake, in 1755, the waters of Lochs Lomond and Katrine in Scotland, and of the great lakes in America, rose and fell in a similar manner. It is not unscientific to believe that these phenomena were linked together. Now let us connect the preceding with the following facts. First, the Sunda or Krakatoa eruption in 1883. Second, the comparative quiescence of the largest volcano of the world, Kilauea, the crater of Mauna Loa, in Hawaii. Third, in the latter part of 1885 the unusual energy of the White Island Sulphur volcano. Fourth, a return of great activity in Mauna Loa. Fifth, the sudden outbreak, in June, 1886, of a new volcano, Tarawera, in New Zealand. Sixth, the formation of a volcanic island by a submarine volcano that suddenly appeared on the 30th August, 1886, at Niuafu in the Tongan Islands, S. lat. 17°. We may conclude that a subterranean and subaqueous wave passed along the fluid belt beneath the earth's crust and affected all these widely distant points with seismic and eruptive disturbances. A quiescence at one vent of volcanic energy is compensated for by increased activity at another focus.

Undoubtedly the surface of the North Island of New Zealand has been upheaved by volcanic action in times not so very remote, from a geologist's point of view,—that is to say, in the Recent and Tertiary periods, to which belong the basaltic and rhyolitic rocks, which constitute at least one-third of the area of this island. Within ten miles of Auckland city Dr. Hochstetter counted no less than sixty-three extinct craters. I have studied with great interest the ridges and fields of solidified lava which in ages past flowed down from Mounts Eden, Albert, and Hobson, now forming the healthiest suburbs of Auckland. Often when driving over these lines of lava, the hollow rumbling sound made by the wheels of the carriage told of the large bubbles of air imprisoned by the rapidly cooling fluid ages ago. As one would expect, these lava ridges make the roads so "hummocky" (to use a colonialism) as to be costly to maintain in order. On the island of Rangitoto we can study the latest forms of black lava and brecciated tufa. The accompanying map, drawn by Mr. S. Percy Smith, now Surveyor-General of New Zealand, to whose exhaustive and thoroughly scientific official report on the Tarawera eruption I am much indebted, displays the whole of the Taupo volcanic zone. This zone covers an area of 4725 square miles, over which none but volcanic rocks or their derivatives are to be found; and it includes all the late and present active manifestations of thermal and Plutonic energy, the hot springs and geysers being marked in red. The longer axis of this volcanic zone runs north-east to north-west, and nearly coincides, it is thought by Mr. Smith and other competent geologists, with a great fissure in the earth's crust from which in Eocene times the islands of New Zealand were thrown up so as to appear above the surface of the sea. This scientific theory is in curious agreement with the legend of the god Maui, and his fish, Te Ika o Maui, alluded to in chapter iii. The general direction of this deep-seated fissure is parallel to the chief mountain chains of both islands. As in Italy so in New Zealand, the more recent and still active volcanic energy is confined to the districts nearest the equator. In chapter ii. I have compared the district north of Auckland to southern Italy.

The area of country covered with pumice mixed with a rusty-coloured arenaceous loam is about 10,775 square miles. The pumice varies from blocks containing 1000 cubic feet down to grains the size of coarse sand. In the Auckland Museum is to be seen a series of specimens finely illustrating the transition of pumice-stone to obsidian, with which it is chemically identical. Changes of the surface are always going on in this volcanic zone; chemical decompositions; sub-aërial denudation; the dissolution of soluble *ejecta*; and the deposition of many substances (silica, lime salts, sulphur, alum, clay, &c.) by countless thermal springs. No less than six extinct volcanoes, namely Tongariro, Kakaramea, Pihanga, Tauhara, Mount Edgecumbe, and Mayor Island, containing among them twelve more or less perfect craters, and having hot springs close to their bases, exist within this Zone. This state of things shows that the volcanic *forces* are not really extinct; they have simply changed the places and the character of their manifestations. We must not forget that volcanic energy is world-wide; for even in steady old Britain we have an earthquake now and then; hot springs exist at Bath, Strathpeffer, and elsewhere; while the Isle of Skye offers a most interesting field for the study of extinct volcanic phenomena. We now proceed to the detailed consideration of the eruption of Mount Tarawera on June 10, 1886.

Mount Tarawera (3650 feet) on the shore of the lake of that name, resembled Table Mountain, Cape of Good Hope, when I saw it in 1880. It is wonderfully changed now. It is composed of rhyolitic and trachytic rocks, and is (Mr. Smith thinks), of igneous origin, but not an extinct volcano; nor does it possess any trace of a crater. The three summits mentioned in chapter vi. are, in order, from north-east to north-west, Wahanga, Ruawahia, and Tarawera. So free was Tarawera from even the tradition of ever having been a source of eruption that the Maoris of the Arawa tribe had buried their chiefs there for centuries. The Maoris of the Tuhourangi tribe, the same who had monopolised the Terraces so covetously (see chapter vi.), had removed to a place called Te Ariki, on a little bay in Lake Tarawera, close to the mountain that broke out. These all perished to a man. An old chief, Rangiheua by name, with about a dozen of the Maoris of the Tuhourangi tribe, had encamped on two islets in Lake Rotomahana for the purposes of sanitary bathing; and these shared the same fate. The total loss of life is reckoned at 111 lives—six Whites and 105 Maoris.

Premonitory Signs.

June in this latitude corresponds to December in the northern hemisphere. The rains of winter had just begun to fall when the eruption took place, after a very dry summer. But the evening of the 9th of June was fine, permitting the visitors at Rotorua to see distinctly the occultation of Mars by the moon at 10.20 P.M. Most fortunate it was and a cause of deep thankfulness that the event I am about to chronicle took place in winter, when there are very few visitors to the lakes and Terraces, and before the establishment of an hotel on the shores of Lake Rotomahana, which was planned for the following summer season. The loss of life would then have been terrible, involving persons from all parts of the world, who in rapidly increasing numbers have been attracted to these beauties of nature. Various changes in the level of Lake Rotokakahi; increased violence of the geysers of the White Terrace, of Wairakei, and of Toka-anu; together with the new phenomenon of steam issuing from the extinct crater of Mount Ruapehu (the Mont Blanc of the North Island), had been noticed by competent observers. The last scientific visitor of note to the Terraces, Dr. T. S. Ralph, of Melbourne, on the 1st of June, describes a peculiar and unusual wave on Lake Tarawera, which caused a temporary rise of the water to the extent of one foot. The guide of his party, Sophia, was alarmed, stating that no such wave had been seen on the lake for fifteen years. There was no wind at the time. At the Pink Terrace it was noticed that there had been a very unusual ejection of mud from that geyser. It was on this 1st of June that the Maori boatmen started the story of the spectral canoe of ancient shape, filled by warriors of the Arawa tribe, which, they said, they saw crossing the Lake Tarawera. Mr. Edwin Bainbridge, one of the victims of the eruption, told Dr. Ralph that on the 1st of June, about the hour that the tidal wave had been seen, he was riding towards Wairoa, and heard a report like the boom of a cannon. In view of subsequent events, it is concluded by scientists that this lake wave was due to an earthquake, or to a subsidence of the shore, marking perhaps the first significant fracture of the rock-masses superimposed on the imprisoned steam, which shortly afterwards was to work such destruction. It is strange that the barometer (self-registering) at Rotorua showed no sign of atmospheric disturbance, either before, during, or after the eruption.

The Eruption of Tarawera.

About 1 A.M., on June the 10th, slight earthquake shocks were felt by the inhabitants of Wairoa, a village eight miles from and due west of Mount Tarawera and by those of Rotorua (eleven miles north-west of Wairoa), where the shakings were accompanied by rumbling noises. At 2.10 or 2.20 A.M. this rumbling noise had increased at Rotorua to a continuous and fearsome roar, and a rather heavy earthquake occurred, felt also at Whakarewarewa, Maketu, Opotiki, Oropi, and Tauranga. At the same time three enormous columns of fire and smoke were seen to rise from the flat summit of Tarawera and to shoot up into the air to an immense height. From this great cloud flashes of electricity and balls of fire darted in all directions, accompanied by loud crackling noises, such as are heard in auroral displays and in the discharges of the static electrical machines. Repeated and very loud claps of thunder were heard. Fireballs, that is, red hot lumps of scoria, and other stone, rolled down the sides of Tarawera or were projected into Wairoa, setting on fire some of the houses and huts. From 3 A.M. to 6 A.M., as the great black cloud worked its way towards the west, north, and south, showers of stone, of mud, and of rain overwhelmed Wairoa, Te Ariki, and the whole neighbourhood of Tarawera and Rotomahana. From Rotomahana, shortly after the outbreak at Tarawera, rose a column of steam, with loud explosions at intervals, and ejections of mud, sand, and ashes. In Auckland two loud explosions were heard at about 2.30 A.M., waking people from their slumbers, myself among the number. The detonations were interpreted by the morning paper to be the sounds of signal guns of distress fired by some large ship aground on the dangerous Manukau bar, but by 9 A.M. telegrams from Rotorua disclosed their real origin. These explosions were heard also at Hamilton, Cambridge, Te Aroha, New Plymouth, Helensville, Whangarei, Waiapu, Taupo, and Wellington, in the North Island; and at Nelson, Blenheim, and Christchurch, in the Middle Island.

The earthquakes were felt at Te Aroha, Cambridge, Lichfield, Waiapu, Taupo, and other places in the North Island. At Rotorua they recurred every ten minutes or so during the 10th of June, and at frequent intervals for days afterwards.

The flashes of electricity were distinctly seen at Auckland, 130 miles distant in a straight line. The vast cloud arising from the new volcano was highly charged with lightning, flashing and darting across and through it, sometimes shooting upwards in long streamers, at other downwards or horizontally, often ending in balls of fire, which burst into thousands of rocket-like stars. The immense cloud of ashes and dust shot up to an almost incredible height in the air, driven first by the south-easterly wind in a westerly direction, and then by the south-west wind towards the north and east. I saw it among hundreds of people at Auckland from the hill called Mount Victoria, North Shore, on the 12th of June, and its height was ascertained by surveyors to be 44,700 feet, or a little over eight miles above the sea level! It quenched the bright moonlight on that fatal night, and darkened the sky until 11 A.M. over all the country around. Charged with ash, dust, sand, and small stones, it spread over 5700 miles of land, dropping these as it went, places 160 miles apart being covered with the material; and it passed far out to sea also. The farms along the coast-line of the Bay of Plenty, from Tauranga to Opotiki, suffered heavily by the destruction of the grasses and vegetation, which caused the death of cattle and sheep from want of food, many of the settlers not having hay or the means to procure it. But the country was not permanently affected, for the rains of the winter washed the deposited dust into the soil, and it proved a fertilizer to the more barren places in the district, while somewhat deleterious to the fertile soils. This volcanic dust consisted, *according to its proximity to or remoteness from the focus of the cloud*, of the following ingredients: silica 66·5 to 55·7; alumina 14·5 to 13·8; iron oxides 4 to 8·3; lime 2·9 to 6·35; magnesia 1·60 to 1·40. In addition there were, on testing it with dilute hydrochloric acid, the following substances: soda, potash, chlorine, phosphoric and sulphuric acids, and organic matter.

Results of the Eruption.

The eruption was practically all over in six hours as far as Tarawera Mountain was concerned. But the craters formed on the site of Rotomahana continued active until the 6th of August. The magnitude of the eruption must not be gauged by the time it lasted, for a marvellous amount of volcanic energy was compressed into a short space of time. The eruption-effects began to be observed from the 13th of June onwards, for exploring parties started off promptly on hearing the news from Auckland, Napier, Taupo, and Cambridge.

Mr. Percy Smith, on the part of the Government, reports in his official pamphlet—1st, that the eruption has formed a great fissure in the earth's crust (marked in red on map 3), nine miles long from north-east to south-west, of a mean width of a furlong, but at Rotomahana a mile and a half broad, 900 feet deep at the northern, and 300 feet deep at the southern end. 2nd, that Rotomahana has become a great crater of one and a half miles in diameter. This crater is encircled by precipitous walls from 200 to 300 feet high. Below the walls the ground slopes by ridges and hollows to the central cavity now filled by water, which is only 565 feet above sea level, or 515 feet *below* the former level of Rotomahana Lake. In this large crater are geysers vomiting steam and mud. Its sides are branded with various colours, the yellow of the ferrochlorides, and the white of the silicates and lime oxides predominating.

Both Pink and White Terraces have disappeared so completely that even their sites can only be guessed at by the native and half-caste guides, who are so familiar with the locality. The conjecture, most probably accurate, judging from the fragments of white silicious sinter found scattered about the northern side of the Rotomahana crater, and the damming up of the Kaiwaka creek to the depth of eighty feet, is that the Pink Terrace has been overwhelmed by a great mass of mud and stones, and that the White Terrace has been partly blown to pieces, and partly has been sunk down far below the ground. A great many cracks in the ground, varying from a few inches to forty feet wide, made by earthquakes, exist in this district. The general direction is parallel to the great fissure. The desolate hue of the whole district round where the bluish-grey mud still lingers can be better imagined than described; but there is still much scenery of great interest for visitors to explore, as I shall describe later on.

The ashes and mud that covered the country over so large an area (p. 127) have now been to a large extent carried off by the streams and rivers; the river Tarawera (which before the eruption had perfectly clear water), ever since the eruption having had its stream made milky-white, and even whitening, the sea for a mile or two near its mouth (see Map 3), throughout the summer of 1886–7. The Government have made new roads, practicable for buggies and light carriages, nearly up to the edge of the great fissure, and to Wairoa, from which points one can plainly see the great gash, as it were, in the side of Tarawera. As the activity of the three craters of this mountain has now (July, 1889) ceased, Mr. Smith is of opinion that the eruption of June the 10th

1886, was an incomplete effort to form a permanently active volcano like Vesuvius or Ætna, only the first stage of the formation being actually attained. Further developments may be looked for; and we in Auckland, being absolutely free from earthquakes, and from other manifestations of disturbance, ascribed our continued immunity to this safety-valve of Tarawera. The alarm felt for some months about the stability of Rotorua and Whakarewarewa, where the geysers have played more vigorously since the eruption, has passed away; and, as the bath accommodation there is very much improved and enlarged, visitors and invalids have resumed coming in large numbers.

The Loss of Life by the Eruption.

Two native settlements, Te Moura and Te Ariki, were destroyed, and every life lost (including a white man), except one. At Wairoa several natives were killed by the falling stones, or smothered in their huts by the mud, scoria, and stones together. This result of the Tarawera eruption reminds us of the sudden destruction of Herculaneum and Pompeii, by the eruption of Vesuvius in A.D. 79, by the ashes and scoria; but the entire absence of molten lava from the former outbreak marks a distinct difference. The most pathetic incidents were the deaths of Mr. Haszard, the schoolmaster, and his three children; the injuries of Mrs. Haszard, who was dug out of the burnt and crushed house, with a dead child lying on her lap; and the death of Mr. Edwin A. Bainbridge, of Newcastle-on-Tyne, at Macrae's Hotel. A touching little memoir of the latter, who was an eminent young Christian, has been written by Mr. Darlington (published by Morgan and Scott), from which I take the following details, as they give the reader a vivid picture of the horrors of that fatal night.

Mr. Bainbridge had visited the Terraces on the 8th of June, and was staying at the Te Wairoa Hotel, kept by a brave Scotchman, Macrae, on the night of the 9th.

He was awakened about 1 A.M. by the landlord, who was the first in the house to be roused, by a severe earthquake and a roaring wind which suddenly sprang up. Mr. Minett, one of the twenty persons staying in the hotel, thus records the events of the night (I condense his narrative):—" I could see the Tarawera mountain belching out flames thousands of feet into the air, and illuminating the whole heavens, clouds of steam and smoke rose above this and a molten shining mass rolled down the sides. The wind increased; it began, as we thought, to rain heavily. The windows were smashed in and we found that what we had taken for rain was scoria and stones. The wind, blowing violently, was veering and shifting in every direction; stones and scoria were dashing on the house with deafening noise; and the roaring of the crater was tremendous. The roof of the house now began to fall in various places; dust, tons of sand, came thundering through the roof, clearing all before it, and lodging in the staircase within a yard of where we were assembled. Looking out, we perceived a fire on the opposite side of the road, which reminded us of the danger we were in from the same cause, and in about five minutes we saw a still larger fire to our right, which we made out was Mr Haszard's house in a blaze. . . between earthquake and fire we stood expecting death. Mr. Bainbridge now, by consent of Mr. Macrae and the rest of those present, read a chapter from the Bible, about the penitent thief on the cross and his forgiveness, spoke a few words of solemn exhortation, and offered a beautiful and touching prayer. We were all silent—expecting death at any moment—either by being buried alive by the sand, mud, and stones that were overwhelming the house, or by suffocation by the sulphurous gases that pervaded the air, or by being crushed under the falling timbers; or swallowed up by the opening ground as it trembled under our feet. Mr. Bainbridge, though calm, seemed to feel that he would not survive the night. He said that whether he lived or died the disaster would have a great effect on his family, as his brother

Cuthbert had been accidentally shot, and his sister May had lately died suddenly from disease. . . It was determined to make a start for Sophia's *whare* (whose highly sloped roof effectually prevented the mud from burying it, and thereby saved the lives of many); the crashing of the house in all directions and the roaring of the volcano prevented any one from hearing the sound of the falling verandah, which must have collapsed just at this time . . . When Mr. Bainbridge's body was found, it appeared that while in the act of leaving the hotel he had been caught and crushed by the verandah. His last words written in his diary on the night of his death were full of trust and faith: 'This is the most awful moment of my life. I cannot tell when I may be called on to meet my God. I am thankful that I find His strength sufficient for me.'"

Kind Auckland friends buried him at Rotorua and erected an obelisk with a suitable inscription. Thus died a Christian hero at the early age of twenty, a simple, gentle, fearless, and pure character, beloved by all who knew him.

Another victim of the eruption was a very different character, old Tuhoto, one of the last, if not the last, of the Maori *tohungas*, or priest-sorcerers, reputed to be 104 years old. He was imprisoned in his *whare* for four days by the mud, and dug out alive! He would have been lynched by the Maoris, who believed that his spells (*karakias*) had caused the eruption, but that his white friends hurried him off to the hospital at Rotorua, where he died in a few days. In times of great excitement Maoris sometimes lose the Christianity they are supposed to hold, and go back for the time to their ancient superstitious belief.

The Wonderland that Remains.

Readers must not think that the catastrophe of the 10th June, 1886, has obliterated all that is worth seeing in the Hot Lake Country. Not by any means, for new places of great interest, hitherto unknown, have been opened up since that event.

Between the Paeroa Range on the west and the Kaingaroa Plain on the east lies the Wai-o-tapu ("sacred river") Valley, stretching from Lake Ngahewa to Ohako. Guarded at its northern end by two grim giants, Mounts Maungaongaonga ("the mount of the stinging nettle"), 2764 feet, and Kakaramea, of the same height. This valley abounds in steam holes, fissures, cauldrons, natural hot baths, lakelets, and terraces in an early stage of formation. The view from the summit of Maungaongaonga is indescribably grand. Far down the valley you see Mount Tauhara, the "Lone Lover" of the Maoris, on which there is a splendid (extinct) crater; beyond, the broad waters of Taupo glisten in the sun; and in the background Tongariro and Ruapehu, mantled in whitest snow, stand out in relief against the blue sky, while the cloud of steam and smoke from Ngauruhoe, reminds you of Vesuvius in its usual aspect. Small lakes, the Green and the Blue, framed in dark-green foliage, glitter in the valley. The Kaingaroa Plains, fifteen miles wide, and seamed with many valleys, lie on the east, with a mass of wild broken country beyond them, extending as far as the eye can reach.

The present chief attraction of Wai-o-tapu are the Pink Cauldron on the side of Maungaongaonga, and the White Terrace. The "Pink Cauldron" is a deep basin coated along its sides and bottom with cream-coloured silicious sinter, tinged with green, yellow, and pink hues, the latter predominating. In one corner of the basin a boiling pool gurgles and splutters, while loud thuds, as of a steam hammer at work, are heard at frequent intervals. On the uppermost side of the basin are three geysers, each about six feet in diameter, arranged one above the other, and filled with boiling water of the purest blue, which, as it rises, flows over the beautiful incrustations of pink and white silica which fringes these cups, and is gradually building up a tier of exquisitely designed steps. Close to these steps is a semicircular fissure, from which dense volumes of steam arise. Higher up the mountain side a jet of steam issues from a small hole with a noise like a locomotive-engine letting off high-pressure steam. About four miles from the northern entrance to the valley is the "White Lake," so called from its sides being formed of milk-white silica, which has assumed a variety of fantastic shapes, and presents an indescribably beautiful appearance. Close to this is the White Terrace, the Te Tarata of the future, now in process of formation. In years to come this piece of fairy-like workmanship will compensate for the loss to the world of the original model. At Wairakei also, six miles from Lake Taupo, there are a series of most curious geysers, one of which called the "Crow's Nest"—from the peculiar nest-like form of the incrustation deposits, which include sticks, branches, and ferns, all silicated over and massed together, that enclose the funnel of the geyser—is the subject of very great interest. The hot sulphurous baths here are of great efficacy. The growth of fruit-trees at this place is extraordinary, the peach and apple bearing luxuriantly after the first year. Most other fruit-trees flourish well, and the Australian gum-tree shoots up faster here even than elsewhere.

The mountain of Horo-Horo, on the road to Wairakei from Rotorua, has a crag projecting from it resembling a veiled female; the Maoris called it "Hinemoa—turned to stone." Some miles from this is a rock called Dickens's Head from a supposed likeness to the novelist. At Ateamuri the road crosses the Waikato at a romantic spot, and the Huka Falls on this large river are most imposing. Lake Taupo, 241 miles square, affords the painter and the lover of scenery a perfect treat; but its waters are treacherously stormy, and much care must be exercised in venturing across it or coasting in a boat. In due time the grand tour of the North Island will be through the country shown on map 3., taking first Te Aroha, then Rotorua, next the Terraces, Waiotapu Valley, and of Orakei-Korako on the Waikato River; the Alum Cave in the same locality;

then the Wairakei geysers, the Huka Falls, Joshua's Baths, near Taupo township; Lake Taupo itself, with Tokaano on its southern shore, where there are numerous geysers and hot springs; the place where the chief Te Heu Heu, with a great number of his people, were overwhelmed by a landslip; thence along the road by the Poutou Valley, skirting the northern base of Tongariro (which now may be ascended without obstruction by the Maoris); by picturesque Lake Roto Aira, for twenty miles or more along the eastern bases of Tongariro, Ngauruhoe, and Ruapehu; or through most beautiful woodland and park-like plains to Waimarino, a Maori *kainga* on the line of the Central Trunk Railway, about midway between Auckland and Wellington, a little over 200 miles from each city. The falls on the Upper Wanganui River are also very well worth a visit, and Mount Egmont (Taranaki) affords one of the most satisfactory Alpine ascents in New Zealand.

CHAPTER VIII.

SELF-GOVERNMENT AND THE SETTLEMENT OF THE LAND.

History of the colony—Treaty of Waitangi, 1840—No convict element at any period—Several centres of colonization—Changes in the constitution—Responsible self-government granted in 1853—Governors of New Zealand from 1840 to 1889—Premiers since 1853—Premiers I have known—Beneficent Acts of Parliament—Colonial debt, how incurred—Absolute solvency of the colony proved by statistics—Laws regulating sale, lease, and transfer of Crown lands—Success of perpetual leasing and of village settlement.

THE colony of New Zealand can justly boast that it was founded by free men, of their own will, and that it has never been the seat of convict establishments. In the first instance New Zealand was a Crown colony, having been so constituted at the time when the treaty of Waitangi was signed in February, 1840, by the leading Maori chiefs and by Captain Hobson, R.N., on the part of her Majesty Queen Victoria. By this treaty—the Magna Charta, so to speak, of the Maori to this day—the sovereignty of New Zealand was given up to the Queen, and the right of pre-emption of any lands the natives wished to sell was given to the Crown that is, the *de facto* government of the colony for the time being. But, in return, all their tribal rights and customs, their land, cattle, and other possessions, were retained by the Maoris, and they became British subjects, with all the privileges attaching to that proud position. The treaty was drafted by Mr. Busby, and fully interpreted by the Rev. Henry Williams. The chief, Tamati Waka Nene, afterwards our faithful ally in the wars, was largely instrumental in determining the waverers among the chiefs to sign. Practically the Maoris have never been liable to direct taxation since this treaty, and their lands were by its Art. II. saved from the depredations of unscrupulous speculators. In fact, the scrupulous desire of the colonial authorities, all through the history of New Zealand, to carry out this treaty in its integrity, and to specially safeguard the rights of the natives has retarded the settlement of the country. For so long as one adult Maori of the *hapu* (tribe) withheld his or her signature from the deed of transfer of any land held by the tribe, even though honestly sold and purchased, the white man's title could not be validated. The tedious delays, repetitions of Maori genealogies, old stories of how this or that piece of land passed, by conquest, inheritance, or communal ownership from hand to hand; and the cross-swearing, have caused many hundreds of honest settlers to curse the Treaty of Waitangi and the Native Lands Court Act, and some have even given up the intention of settling on native land, in despair of ever obtaining a clear title. The famous treaty was hastily drawn up because of the race between the English and French commanders to plant the flag of their respective countries first in New Zealand, and thus claim it as a colony.

Of late years the procedures of the Native Lands Courts have been shortened and simplified, and, through interpreters, and their own increased knowledge of the English language and ways, the Maoris have come round to understand what an advantage it is for them to sell or lease their land at a good figure to men who will cultivate it, live upon it, and hire their labour also. I understand that Maoris work well for wages, though not for long at a time. Their railway sub-contracts are also faithfully performed. The Government has been a "paternal" one to the natives. From time to time special Acts of Parliament have been passed, providing for the equitable lease, sale, or transfer of their lands; for their free education; their Parliamentary representation, medical attendance, food and shelter; and the Maoris since the last peace have appreciated this kindness. The first Maori war was caused by the misunderstanding on the part of several Maori chiefs (who did not sign the treaty) of the provisions and binding character of that document. But in all their wars of independence it was only a minority of the natives who took up arms against us, the large majority either remaining peaceable, or assisting us actively. The *Hau-hau* or "*Pai-marire*" fanatical outbursts were confined to a small district, and soon were suppressed. As was remarked in chapter iii., the Maoris have always behaved honourably in open war, and while the "civilized" French were suffocating Arabs, men, women, and children, in caves in Algeria, the "savage" Maori was exchanging all the courtesies of war with the British who were conquering his country. And now all New Zealand, even the "King" country, is open to the traveller—the remark made on p. 38 about the inaccessibility of the latter region only applying to the absence of roads, accommodation, sign-posts, and so on. If New Zealand were to be invaded, I am sure that the Maoris would enrol themselves as soldiers of the colony and fight to the last man for us, with all the bravery of their ancestors.

The first Governor of New Zealand was Captain William Hobson, a just, humane, and prudent man, who kept faith with white man and Maori alike, and gave the "tone" to some who succeeded him which is so beneficial to the administration of a young and mixed community consisting of dominant and subject races. In 1840 he founded Auckland, and in the following year made it the capital of New Zealand. He died in 1842; and after Lieut.-Colonel Shortland had carried on the Government for a year, Captain Fitzroy was appointed. After two years he was succeeded by Captain G. Grey (made a K.C.B. in 1848), who in September, 1852, had the dignity of his office increased by the abolition of that of Lieutenant-Governor.

Meantime colonization was going rapidly on from

four or five different centres. In 1840 Wellington, the present capital, was founded by the New Zealand Company of London. In 1841 New Plymouth and Nelson were commenced. Dunedin and the province of Otago were settled in 1848 by a band of Scottish Presbyterians, and in 1850 Christchurch and the province of Canterbury were founded by a Church of England association. Thus it was that the proverbial Presbyterian ruling element in Dunedin and the Episcopalian sentiment of Christchurch came about. With the exceptions, however, of a German settlement at Puhoi, near Waiwera, and the Scandinavians at Norsewood and Dannevirke, all of which are thriving, there is no predominance of either one religion or one nationality in any town or district in the colony. When at Tromsö within the arctic circle, this summer (1889), I saw with much pleasure a party of hardy Norsemen ready to go out to New Zealand—a change indeed from a winter temperature (the mean average) of 23° to one of 56°!

The colonization from four great centres has made New Zealand very different from the Australian colonies, each of which grew from one centre only. This fact also increases the difficulty of governing New Zealand effectively from one point. Decentralization has had its day, and now the tendency is to too great centralization. The reason why so large a salary and allowance, amounting to £7500 per annum, has been hitherto paid to the Governor by a colony so small in population is that, in order to be useful throughout the whole colony, the Governor must visit and stay at all the four "capitals" during his term of office, although his permanent official residence is in Wellington.

Up to the year 1853 New Zealand remained a Crown colony. In that year responsible government in the shape of a popular Constitution, on a plan drawn up by Sir George Grey and adopted by the Imperial Government in 1852, was granted to New Zealand. The Governor, appointed by the Queen for five years; a Legislative Council composed of members nominated for life by the

Crown; and a House of Representatives elected by the people on a liberal franchise for five years constituted the legislature of the colony. Power was given to the legislature to make laws, to raise loans, to levy duties and impose taxes, and to modify the constitution of the colony. New Zealand was divided into six, afterwards nine, provinces:—in the North Island the provinces of Auckland, Hawke's Bay, Taranaki, and Wellington; in the Middle Island the Provinces of Nelson, Marlborough, Westland, Canterbury, and Otago. Each province was administered by an elective superintendent and an elective council; and each province sent a certain number of representatives to the Colonial Parliament. Twenty years of this mode of government sufficiently proved its impracticability, when such hotly disputed subjects as land endowments, the construction of railways, roads, and bridges, and the apportionment of the money raised at home, came under discussion. Each province tried to grasp the largest share of the good things dealt out by the central colonial Government. After several years' discussion a sweeping reform was carried out in 1875, whereby the whole Provincial System of administration was abolished, and the colony was divided into sixty-three counties, each provided with an elective county council armed with full powers of local self-government, including rating. From time to time enlarged powers have been granted by the Imperial Government to the New Zealand Parliament; in fact, the whole tendency of imperial legislation, as it affects this colony, for the past thirty years, has been to give the colony *absolute self-government in its domestic matters.* The Governor has the power of assenting to or withholding assent from the Acts passed by the colonial legislature, or he can "reserve them for her Majesty's will and pleasure."

Two facts in the parliamentary history of New Zealand speak well for the right-mindedness, loyalty, and common sense of its legislators: *first*, there has never been in New Zealand a "dead-lock" between the two Houses of Parliament, as in several of the Australian colonies; and, *second,* that out of more than two thousand Acts passed in New Zealand there have not been more than six instances of disallowance (veto) by the Queen.

It may be of interest here to enumerate in chronological order the excellent Governors who have filled the New Zealand appointment — now a first-class governorship at the Colonial Office — from the death of Captain Hobson in 1842 to the present time, omitting only the temporary administrators. In the absence or resignation of the Governor the administration of his functions devolves upon the Chief Justice of the Supreme Court. The list is as follows :—Captain Fitzroy; Sir George Grey; Colonel T. Gore Browne; Sir George Grey (second term); Sir G. F. Bowen; Sir James Fergusson, Bart.; The Marquis of Normanby; Sir Hercules Robinson; Sir Arthur Gordon; Sir W. F. D. Jervois; Lord Onslow. These have been all able men, and as a rule the rank that New Zealand holds in the classification of colonial governorships entitles it to obtain the services of experienced administrators.

In New Zealand great legislative experiments are being tried and worked out which are carefully watched by both political parties at home, and by the Americans and foreigners who visit the country. Parliaments are triennial; all members are paid; practically manhood suffrage exists; petitions to Parliament and objections to parliamentary elections have a careful consideration accorded them; the conduct of Government officials and of public men is freely ventilated by the press; and on the whole the government of New Zealand, with all its faults, comes as near as may be to the democratic ideal of a "government by the people and for the people." At the present time, owing to the heavy burden of interest payable on the colonial debt (£35,196,000 on March 31, 1888), large reductions are being made in all branches of the Government. The Governor's salary is reduced to £5000; the salaries of Cabinet ministers are largely reduced; the number of representatives is decreased from 95 to 74, thereby saving twenty-one *honoraria* of £210 each paid to members; and the civil service has been so cut down that in the executive departments of Government the saving already effected amounts to £233,000. In chapter ix. I have summarised briefly the financial and economical position of the colony, and need not further enlarge on this important subject. These Radical principles of representative popular government above enumerated seem to tend to frequent changes of the Ministry—the real Government of New Zealand. In my comparatively short residence in the colony I have witnessed the entrance and exit of six ministries (in nine years), each change being accompanied with a certain amount of disturbance in the steady working of the public services, and a variation of the financial policy of the preceding Cabinet, so far as regards the mode of raising money. The incidence of taxation is, of course, the "burning question" of the last nineteen years, for at the present time the six hundred thousand white people of New Zealand have to pay the enormous interest, annually, of the sum of £1,767,200—at least, not having the legerdemain skill of Sir Julius Vogel, K.C.M.G., in figures, I cannot make it less, after a diligent study of all the latest statements and statistics. But, from what has been stated above, the reader will understand that the Government is manfully economising in every possible way, and so good is the credit of the colony in the Home money market that the last (1888) four per cent. loan of two millions was subscribed for *four times over*.

In chapter ix. I have clearly stated the process, reasons, or excuses for, and results of, the "borrowing policy;" and sketched candidly the present position and future prospects of New Zealand.

On looking over the list of Premiers and Ministers since 1853, I have been struck with the fact that even this changeful Parliament of colonists chooses the same men, over and over again, to lead them and guide them. I consider it a high testimony to their character and ability. As a chronological table would occupy too much space, I will merely enumerate the names of the premiers since 1856, when Mr. Henry Sewell took office on the 7th of May. On the 20th of May he was succeeded by my friend Sir William Fox, who has four times served his country most ably in this responsible position. Next in order comes Sir E. W. Stafford, who has thrice been premier; next Alfred Domett, author of that charming poem "Ranolf and Amohia;" Sir Frederick Whitaker, whose honourable *sobriquet* is "the Nestor of politics," twice premier; Sir Frederick A. Weld, whose successful career as governor of various colonies (Tasmania, Straits Settlements, &c.) is well known; G. M. Waterhouse, Esq., who bears a striking facial resemblance to Charles Kingsley; Sir Julius Vogel, the celebrated financier, twice; Daniel Pollen, Esq.; Sir George Grey, K.C.B.; Sir John Hall; Sir Robert Stout, a clever advocate, the head of the colonial bar, twice; and Sir Harry Atkinson, who *five times* has been chosen premier, and is now (1889) holding that arduous position. I have sometimes mentally compared him to Ciucinnatus, for the honourable gentleman is an ardent agriculturist and raiser of choice breeds of fowls and ducks in the sylvan glades and breezy downs of Taranaki.

The five premiers whom I have the honour of knowing personally are men of vigorous intellect, of learning and culture, of knowledge of men and statecraft, frank yet dignified in bearing, courteous in demeanour, having "fads" no doubt, but not injurious ones. There is much to be said, *e.g.*, for Sir Harry Atkinson's "fad" of national insurance, and for Sir George Grey's "fad" of land nationalization; and all these five are men who would not only do credit to the British Houses of Parliament, either as Peers or Commons, but even to the Imperial Ministry.

A Cabinet minister in New Zealand, as in other free colonies, must learn to be pachydermatous, yet conciliatory. While in office everyone may worry them with letters, petitions, interviews, and so forth, while the opposition newspapers continually accuse them of idling, pleasuring at the country's expense, nepotism, promise-breaking, bribing partisans, voting themselves extra allowances, and all that sort of electioneering calumny. I used to feel hurt sometimes, when I *knew* for a fact that none of these gentlemen had done these things, nor had they enriched but rather impoverished themselves by their tenure of high office. Out of those five premiers, one has immortalized his name by the magnificent gift of a library of rare literary gems to the city of Auckland; another has employed for many years his rare legal acumen to draw up with accuracy wise, just, and beneficent Acts of Parliament; and a third has proved himself the most economical minister the colony ever had.

Quite recently the entire colony has been divided into equal electoral districts, and a modification of the Hare system of cumulative voting is to be introduced—another important experiment in Representative Government.

And now, bidding adieu to colonial politics, I will come to the chief object of this chapter, which is to give the intending immigrant some idea of the land laws of New Zealand, and of the kind of land that he will find still unappropriated.

The colony is filling up more slowly since the public money used in granting free or assisted passages came to an end. But already about one in every five of the adult males of New Zealand occupy and work land. The number of holdings of one acre and upwards in February, 1888, was 34,743. Of land cultivated or broken up ready for cultivation there are twelve acres for each person (man, woman and child) in the colony. In Great Britain and Ireland the proportion is not quite $1\frac{1}{2}$ acres per head. Upwards of thirty-three million acres of land belonging to the Crown are still unsold in the colony. Of these acres fourteen millions are open fern or grass land, ten millions forest, and nine million barren mountain-tops, lakes, and worthless country. The Crown lands of the colony are administered under two laws called "The Land Act, 1885," and the "The Land Act Amendment Act, 1887."

The large tracts still owned by the Maoris, however, are dealt with under another law, "The Native Lands Act, 1888," whereby every precaution possible is provided to cheapen and facilitate the sale, lease, or transfer of native land, and to establish firmly the title of the purchaser. In no country in the world is the transfer and registration of land more inexpensive and complete than in New Zealand. Oh that we had such a state of things in England, where a simple lease of a house costs £10! There are Crown Lands Offices in the following thirteen cities and towns in New Zealand (possibly others may have been opened since these lines were written): Auckland, Tauranga, Gisborne, Napier, New Plymouth, Patea, Wellington (North Island), Nelson, Blenheim, Christchurch, Hokitika, Dunedin, and Invercargill (Middle Island). Crown lands are divided into three classes:—

1. Town and village lands, being the sites heretofore reserved or which shall be hereafter reserved for towns and villages.

2. Suburban lands in the vicinity of the above.

3. Rural lands, comprising all other land, whether forest, pastoral, or agricultural, except mining ground.

These lands can be purchased direct from the Crown, thus rendering all swindles by land agents either at home or in the colony impossible. They are sold by public auction from time to time, as the demand varies, or on application by intending purchasers at the Land Office of the district, at prices varying from five to forty shillings per acre, according to one or other of the following plans:—

I. Immediate and Full Cash Payment at the "upset price," thus securing the freehold of the land without any further liability. The area purchaseable by one adult is wisely restricted by law to 640 acres of first-class or 2000 acres of second-class land, in order to discourage the formation of large estates belonging to one individual. Of course companies can purchase to a larger amount.

II. The Deferred Payment System, (area not more

L

than 320 acres per head). Suburban lands are sold at £4 10s. per acre; rural lands at not less than £1 per acre, except in certain parts of the colony, where the price may be less. The payments are made in equal instalments every six months, and are spread over a period of five years for suburban and ten years for rural land. The selector binds himself to reside on the land for at least six years, and to fence and cultivate a certain amount of ground each year. If more than one person applies for the same land on the same day it is put up for competition by tender, *limited to the applicants.* Supposing a piece of rural land is priced at £1 per acre, the purchaser pays only one shilling every six months for ten years, at the end of which time the freehold of the land becomes his own. Another convenient arrangement is provided by the Government: any purchaser under this system who has paid his two first instalments, and has complied with all the conditions of cultivation, may have the amount of the unpaid instalments capitalized, at the then value of an annuity of the same amount as the payments then due to complete the purchase. The settler then begins to pay semi-annually, instead of the original half-yearly instalment of the purchase money a sum which is fixed at five per cent. upon that capitalized amount until the whole of the balance is paid to the Government.

III. Perpetual Leasing. To a *bonâ-fide* occupier lands in certain districts are leased at a fixed rental of five per cent. on the capital value, which is usually £1 per acre, for thirty years, with right of renewal for twenty-one years, and so on for ever. The area of land per head leased in this way is restricted to 640 acres. The first lessee has the right of purchase after six and within twelve years if he elects to buy. At the end of the first lease, should the occupier wish to sell the lease to anyone, the incoming tenant is bound by law to pay the full value of all improvements made on the estate by the first lessee. He is also bound to carry out the original conditions made by the Government. By the

Act of 1877 the freehold of land held in this way may be acquired on certain easy terms. This is the first practical attempt that I am acquainted with towards land nationalization.

IV. The Homestead System. This method of taking up land is specially adapted for poor settlers. No payment is required except the cost of survey. On the completion of the conditions, namely, the erection of a house, and the cultivation of one-third of all his holding if open land, or one-fifth if bush land, the settler will receive his freehold and title from the Crown. Each person of eighteen years of age may take up fifty to seventy-five acres, and if under eighteen years, twenty to thirty acres. It is possible for a man and his family (the wife not being eligible as a selector) to take up as much as 200 acres of good open land and work it so as to make a decent living out of it in three or four years.

V. The Village Settlement Act provides that any person can select fifty acres of land in a particular locality reserved for a village settlement, on perpetual lease, with right of purchase. The rental charged is five per cent. on the purchasing price. The great advantage is that a small proprietor can find work for wages among his neighbours, and can on his leisure days be constantly improving his own farm.

VI. Special Settlements. Any number of persons, not less than twenty-five, of approved character, may obtain the privilege of selecting a large block of land, subject to all the conditions of deferred payment, or perpetual lease, as the case may be, on which they can all settle adjacent to each other. Many flourishing villages have thus been formed, in the North Island especially, some by Englishmen of the same religious denomination (Port Albert), some by Germans (Puhoi), some by Scandinavians (Norsewood). And it has been found that those special settlements flourish best where public-houses have been religiously excluded from the block. Some, it is true, have failed, because of the poverty of the land selected, or because of internal squabbles, or of unsuitability of some of the settlers for farming or agricultural work. But the scheme of every one of these six modes of land settlement is well thought out and thoroughly workable, being fair to both buyer and seller, and safeguarded against abuse by the capitalist.

VII. Small Grazing Runs, not exceeding 5000 acres. These are let from time to time by public auction for a term of twenty-one years, with right of renewal for a second term of same length, at an upset price of $2\frac{1}{2}$ per cent. on the capital value. Recent sales (1888) realised from threepence to one shilling and eightpence per acre, annual rental. The lessee has the exclusive right of the natural pasturage, and may cultivate any or all of the area leased. Full valuation for improvements is allowed to the tenant at the end of each lease.

VIII. Pastoral Runs. These are let by auction on leases for terms not exceeding twenty-one years, in large areas of 5000 acres and upwards. The average rental is about fourpence per acre per annum. Any number of runs may be leased by one person or by a company. Valuation to an amount not exceeding three years' rental is allowed to the outgoing tenant for any improvements he may have made. In the Middle Island about eleven million acres of natural pasturage are leased in this way.

Special provisions are made by the laws of the colony for agricultural leases of land containing minerals, and for gold-mining or Crown lands.

Success in New Zealand, as I have hinted in the opening chapter, as indeed everywhere else in the colonies, depends on the character of the immigrant and the right choice of his place of settlement. No other colony can show a greater number of families who by steady industry, thrift, honesty, and perseverance have raised themselves from poverty to comfort or even wealth. There is hope, therefore, for all immigrants who can and will diligently and intelligently work the land; but let the foolish idea that anyone can without previous training become a successful farmer be dismissed from our minds. The home-bred agriculturist is more likely to succeed in New Zealand at farming than he who has previously followed a different trade or occupation. The excellence of Systems III., IV., and V., consists in the economy of capital, and the wise expenditure of labour by the humblest, poorest, and least educated of settlers. Many of these men have far surpassed Jesse Collings's ideal of "three acres and a cow" by the acquisition, entirely through their own toil, of well-improved farms of from 200 to 400 acres, a score or two of cows, numerous sheep, orchards, vegetable gardens, and a comfortable frame-house. And, what is most important of all, the settler has a ready sale for his lambs, sheep, and agricultural produce, as will be seen by the statement in chapter x. Every year more lines of road and rail are being opened up from the interior to the coast, and from the large towns into the country. At the end of March, 1888, seventeen hundred and seventy miles of railway were open and 8478 miles of road in the colony. By sea the communication between ports is frequent and regular, but the freights are too high for the small farmer because the coast of New Zealand is very dangerous and the Union Steamship Company have practically extinguished all competition. We must acknowledge, however, that no steamship company has done as much as the Union Company to develop and extend the coastal and inter-colonial trading facilities of New Zealand.

CHAPTER IX.

PUBLIC WORKS AND INSTITUTIONS.

Their growth—Nourished on loans—Reaction and commercial depression — Improving prospects and returning prosperity—Churches—Education: Primary, Secondary, and University—New Zealand University—Its statutes, meetings, &c.—Auckland University College—Technical education—Otago Medical School—Lincoln School of Agriculture—The Press of New Zealand—Hospitals, refuges, asylums—Police, gaols, public works, post-office departments—Government Insurance—Government trustees, assignees in bankruptcy—Friendly and Building societies—Sailors' Homes and Rests.

THE multiplication and growth of the public works and institutions of New Zealand, using the word "institutions" in its widest or American sense, have been so rapid since the inauguration by Sir Julius Vogel, in 1870, of the daring 'public works and immigration policy' as to excite the apprehension of thoughtful colonists, that the country was "going ahead" too fast. The policy of developing a new country on borrowed capital, apparently imitated by this astute but too sanguine financier from the example of the United States and the South American republics is a dangerous one. As long as the public money was circulated freely the colony was prosperous, but this prosperity resembles that of the "remittance men" described in chapter xi., a seeming and temporary, rather than a real and permanent prosperity. When the expenditure of the loans so freely spent on the public works of the Government came to an end, the whole of New Zealand felt the pinch, and a state of commercial depression set in about the year 1885, which is only now passing off.

Each of the last four ministries of the colony has come into office pledged to "economy and retrenchment," but Sir H. Atkinson's ministry alone has been successful in grappling with these Herculean and unpopular labours. The stoppage of all money help from the Government to immigrants, the imposition of a direct tax (the property tax); the cessation of half-finished works, throwing out of employment hundreds of workmen, and the dismissal of numerous officials, came upon the community almost simultaneously with a falling-off of exports, a diminished production of gold from the mines, and a lessened influx of tourists, the travelling world having heard that the great attraction of New Zealand, the Sinter Terraces, had been destroyed (chapter vii.).

The problem of how 600,000 people are to pay the annual interest and sinking fund due on a debt of over £35,000,000, while continuing in a state of efficiency an overgrown civil service—of which the costly Education Department is really a branch, and the payment of representatives in Parliament an offshoot—is one that taxes severely the ingenuity of our colonial Chancellors of the Exchequer. Doubtless, on reviewing the colony's history, it is to be regretted that this huge borrowing was not delayed until, by natural and not artificial processes, such as free immigration, the population had increased to four or five times its present number, so that these financial burdens would have been more easily borne, being distributed over a larger number of tax-payers. But those who accuse New Zealand of having not only borrowed recklessly but spent extravagantly upon unremunerative or unnecessary works—and there are many such critics at home I find—must remember that (1) more than twenty-four and a half millions have been spent on public works of a *permanent value*, which have greatly improved and opened up for settlement the interior of the colony; (2) that since 1870 large numbers of people have been attracted to the country, many of whom have become useful colonists; and (3) the present inhabitants of a young country are now enjoying all the conveniences of the most advanced civilization—in some matters, such as cheap telephones, surpassing the mother country. In order to remove the too prevalent but erroneous impression in England that New Zealand is hopelessly sunk in debt, I have collected the following facts, which, being official, are absolutely correct, and, when connected with the chapter on productions and industries (chapter x.), should go far towards establishing a confidence in the solvency of this vigorous colony.

1. The surplus assets over all liabilities of all public and private property in New Zealand amounted in May, 1887, to no less than £128,803,635.

2. With the exception of France and Switzerland, no country in the world can show so large a proportion of savings bank depositors to the general population as New Zealand, viz., *one in six*. This fact shows that there is a thrift among the colonists which one would not have expected to find among a people of such wasteful habits as regards food, and so lavish as regards expenditure on amusements. At the end of March, 1888, after three years of great commercial depression, the moneys deposited in the Government and seven other savings banks amounted to no less than £2,462,304, standing to the credit of 99,277 depositors. The *stability* of the population is shown by the fact that there are 80,527 owners of land in the colony.

3. The stern but necessary reductions in the Government offices are keeping down the cost while not diminishing the efficiency of the collection of the public revenue.

4. The exports of the colony, by the latest returns, show a substantial increase.

5. Capital is flowing into the colony from Australia, an instance of which is the recent purchase by a syndicate, largely composed of Australians, of all the Kauri forests, mills, and machinery in the North Island.

6. The surplus of revenue over expenditure for the

past financial year (1888-9), shows an increase of no less than £453,000.

7. The land sales are greatly improved, 330,817 acres having been purchased by 1893 persons on one or other of the plans described in chapter viii. during the year ending March, 1889.

The reader, then, or his friends who may chance to hold New Zealand bonds need not fear either the loss of principal or the suspension of payment of interest.

The following brief account of the most important public works, institutions, and societies of New Zealand must be premised by stating that the latest complete census of the colony is that of 1886; that the statistics for 1888 and 1889 are not yet available; and that there are many smaller institutions and societies useful to the colony which cannot be included for want of space.

1. *Religion.*

In New Zealand, there being no connection between Church and State, and no one religious body having any social or political pre-eminence over another, one fruitful element of discord in the old country does not exist in the new. The very few endowments that exist have been presented by the early native converts to the missionaries, or acquired by the latter for their churches by subscription. The non-existence of either Establishment or State endowment seems to give exactly that stimulus to the free Church of England in New Zealand which is lacking in many quarters at Home. The new-comer notices an activity and aggressiveness about its organization, a freshness and vigour in its preaching, and a personal knowledge and regard existing between clergyman and congregation, that are not by any means universal in England.

By the latest religious census, that of 1886, it appeared that there were then in New Zealand 1499 buildings open for public worship, with accommodation for over 256,000 persons, being an increase of 385 on the number of similar buildings in 1881. Out of the entire population of 578,482 persons, exclusive of Maoris, there were—

Protestants	461,340
Roman Catholics	80,715
Of no denomination	9,888
Jews and others	6,650
Objected to state their religion	19,889

Analyzing the first division of the foregoing official classification (which is singularly expressed), we find under the term "Protestants"—

Church of England	229,757
Presbyterians	130,643
Wesleyan and other Methodists	45,164
Baptists, Congregationalists, Salvation Army, and other denominations	55,776

The number of children attending Sunday-schools was found to be 99,884, an increase of 20,993 over the attendance in 1881.

I leave readers to draw their own conclusions from these official figures. I have no means of ascertaining how the different denominations have varied in numbers since 1886, the next census being not due till 1891.

There is much Christian work being done by all denominations in New Zealand. The laity make much personal sacrifice to maintain the edifices and services of their churches, and to evangelize rather than proselytize the community at large, among whom a certain amount of combative atheism and a large amount of indifference to religion exist. The stipends of clergymen and ministers are very moderate, and are raised with some difficulty in unprosperous times. Their incomes are derived from pew rents, grants from missionary societies at home, small endowments, and voluntary subscriptions. A bishop's income rarely exceeds £900, a clergyman's would average £300, and a curate's £120. My clerical readers must not take these rough estimates as "gospel," but as approximations to the truth.

It is very pleasing to one who has witnessed something of inter-sectarian bitterness (so utterly opposed to the spirit of Christ's teaching) in old England, to see, in this free country, that in settlements where no one religious body is strong enough to support a resident minister, a hall or schoolroom is hired and shared by the Episcopalians, Wesleyans, Presbyterians, and others, who hold their services in rotation, in perfect harmony, by mutual arrangement.

In Christchurch, founded by the Church of England Association in 1850, there is a preponderance of Episcopalians; and in Dunedin, first established by Presbyterians, there is a predominating element of that creed; but in Wellington, Auckland, Nelson, and the other large towns, sects are pretty equally mixed. Albertland, ninety miles north of Auckland, was founded by Congregationalists, and Roman Catholics pervade the Pensioner settlement of Howick.

Most of the places of worship are built of wood, but Christchurch boasts of a fine stone Anglican cathedral, and Dunedin of her stone Presbyterian churches. Notwithstanding the commercial depression having temporarily limited the power of giving, there has been a steady increase, since the last census, of places of worship and of evangelistic services in halls and schoolrooms. The missions among the Maoris are heartily maintained, and, now that the whole body of natives are Christianized, there is no difficulty in supplying them with trained *native* clergymen and evangelists.

The Church of England in New Zealand takes the lead, naturally enough, in numbers, and in influence, throughout all the provincial districts, except Otago and Southland. It is free, as I have stated, from all State control, and has the advantage of an excellent working Constitution, mainly drawn up by that great and good man, George Augustus Selwyn, first Bishop of New Zealand, whose memory is to the present hour very dearly cherished.

After the disestablishment of the Church of Ireland, that church was remodelled on the plan of this very

Constitution, in its main principles—the greatest respect that could be shown to it. The General Synod of the Episcopal Church is the ruling body; and each diocese has its diocesan synod, presided over by the Bishop of that diocese. The Diocesan Synods meet once a year, the General Synod once in three years, taking the principal cities in rotation. Standing committees conduct the business that may accrue between the synodal meetings. So well do these committees attend to their business, and so admirably is the voting power distributed among the three orders of the Church—bishops, clergy, and laity—that never since the first meeting of the General Synod in Wellington, March 9th, 1859, has any serious discord or quarrel occurred in this branch of the Church of England. The memorable date of the adoption of this constitution at Auckland was June 13th, 1857. Presided over by hardworking bishops, on whom much of the spirit of Selwyn has fallen (as in the case of our Bishop Cowie of Auckland); officered by a clergy filled with a zeal almost free from Ritualism; and filled with lay members who liberally respond to the calls made upon them; the Church of England in New Zealand is a power for good in the land. All the other Protestant denominations are active and doing much good, and it behoves them to be aggressive in the new country, for new-comers too often not only desert their home Church, whatever it may be, but also throw aside all external observances of religion, and sometimes drift away into absolute indifference, or into atheism, if a helping hand is not extended to them by the churches.

2. *Education.*

The educational system, which is estimated to cost the colonists not less than £400,000 per annum, is the pride of the average New Zealander. It is free, compulsory, and absolutely secular. The burden of supplying free Primary education to 110,000 children of school age—seven to thirteen—scattered over a hundred thousand square miles of land, falls upon a population rather less than that of Liverpool and Birkenhead, and is indeed heavy. For the authorities, in their zeal to carry out the Act, have built "full" or "half-time" schools in every place, however remote, where there are a dozen settlers or so. While the English tax-payer pays one shilling and eightpence every year for public education (not absolutely free in England) the New Zealander pays no less than eleven shillings and sixpence. The principle of popular control over the schools is carried out thus. In each city, town, or country district, a School Committee is elected annually by those persons who are on the electoral roll. This Committee manages all the business of the schools in its district, hears complaints, supervises the teacher, but has no power either to appoint or remove him. This power, along with the regulation of the course of study, school-books, furniture, pay, appointment, removal, or censure of teachers, is reserved for the School Board of the province, to which each School Committee sends a delegate. Representatives of the higher educational institutions have also seats on these School Boards, which have permanent secretaries, and appoint the Inspectors of schools. The head of the whole department is the Minister of Education.

The teachers in the Primary schools are carefully selected, according to merit, by the boards from men and women who (1) have had large experience at home and have a university degree; (2) or who have passed creditably through the training colleges of the colony; or (3) who have taken the B.A. degree of the New Zealand University. The four standards for examination in the primary schools are similar to those of the Education Code of Great Britain; and the teaching is thorough, for payment by results forms the larger part of the teachers' salary. In 1887 there were 1093 primary schools, with 110,919 pupils on the rolls, the mean average number attending each school being 82. The number of children on the rolls had increased over that of 1886 by 4591, in a larger proportion than the increase in the population during the year. The actual daily average attendance during the fourth quarter of the year 1887 was 89,589 children. There were also 13,437 children attending private and denominational elementary schools. Counting in the latter we find that New Zealand possesses one school for every 470 inhabitants, which is the *largest proportion of any nation in the world*, France coming near it with one school to 500 inhabitants. The fact that young Australia and young New Zealand are well educated is beginning to strike travellers. Out of 10,000 children, in any part of the Australian colonies, it is found that 9481 can read, and 8535 can write and read, showing that colonial parents freely avail themselves of the free schools. The only charge is one shilling per quarter for school requisites, and even this is remitted where poverty is proved to the board's satisfaction. The figures relating to New Zealand abundantly show the appreciation by the New Zealand parent of the present system of education.

But here let me say as a *paterfamilias*, and as a sincere well-wisher to New Zealand, that in my humble opinion the framers of the Education Act have made too much of the so-called "religious difficulty," in absolutely excluding not only the simple reading of the Bible without note or comment, but also even hymns, prayer, or any form of recognition of the Deity from the public schools. I cannot, for the life of me, see why these simple and comprehensive elements of worship—the prayer or hymn being of course so drawn as to contain no disputed doctrinal teaching—such as are used daily in Great Britain, most of the United States, Ireland, and New South Wales—I cannot understand, I repeat, how or why this procedure should be stigmatised as "denominational endowment," or "teaching religion at the expense of the State." After all, in training a young nation, it should be remembered that it is "righteousness," not mere education, that "exalteth a nation;" and that education, properly conducted, may be made the handmaid of righteousness. That the heart and intellect of man require the moral teaching and Divine truths of the Bible to preserve him from degradation, the facts of colonial life (as of life, indeed, everywhere) abundantly testify. The "larrikinism" commented upon in chapter xi. might have been checked in its origin had the Bible been read in the Primary schools from their first start.

Proceeding, after this digression, step by step higher in public education, we come to the Secondary schools, called "Grammar schools," "High schools," or Colleges, all of which, while State aided by money grants, or State-endowed by lands, charge moderate fees to parents, in addition. In 1887 these schools numbered twenty-two, teaching 2242 pupils. From my son's experience I can bear witness that the curriculum and teaching of one of these, the Auckland College and Grammar School (Headmaster, C. F. Bourne, Esq., M.A.), are fully equal to what exist in similar schools in England. The fees there are only eight to ten guineas per annum. School text-books are, naturally, more costly—about fifteen to twenty-five per cent.—than at home.

Next come the University Colleges, of which there are three, namely, Auckland University College, Canterbury College, at Christchurch, and the Otago University, at Dunedin, all affiliated to the New Zealand University. A movement is on foot to establish a Wellington University College, so that each of the four great centres may have this higher education brought into their midst, but the pressing necessity for economy prevents the present Government from granting the money for it. These Colleges are teaching, not degree-granting institutions, and are governed by Councils, partly nominated by the Government, and partly representative of other educational bodies. The College Calendars of 1888 showed that 580 students, of whom 266 had matriculated, were attending these three colleges.

The apex of the educational pyramid is formed by the New Zealand University, founded in 1870, and empowered by Royal Charter, in 1876, to grant degrees in all branches of knowledge. I find that little is known of this promising institution in England, so will give a few details. The Constitution of this University, its courses of study, examinations, and council, are all modelled upon those of the University of London. Its governing body, the Senate, composed of some of the most eminent men in the colony, meets annually in some city where higher education is cultivated; and are cordially welcomed wherever the reunion is held. Every meeting of the Senate is followed by an increased impetus given to the educational resources of the district where it has met.

All degrees of this university are open to women as well as men. The special adaptation of its rules to colonial requirements is exemplified by the following admirable provision for wage-earning students made in chapter vi. of the Statutes: "Any student who is engaged in acquiring a profession or trade, or earning a livelihood, may keep terms without attending lectures." ... He "must have his name on the books of an affiliated college, and must pass its annual examination in order to keep the terms of the year." Thus, a clerk, mechanic, or agriculturist may study at home, pass his various examinations, and obtain his degree, while still all the while earning his bread. The whole course of study at any of the affiliated colleges, including examination fees and the cost of books, for the degree of B.A. need not exceed £30. And further, by an excellent system of free scholarships from the Primary to the Secondary schools, and from these to the University Colleges, a youth of talent and industry may obtain a complete education, finishing with a University degree, at little, if any, expense to his friends.

Most of the lectures at these three affiliated colleges are delivered in the evenings, in order to suit the convenience of those students who are employed throughout the day. The Professors are carefully selected from the best university men at Home, and the lectures, therefore, are of a high order of merit. The fees for the lectures are very moderate, averaging ten to fifteen shillings per term.

As it would unduly extend this section to enumerate the staff of all the three colleges, I will briefly mention some details of the college best known to me and latest established, namely, Auckland University College, opened in 1883. Forty applications from some of the best scientific and literary graduates of English universities were sent in to the Agent-General for New Zealand for the four professorships then established. Four very superior men were chosen: Professors F. G. Walker (mathematics and physics); F. D. Brown (chemistry and experimental physics); F. G. Tucker, senior classic and Fellow (classics and English); and A. P. W. Thomas (biology and geology). Of these Professor Walker was drowned shortly after his arrival, to the great regret of those who knew him; and Professor W. S. Aldis, who was senior wrangler of his year at Cambridge, was appointed to the chair, which he still occupies with much acceptability. After some years Professor Tucker removed to Melbourne University, and was succeeded by Dr. H. Macaulay Posnett, LL.D., Senior Moderator in Classics, Trinity College, Dublin, &c., author of "Comparative Literature."

On the first opening of this College, the newspapers of Auckland eulogised it, but when the depression began to be felt, the institution was denounced as being an expensive and premature luxury. A life of six useful years, however, has amply justified its foundation, for the following, among other benefits, have been conferred upon the Auckland provincial district: the standard of education, training, and qualification of public school teachers has been distinctly raised; a technical school has been founded; frequent "popular science" lectures on subjects useful as well as interesting have been delivered by the professors; a body of students—numbering 107 (68 men and 39 women) in the year 1887 has been formed, who are not only fostering a love for learning and research of all kinds, but diffusing "sweetness and light" through that utilitarian community; and lastly, eminent men of the very highest qualifications for teaching their respective subjects have been attracted to New Zealand.

As an incentive to Technical Education, hitherto very deficient in the colony, the council of this college have lately opened a School of Applied Science, wherein instruction during a three years' course is given in the following subjects: mathematics, astronomy, chemistry, drawing, surveying, mechanics, architecture, metallurgy, mining, engineering, and mine surveying. I hail this new addition to the advantages of the college as a great boon to the Auckland district, where the mines of gold and other minerals need a more *scientific* and economical mode of development than they have hitherto had. Professors Black, of Otago University, and Brown, of Auckland University College, have awakened the public mind to the immense importance of *scientific mining* and assaying, and all the science professors of the three colleges have continually advocated the teaching of science in schools, especially as applicable to the wants of colonial life.

In connection with the Canterbury College—which, by the way, has just lost one of its chief ornaments, Professor Sir Julius von Haast—a very useful institution, called the School of Agriculture, was opened in 1880 at Lincoln, near Christchurch. The director is Mr. W. E. Ivey, who, with a competent staff of assistants, gives a practical and scientific training to those who intend to make farming their livelihood, upon a large farm of 660 acres, containing soils of all kinds and conditions. The exhibits of wool and cereals sent from this farm to the Indian and Colonial Exhibition of 1886, were most favourably reported on by the judges. It is probable that young Englishmen who choose New Zealand as a place for settlement would get a better idea of the actual peculiarities of New Zealand farming by spending a year or eighteen months at this very excellent School of Agriculture than they would by this same length of time passed at Hollesley Bay, Suffolk, well planned though that institution seems to be. The special advantage offered by the Otago University is the

Medical and Surgical school their Council have formed. There is an operating theatre in Dunedin Hospital, a dissecting room, a well-appointed chemical laboratory, and the Museum of the province is under the Council's management. The course of study at this school, as will be gathered from the remark on p. 7, does not qualify for the degree of M.D. of the New Zealand University, but it is recognized by the Royal Colleges of Physicians and Surgeons of England. There can be no doubt that university education is rapidly becoming popular in New Zealand.

The New Zealand Institute, established at Wellington in 1868, is the central scientific association of the colony. It consists of seven local Scientific Institutes, having their meetings in Auckland, Napier, Wellington, Nelson, Christchurch, Dunedin, and Invercargill respectively. In 1887 the membership of the New Zealand Institute was 1156. The governors of the Central Institute are elected annually from the councils of these local Institutes, and the permanent secretary is Sir James Hector, K.C.M.G., director of the Geological Survey and of the Colonial Museum. The objects of the New Zealand Institute are the encouragement of the pursuit of science in general; the investigation of the geology, *fauna*, and *flora* of the whole colony; and the collection of the history, traditions, and antiquities of the Maori race. It seeks to effect these objects by collecting, recording, and criticizing papers and essays upon any of these subjects at the winter meetings; by the annual publication of a volume of Transactions, which it exchanges with other similar institutions all over the world; and by grants of money to scientific and literary workers in various departments. Already the institute has published twenty-one volumes of Transactions, which are of considerable value to the scientific world, the Government assisting in the expense of production by an annual grant of £500.

The great value in the education of the public attaching to Free Libraries is wisely recognized by the Government by an annual parliamentary grant in aid of their funds;

this sum being distributed in proportion to the income derived by the libraries from other sources, generally voluntary; the sole condition qualifying a library to share in the grant being that the library must be open *free to the public*. In 1887 three hundred and sixty-one libraries, distributed through all parts of New Zealand, shared in the grant. But the stern hand of retrenchment has swept this aid away for a time.

In connection with the education of the public, we must not forget that powerful agent, the newspaper Press of New Zealand. There are in the colony more than twenty daily and a large number of weekly newspapers, which circulate to the remotest parts of the country. Every little town has its daily or tri-weekly newspaper. On the whole the Press of New Zealand is creditable to its conductors, the chief blemish of the average New Zealand newspaper consisting in vituperative attacks upon the other towns or districts in the colony. When a Dunedin paper calls Wellington " the windy, shaky, metropolis of matchboxes," one cannot help laughing at the grain of truth contained in the farcical epigram; but it is not fair to the Wellingtonians to hurt their feelings thus, for *they* are not responsible for either storm or earthquake, and their wooden houses are incontestably the safest and best for these conditions of habitation. An Auckland resident, again, cannot feel kindly to the Wairarapa people when their newspaper, the *Star*, àpropos of the great disappointment felt in Auckland at the gist of the parliamentary committee's Report on the North Island Trunk Railway, which was that the Central instead of the Taranaki route must be adopted, writes: " Visions of wrong inflicted upon the people of that warm and unhappy region of volcanic *débris* began to dance in the bosoms of her devoted banks, and more devoted insurance companies, embalmed by faithful directors of money rings, South Sea kidnappers, *Pakeha-Maoris*, native land-sharks, and ladies of the period enshrined in matchbox hotels and suicidal boarding-houses, surrounded by speculative villas that, like Mounts Etna and Vesuvius start occasionally into flame. The scoriacity of Mount Eden would make the city lead a dreamy somnolent kind of existence, were it not that the weight of its iniquities, lying heavily across its chest, causes its slumbers now and then to be disturbed by frightful nightmares."

I have numerous other specimens of journalistic objurgation, but refrain from quoting any more, for their local flavour would scarcely be appreciated by Home readers. On the other hand the leading newspapers of the colony display in their editorial articles a bright intelligence and sturdy common sense in commenting upon British and foreign politics such as are not always found in the organs of the extreme political parties at home. The Home Rule question, for instance, is fairly and independently discussed ; a loyal tone pervades all references to our august Sovereign, and to the Royal Family; while the excessive expenditures on Court sinecures are unsparingly assailed. Isolated passages in some newspapers would lead the casual reader to imagine that there was a republican feeling in New Zealand, but the whole spirit of the press displays a steady loyalty to the existing British Constitution, and a love for the dear Old Country. Interesting letters from London, from the United States, and from special correspondents in the Pacific Islands convey to New Zealanders accurate and condensed information of what is passing all over the world. The serial tale is now a regular part of the eight-page daily; and the Saturday supplements of newspapers like the *New Zealand Herald* and *Evening Star* of Auckland contain capital selections of scientific, critical, and light reading.

3. *Hospitals, Refuges, Asylums, and Poor Relief.*

There is no such complete poor-law in New Zealand as we have in England: there are no workhouses or casual wards. Pauperism, and the formation of a pauper class, is greatly dreaded. But there is a system of outdoor relief, in the shape of a weekly dole of food given to necessitous persons and their families, until employment is found for the bread-winner, or the whole family leave the colony. Money is seldom given, except for house-rent. The Relieving Officer was until lately a Government official, now he is appointed by the "Hospital and Charitable Aid Board" for the City or District. The local Benevolent Societies co-operate with the board's officers in the distribution of relief, so as to prevent imposture and deception. There is urgent need now for a tramp or casual shed in each of the four large cities of the colony; but long distant be the day when a workhouse shall be a necessity for New Zealand!

The Government have hitherto given £1 for £1 on the sum raised by the contributions made from the rates and by voluntary subscriptions towards the maintenance of the outdoor relief fund, the benevolent asylums or refuges, and the public hospitals, all of which are now under the control of this new "Hospital and Charitable Aid Board." Hundreds of men, women, and children avail themselves of the temporary but timely relief thus given; but though there are some "old soldiers," who hang along for years on charity, there is no inert mass of helpless, hopeless, pauperism as yet in New Zealand, and I devoutly hope there never will be. The eight benevolent asylums during the year 1887 maintained 972 persons, and the amount expended on them was £32,183. The six orphanages and four industrial schools during the same year contained 270 inmates, on whom £7678 were expended. The Institution for the Deaf and Dumb is a private one, well conducted.

The Hospitals of New Zealand are now placed under the management of the "Hospital and Charitable Aid Boards." They are conducted in different ways in different parts of the colony, some not altogether satisfactory, judging by the frequent changes in the medical and surgical staff, and the numerous attacks in the press. In most of them payment by patients is compulsory—generally 12s. per week for a bed in the general wards, or one guinea in a private ward; but if absolute want of means can be proved to the hospital board, the payment is remitted. There are thirty-seven hospitals in the colony, in which beds are provided for 870 male and 333 female patients. A dispensary, or out-patient department, is usually attached to each hospital, where both advice and medicine may be obtained gratis. The total receipts of these hospitals during 1887 amounted to £77,668, and the expenditure upon them to £75,313. The number of patients admitted into them during this year was 6681.

In the Auckland, Wellington, Christchurch, and Dunedin hospitals the nursing is first-class, and probationers are trained under the supervision of a lady-superintendent. Our matron, Miss Crisp (now Mrs. Dr. Bond), in Auckland, was a distinguished army nurse, who had medals for service in Egypt and in South Africa, and was presented with the new Order of Merit devised by the Queen for nurses by the Governor, Sir W. F. D. Jervois, at a distinguished gathering at Government House, Auckland. The ventilation and internal arrangements are usually good in these hospitals. The smaller country and town hospitals are attended by one medical officer, who calls in his colleagues' aid when deemed advisable. In the larger hospitals there is one resident doctor, or two, and an honorary staff. If the best practitioners of the city do not join the staff (as is sometimes stated) it is because the relative duties and departments of the medical staff and committee of management are not as clearly defined as in England. This matter will in due time right itself, however. The recent legislation respecting hospitals has been rather hasty and crude; for it is not wise *suddenly* to throw their support upon the rates, and thereby discourage voluntary subscriptions, which in many cases formed the chief source of income. Some years' trial is necessary before we can pronounce the change beneficial or injurious to the community at large.

There are seven public Lunatic Asylums and one

Private Licensed Asylum in the colony. At the end of 1887 these contained 1695 inmates (1053 males and 642 females). During that year 415 lunatics had been admitted, 226 discharged, and 101 had died. In chapter xii. I have demonstrated that mental diseases are not so prevalent in New Zealand as in some other Australasian colonies.

One Home for Inebriates, under private management, exists in the colony.

4. *Gaols and Police.*

Justice is administered in New Zealand by a Supreme Court, consisting of a Chief Justice and four Puisne Judges; by District Judges; stipendiary Resident Magistrates, and unpaid Justices of the Peace, proceedings being in most respects the same as in England. In addition there are some procedures not known in England, such as the coroner's inquest on a fire when arson is suspected.

In criminal statistics it is gratifying to state that for seven years past there has been a gradual decrease in the proportion of charges and convictions to the whole population. It has been remarked that this decrease has been simultaneous with a steady diminution in the consumption of spirits and beer per head during the same period. The percentage of convictions to charges is somewhat lower than in England and Wales.

There is a gaol in each provincial district, generally situated in the capital of that district. The prison management, fare, and discipline are good; good conduct marks are given, and the health of the prisoners is well maintained by the work they do for the Government on roads, streets, parks, &c. Free access to the prisons is permitted to all ministers of religion who desire to visit the prisoners. Careful periodical inspections of the prisons are made both by the Inspector-general of Prisons and by the Visiting Justices. Since the year 1881 the number of prisoners incarcerated in the gaols throughout the colony has been about 5500 in the year; the daily average was about 600.

The police force is a centralized body under the direct control of the Minister of Justice. It is now (1889) under the retrenchment scheme, cut down to 500 of all ranks, a proportion of one to 1220 of the population of New Zealand, which is a contrast to the one to 571 of Great Britain. For intelligence, sobriety, and common sense the New Zealand police officer surpasses his British *confrère*. The Superintendents of Police have to perform in many criminal cases the difficult and delicate duty of prosecution. The Government, therefore, every two or three years changes their districts, so as to keep them as free as possible from local bias.

The " First Offenders' Probation Act, 1886," whereby a person of previously good character, convicted of a first offence, may be liberated by the judge, on condition of a surety, approved by him, undertaking to keep the accused under surveillance for a certain period, has worked so well that I observe a similar Act has been recently passed by our Imperial Parliament.

The Registrar-general, in his report on the census of 1886, gives the number of persons living on charity and at the expense of the State as 4202, including 599 belonging to the "criminal class."

The temperance societies of all sorts and descriptions are strong in numbers and energy in New Zealand, and influence many votes in the parliamentary elections. The principle of local option is now carried into practice in New Zealand, and has proved on the whole beneficial to the community.

5. *Public Works.*

These comprise roads, railways, bridges, docks, harbours, Government buildings, and other works of a permanent value to the colony, the expenditure on which since 1870 has amounted to £24,669,000.

When New Zealanders are twitted with their large public debt of thirty-five millions, they can point to saleable and more or less reproductive assets, in the shape of 1770 miles of railway; 4746 miles of telegraph; 8478 miles of road; 791 bridges; lighthouses, harbour works, and harbour defences to the value of £826,000; public buildings valued at £1,652,000; waterworks on the gold-fields, £510,000; and land purchased from the natives to the value of £1,145,000. The surface of New Zealand being unfavourable to railway construction, it is creditable to the engineers who laid out the lines that both the *original cost* of making the railways has been less than than that of the cheapest railways of other British colonies (Cape Colony, for instance) by £1242 per mile; and that the *cost of maintenance per mile* (£141) is £2 less than in Cape Colony, £9 less than in Victoria, and £9 less than in New South Wales. On the 31st March, 1888, the net earnings of all the railways in New Zealand, some lines paying better than others, amounted to a sum equal to £2 6s. per cent. upon their original cost.

The gauge in New Zealand is narrow—3 ft. 6 in.—as being less costly and better suited to the sharp curves and narrow passes through which the railways have to run in many parts—the Rimutaka Pass and the Manawatu Gorge, for example—than the English standard gauge. The classes are two: 1st, the fare by which averages 2*d*. per mile; and 2nd, where the fare is 1½*d*. The carriages are built on the American pattern, with seats on each side and a passage down the centre, leading to a platform at each end of the car. There is provision for ventilation but not for heating. The new "bogie" carriages on the long main lines are quite comfortable. The ordinary speed, including stoppages, is fifteen miles an hour, and for "expresses" from twenty to twenty-five miles an hour.

The harbours and docks of the colony have been built out of loans negotiated in London on the security of the colonial Government, but borrowed by Harbour Boards and Dock Companies, over which the Government have a control by their auditors. These works are therefore "public" not "private," and are maintained by dues, rates, and licenses levied by the several corporations to which they belong. Complaints are made by shipping and steamer companies of the high harbour and dock dues, but they are in reality reasonable when the great cost of construction and maintenance is considered. When trade is prosperous, the harbour and dock bonds are as good as any investment in New Zealand. When there is a lull in outside sea-going commerce, the smaller harbour boards find it difficult to pay the usual interest and keep up the sinking fund. Hence disputes arise; but the colonial Government invariably keep them to the strict letter of the law. The breakwaters at Timaru and at New Plymouth are now effective, but have been in their time "white elephants," sinking thousands of pounds in the boisterous sea. Eventually, however, engineering science triumphs over nature in all these seaports.

By their perseverance and liberal expenditure the Auckland Harbour Board possess as part of the admirable facilities of the Waitemata, the largest graving-dock (the 'Calliope,' described on p. 61) south of the line. Lyttelton, the port of Christchurch, with which a tunnel connects it, has a deep-water harbour, with quays illuminated by the electric light, large wool stores near the wharves, and a graving-dock 450 feet long by 82 feet wide. During the wheat-shipment season Lyttelton wharves are one of the sights best worth seeing in New Zealand. The Otago Harbour Board have so improved and deepened the tortuous channel of the estuary leading from Port Chalmers to Dunedin that now the Union Company's steamers of 2000 tons can safely come up to the wharves of the city. The harbour of Wellington, the capital, is well supplied with all the most modern appliances.

Too much space would be occupied were I to describe the principal bridges in the colony, some of which, made of iron manufactured in England, such as that of Wanganui, Manawatu, and the Clutha and

Waitaki rivers. The ambition of New Zealand now is directed to manufacture in the colony and put together all her own iron structures, bridges, locomotives, cranes, fencing, &c., from the iron or steel made from the native iron-sand, chrome iron ore, or hematite.

The lighthouses of New Zealand belong to the Government, and are efficient, but are not so powerful or elaborate as in the old country; nor are they sufficiently numerous for so dangerous a coast. As the Government can afford it their number will be increased.

The defences of New Zealand have been skilfully carried out under the able superintendence of the late Governor, Sir W. F. D. Jervois, G.C.M.G., and the colony contributes its share to the Australasian Defence Squadron.

The Government buildings are nearly all creditable to the colony and suitable for their purposes.

6. *Post Office, Telegraphs, and Telephones.*

New Zealand surpasses the rest of the Australasian colonies, taking into account the mountainous nature of the country and the large cost of sea-borne mails, in the convenience, speed, and frequency, of both internal and external postal communications. Though the rates of postage are, generally speaking, double the English rates, there are more letters, and newspapers, and money orders per head of the population sent through the post than in Great Britain. Outside of a city or borough one needs a two-penny stamp for a letter weighing half an ounce; the same letter would go to the Fijis, Norfolk Island, or any part of Australia for the same stamp. The postage for the same weight to England, Europe, or America is sixpence. Yet the great mental activity and home attachments of the New Zealanders is shown by the fact that no less than 39,377,774 letters and over 15,380,000 newspapers were posted or delivered during 1887, at and by the 1118 post-offices then open. The number of inland mail services was 600, and of telephone bureaux 33, to which there were 2042 subscribers. During the same year, 159,597 money orders were issued, for an aggregate sum of £555,744. All the facilities of postal notes, post-cards, &c., of the British post-office are provided, with the convenient addition of "delayed telegrams," which are sent off at any time the wire is unoccupied, at the rate of 6d. for twenty words ; and of telegraphic money orders, which are only this year (1889) being experimentally tried in this country. A foreign parcels post has recently been established, the rates being 1s. 6d. for 2 lbs. and 9d. per lb. up to 11 lbs. the limit of weight. The high rates of foreign postage, parcels post, &c., are due to the heavy subsidies paid to the steamship lines *viâ* America and Cape Horn which carry the ocean mails. A change is impending in these arrangements.

Over the 4746 miles of telegraph line 1,835,394 messages were sent in 1887. The telephone is much used in all the business centres of New Zealand, the Government has the monopoly, but has fixed the rates at a much more moderate figure than have the companies in England. One is charged £10 per telephone for the first year, if within the half-mile radius of the central bureau, and £8 for every year afterwards. Doctors, chemists, bankers, dentists all use them, and merchants and brokers often have a second telephone at their residences.

The post-office savings banks, of which there were 283 in 1887, do a very large business, which varies sympathetically with the fluctuations of trade and commerce throughout the colony. The tide of returning prosperity is accurately shown, therefore, by the facts that (*a*) while the withdrawals from these banks exceeded the deposits by £87,881 in the year 1886, in the following year 1887 the deposits exceeded the withdrawals by £129,741 ; and (*b*) in all the savings banks of the colony, including the seven non-official, £273,995 more were deposited during 1887 than during 1886.

7. *Government Life Assurance.*

This Department, opened in 1870, was the first of the kind established in any British colony. Its success has amply justified the expectations of its founders, the chief of whom, if I mistake not, was Sir J. Vogel. By means of conveniently situated offices in every town, by courteous managers, the most skilful medical referees obtainable, and a host of energetic canvassers, this department, though keenly competed with by the Australian Mutual Provident Association, does a business with which our own Government life assurance and annuity (post-office) business is a mere bagatelle. The Department offers the exceptional advantages of—1st. Inviolable security to the assured, the payment of every policy being guaranteed by the colony under a special Act of Parliament; 2nd. The division of the entire profits among the policy-holders alone. In the first ten years of its existence (1870-1880) these profits amounted to £77,595. 3rd. There are no restrictions on the policy as to trade, occupation, or travelling to other countries; each policy also being unchallengeable after five years' standing. 4th. The premiums are very low; the premiums with profits being as low as the *non-participating* rates in other offices. The very low death-rate in New Zealand—in 1887 *only* 10·29 for every 1000 inhabitants, as compared with 18·78 per 1000 for England and Wales—enables the department to do a safe remunerative business, while keeping the rates of premiums low. Despite the competition of seven other life assurance companies doing business in the colony, the Government assurance holds its own well, though the first to suffer in "hard times" by the lapse of old policies and the slackening-off of new insurances. During the year 1888 the new policies issued were 2957, insuring an amount of £785,692. The total number of policies in force are now 26,168, insuring over £7,700,000. The accumulated funds amount to £1,452,478. I have been thus minute in describing this Department because it is of great importance to the intending settler to know that he can cheaply, conveniently, and securely insure his life in New Zealand; and it is interesting to my medical colleagues to see demonstrated by these hard facts the healthiness of New Zealanders—and hence of their climate.

8. *Other Government Departments.*

1. The Public Trust Office, established in 1872. In New Zealand many persons die by accident or are drowned at sea, or in one way or another meet with a sudden death, leaving no will, nor any relatives in the colony. Sometimes their real names are unknown. In many such sad events, property was left by the deceased, and its rightful disposal was a matter of much difficulty. To meet this difficulty the Government opened this Office, appointing a Public Trustee and Executor, with a Deputy in each provincial district, whose duty it should be to collect all the property of the deceased, and distribute it to the legitimate claimants; to discharge all just debts; and to carry out the provisions of the will, where there was one left by the deceased. He may also administer trusts under deeds and settlements, and may manage the estate of a lunatic. All investments of money are under the control of a Board, consisting of the Colonial Treasurer, the Attorney-general, the Controller and Auditor-general, and the Public Trustee. The Government are directly responsible for the honest fulfilment of the trusts, and the Public and Deputy Trustees have hitherto given satisfaction. That there is need for such an office is proved by the fact that in 1885 the cash receipts of the Public Trustee amounted to £195,000. The expense of management is covered by a tax of five per cent. upon the property of deceased persons.

2. The Assignees in Bankruptcy are gentlemen of honesty, ability, and business experience, appointed in each large town of the colony to carry out the provisions

of the Bankruptcy Acts. In fact, they perform the duties assigned at home to the Registrars in Bankruptcy, and have judicial as well as administrative powers. So far as my experience (as a creditor only) goes in the Auckland district, they perform their difficult and delicate duties with an integrity, firmness, and diligence which leave nothing to be desired.

3. Sheep and Rabbit Inspectors. The former class of officials have to see that no epizootic disease is allowed to spread; that the sheep are properly dipped in some disinfectant when the "scab" breaks out, and so on. The latter class of inspectors do their very best to enforce the law relative to fencing (so as to keep the rabbits from spreading from one farm to another), and to extermination. The extent of the rabbit pest in the Middle Island has necessitated the appointment of these officers.

All the above branches of the Government have a special interest for immigrants. There are numerous other offices which it is not necessary to introduce into a small volume like this.

9. *Friendly Societies*

Are numerous, and called by as diverse names as in the old country. In 1887 they numbered 290 "lodges" and thirty central associations. The number of members then was 21,679, and the value of their property was £335,675. All these societies must be registered, and must submit their accounts to the Public Auditor and Valuer annually. Their weekly allowances to sick and infirm members are more liberal than in the old country, commensurate with the higher rate of contributions.

10. *Building Societies.*

On the 1st of January, 1887, there were forty-eight land, building, and investment societies in the colony. The number of members was 4480. The rules and accounts are subject to revision by Government officials. The shares pay a dividend of from eight to ten per cent. to investing members.

11. *Sailors' Homes and Rests.*

It is to be regretted that these useful institutions are not so numerous in New Zealand as could be wished; but what do exist are very successful. At Lyttelton there is a neat Sailors' Home which cost £2500, and is well managed by a retired captain. In Auckland, as described on p. 65, there is a spacious and handsome building for sailors, in which the Sailors' Rest inaugurated by Bishop Cowie in 1881 is blended with the ordinary work of a Sailors' Home.

Sailors' Rests, that is, free reading and refreshment rooms for the use of those who follow the sea, are to be found at Auckland, Wellington, Port Chalmers, and Dunedin, managed by committees of ladies and gentlemen warmly interested in Christian and philanthropic work.

CHAPTER X.

PRODUCTIONS AND INDUSTRIES.

Natural products evolve certain Industries—The growth of fifty years—Exports now exceed Imports in value—Statistics of production of Wool—Meat—The frozen meat trade—Skins and hides—Dairy produce—Wheat—Timber—Kauri gum—Gold and silver—Other metals—Building stone—Coal—Flax, fungus, tan-bark, petroleum, train oil—Minor Industries—Reasons for the Protective Tariff—Policy of Bonuses for new Cultures and Industries—The working-man of New Zealand and the Chinese—W. N. Blair on Labour and Capital—Patent law—Inventiveness of New Zealanders—Humane legislation for women and children in factories.

FOR a colony which will celebrate its first jubilee in 1890, New Zealand has developed a wonderful variety of industries and manufactures. These are very nearly all based upon indigenous raw products. There can be little question that the grand resources of the colony in climate, water, coal, timber, iron, and other minerals fit her to become a manufacturing as well as an agricultural country. Let but a great market be open to her outside, and let her own children wear and use her own fabrics and implements, and Zealandia need no longer be "pap-fed" by Government bonuses, or bolstered up by excessively high import duties. The 1770 miles of rail open on March 31, 1888, and the yearly increasing coastal steamer facilities are also promoting the industries of the colony by cheaper and quicker communications. All real progress in a new country must depend upon its natural resources, its geographical position, and the intelligence of its people. The discovery of gold has greatly accelerated the colonization of New Zealand, and given rise to mills, smelting works, assay laboratories, and so on. The existence of vast deposits of iron-sand on the coast together with coal in over a hundred places in the interior has given rise to iron-works at Onehunga and Taranaki. The profusion of sheep and cattle have made meat so cheap that meat freezing and preserving works have sprung up in several places. Similarly, fish in prodigal abundance, and fruit in quantities which are too great for home consumption in the fresh state, have given rise to "canneries," and jam factories. The discovery of capital tan-bark trees (*Phyllocladus* and others) has coincided with the extraordinary cheapness of skins and hides to evolve tanneries, where leather is now produced in quality almost equal to the English article. Political economists tell us that that country has a prosperous trade where the exports exceed in value the imports. Upon this theory the balance of trade has been against New Zealand's prosperity up to a recent period. But a turn in the tide has come; for, whereas in the year 1882 the declared value of all the imports was £8,609,270 and that of the exports only £6,658,000, in the year 1887 the value of imports had sunk to £6,245,515, while that of exports had risen to £6,866,169. Of all this trade at least seventy per cent. was carried on with Great Britain.

In this chapter I have given a brief and condensed statement of the principal natural products, industries, and manufactures of New Zealand at the present time. I have taken the statistics of 1886 as the basis, but where reliable figures of later date have been issued by the Government I shall use them. While I do not profess to give a complete list of *all* the products and manufactures of the colony, I think the English reader will see even in this short compendium of the amount and variety of the business done in New Zealand enough to astonish him.

1. *Wool.*

This is still the most important raw product of this colony, the value of the wool exported being treble that of the gold produced. Although individual sheep farmers have in many cases lost their capital in this pursuit, from inexperience, bad management, diseases among the sheep, disastrous winters, or general "ill-luck," yet wool-growing has proved on the whole to be a great success in New Zealand. Not only have the sheep multiplied *ninefold* in the twenty-one years, the breed being continually improved by fresh importations of Southdown, Merino, and Saxon rams, but also the *weight* of the fleece has *doubled*, while the average weight of a "carcase" in New Zealand is as much as 68 lbs., that of an Australian sheep being 50 lbs.; of a River Plate sheep 37 lbs; and a sheep from the Cape Colony only 22 lbs.

New Zealand now provides the European market with exactly the two classes of wool required by the manufacturer—combing wool for worsted goods, bombazines, camlets, &c; and clothing wool for broadcloth, tweed, &c. The Lincoln, Leicester, Cotswold, and Romney Marsh breeds of long-staple-woolled sheep and the Southdown, Shropshire, and Spanish Merino varieties of short-staple-woolled sheep thrive better than in their European *habitats* because of the shorter and milder winters. The Merino sheep seems to adapt itself to every climate. The peculiar excellence of its wool consists in the fineness and number of serrations in each hair, whereby it is enabled to "*felt well*," as it is termed. Thus, under the microscope one finds 2720 serrations in one inch of a saxon Merino hair, but only 2000 in the same length of a Southdown, and 1850 in that of a Leicester sheep.

In 1887 from a little over fifteen million sheep the wool clipped amounted to 90,825,937 lbs. Of this amount over two millions were used within the colony in manufacture of blankets, tweeds, felt, &c; and 88,824,382 lbs., valued at £3,321,074, were exported, this being a large advance in value over that of the previous year. The market price of wool fluctuates very much, for New Zealand competes at an immense distance with wool-producing countries nearer the home market; but let it be noted that a low price in London quotations of New Zealand wools does not indicate a quality inferior to the usual average produced in the colony. Excellent blankets, tweeds, worsted goods, stockings, caps, &c., are now manufactured from native wool at Onehunga, Petone, Kaiapoi, and Mossgiel. So pure and honestly made are the woollen goods of New Zealand that a French manufacturer, visiting the Sydney Exhibition, after critically examining the tweed from our colony and finding to his astonishment that it was "all wool," exclaimed, "Well, these New Zealanders *are* fools!"

2. *Meat.*

A large and ever-increasing trade in frozen and tinned meat (mutton, beef, lamb, tongues, kidneys, &c.) has grown up since 1882 between New Zealand and Great Britain. The great distance between the two countries alone prevents a "live-stock" trade from taking the place of "dead meat" business. The importance to Great Britain of this New Zealand meat, of such excellent quality and sold so cheaply to the actual consumer in this country (4d. or 5d. per lb.) cannot be over-estimated. Our Home population, even after allowing for deaths and emigration, is increasing at the prodigious rate of nearly 1000 a day, while the live stock raised in our own country is not increasing. By the year 1896, Mulhall calculates, our population will have risen to forty-three millions, while the country itself will be producing only enough meat to feed its inhabitants for *five months in the year.* Already we import 600,000 tons of meat from North and South America. But the colony of New Zealand is our latest and best sheep-farm. Even seven years since New Zealand ranked second among the Australasian colonies as a sheep-breeding country; and its juicy meat brought twopence a pound more in the English market than the lean, tough, and flavourless mutton of Australia. The meat-freezing machinery now works to perfection; the voyage from port to port is brought within forty days by direct steamer; and we can now have the delicious grass-fed mutton, beef, and lamb of New Zealand, with the flavour unimpaired, placed on our tables, at a price *fifty per cent. less* than that of English grown meat, yet with a fair profit to the colonial sheep farmer. This kind of freight is now, I am told, the most remunerative of any to the steamship companies, The *Tainui* of the Shaw, Savill, and Albion line, made the voyage from Lyttelton to Plymouth in the autumn of 1888 in 38 days and 17 hours, loaded with 30,000 frozen sheep, which she landed in good condition at Rio de Janeiro and at London. The New Zealand Shipping Company's steamers have done the same trip in 36 days. From the year 1882, when 15,244 cwt. of frozen meat, valued at £19,339, were exported to England, much of it being spoiled through inexperience in the various processes,—the trade has rapidly increased, so that in 1887 no less than 402,107 cwt. of meats of the value of £455,870, were exported from New Zealand. In that year there were forty-four meat-freezing and preserving works in the colony, representing capital sunk in buildings and machinery to the amount of £442,962.

The recent amalgamation and consequent closing of the smaller works will enhance the profits of those still in the trade. If the sheep farmer receives even $2\frac{1}{4}d.$ only per lb. for the carcases he delivers at the works it pays him. So cheap is mutton in the colony that during the year ending March 31, 1888, while 931,526 sheep were frozen and 215,192 were preserved for export, no less than 378,339 were boiled down for tallow.

The value of cured, salted, and tinned meats in the year ending March 31, 1888, was £98,036.

3. *Skins and Hides.*

Over twelve and a half millions of rabbit-skins were exported during 1887, of the value of £111,172—a poor compensation, though not to be despised, for the devastation of the pasturage in the South of New Zealand by the voracity of these *Rodentia*. In that year the export of all descriptions of skins and hides was over fifteen millions in number, of the value of £240,219.

4. *Dairy Produce.*

Australia regards New Zealand as its dairy farm, just as it looks upon Tasmania as its fruit garden and jam factory. India also is now looking to New Zealand for cheese and butter. The fondness of the "mild Hindoo" for *ghee* affords an outlet for the inferior butter of the New Zealand farmer, while the best and medium qualities realize handsome prices in the two great markets above mentioned. The export of butter from New Zealand during 1887 amounted in value to £54,921, and of cheese the value was £54,562. In this connection I may mention the invention by J. A. Pond, of Auckland, of an ingenious enamel for lining butter-boxes, which makes them air-tight and water-tight. Butter may thus be conveyed to any distance without waste or loss. There are about 190,000 cows in New Zealand, and each is estimated to return £5 per annum to the owner. The cheese factories have not been all successful, but have created a new export, which will in due time yield a handsome profit, and cause this new industry to be greatly extended.

Though scarcely a product of the dairy, it is noteworthy that honey of excellent flavour is being produced in the Waikato and other districts of the North Island. The value of the honey exported in 1886 was £1133.

5. *Wheat and other Cereals.*

New Zealand is *first* a pastoral, and *secondly* an agricultural country; but the area devoted to the growth of cereals is every year increasing. The wheat-growing land in 1888 was 337,359 acres, an increase of more than 104,000 acres over the area thus occupied in 1887. In

1888 the production of wheat was 9,424,059 bushels, as against 6,297,638 bushels in 1887.

The yield *per acre* in 1888 was very good, surpassing the annual average. In Auckland and Taranaki it was over 29 bushels; in Otago nearly 30; while in Hawke's Bay it reached the high figure of 31·48.

Of course harvests vary from year to year even in the comparatively steady climate of New Zealand; but it is confessed by all the other colonies to be ahead of them in the *average yield per acre* of all cereals, and of potatoes. For instance, in 1882, according to the best statist of the colonies, Mr. H. H. Hayter, of Victoria, New Zealand produced per acre:—

	New Zealand.	New South Wales.	Victoria.
Wheat	Bushels. 26·28	Bushels. 16·34	Bushels. 9·03
Oats	32·95	24·88	26·17
Barley	26·19	20·55	17·35
Potatoes	Tons. 5·1	Tons. 3·00	Tons. 3·78

New Zealand oats are of high quality, and when there is a drought in Australia their price goes up very high, and is even maintained (as in 1889) for some months after the welcome rain has fallen. In 1887 over three million bushels of oats, of the value of £279,556, were exported; and of barley, maize, and malt 213,969 bushels, valued at £39,799. More land should be sown in these cereals, for they are all of such good quality and weight as to pay better than the produce of grass land. Out of seven and a quarter million acres under cultivation in February 1888 (the latest official statement) nearly six millions were sown with grasses. Grass and clover seed to the value of £45,000, and potatoes valued at £23,700, were exported in 1886. The best-flavoured and best-keeping New Zealand potatoes are those grown in Canterbury.

6. *Timber.*

Extensive forests of useful native woods abound in New Zealand, and are being used up at a prodigal rate. The most valuable tree of all is the *kauri* pine (*Dammara Australis*), of the natural order Coniferæ, to which many of the timber-trees belong. Builders are insatiable in their demand for the *kauri*, whose wood, of a light yellowish brown colour, tough yet silky when polished, and very easily worked, is durable, not readily worm-eaten, and when *long* seasoned does not shrink perceptibly. Unfortunately it is a tree of very slow growth, does not exist south of Mercury Bay, and it is not being replanted anywhere. At the present rate of consumption, in about fifteen years this favourite timber will be extinct. Some *kauri* trees are found 150 feet high with a circumference of sixty to ninety feet.

In 1887 there were produced nearly thirty-one million feet of sawn and hewn *kauri* timber, valued at £127,108, the price being low: during the previous year $29\frac{1}{3}$ million feet had realised £139,905. The woods next in commercial value are: the birch, *kahikatea* or white pine, *rimu*, *totara*, *puriri*, *rata*, white and black *maire*, *rewarewa*, and *pohutakawa*. In the Middle Island, there being no *kauri*, the great demand is for white pine (*kahikatea*) and birch for building. The gum that ages ago exuded from *kauri* trees, long dead and decayed, affords a special industry in the north of the North Island. It is dug up from the ground, being found usually from two to six feet below the surface, and forms, when properly cleaned, a valuable article of export. "Gum-digging" is regarded in Auckland as the "last refuge for the destitute;" for the work is rough but remunerative, and requires no previous training. A spear wherewith to prod the ground, a spade to dig out the gum, a knife to scrape it, and a sack are all that are needed to fit out the "gum-digger." Their camps are one of the sights peculiar to the North Island. "Wastrels," men of education and culture, runaway sailors and shopmen, broken-down speculators, and the waifs and strays of society are to be found in the ranks of the gum-diggers. The *kauri* gum is an amber-resin, and is sought after by coachmakers and others in London and New York because its finer more transparent forms make, when melted, a transparent varnish suitable for carriages. To make the varnish the *kauri* gum is melted in copper kettles and mixed with turpentine and linseed oil. Its market price fluctuates greatly. In 1882 gum was worth £46 per ton on an average of the whole year. In that year 5533 tons, of the value of £240,580, were exported; in 1887 the exportation was 6791 tons, valued at £362,449. This natural and useful product will, like the *kauri* itself, come to an end in no very long time. It is now being searched for with all the ardour that men display in prospecting for gold.

7. *Gold and Silver.*

The existence of gold in the Thames river, near Auckland, in the North Island, was reported by a traveller named Griffe in 1830; but it was not until 1852 that it was discovered in payable quantities, by Mr. Charles Ring, in the Coromandel district. It is now found to be of all metals perhaps the most widely distributed in New Zealand. Gold occurs in three kinds of deposits. 1. Quartz veins (Auckland district). 2. Alluvial drift (Otago). 3. Recent sea-beaches (Hokitika).

From the year 1857, when the Government began to levy a tax of half-a-crown (since reduced to two shillings) upon every ounce extracted from the ore, to the present time, this precious metal has yielded an important item to the annual revenue of the colony. The value of the gold exported up to the end of 1887 was £44,042,576, and of the silver £124,721.

Silver is found as an alloy in Thames gold ore to the extent of thirty per cent; and in galena (sulphide of lead) to the amount of twenty to fifty ounces to the ton.

A few of the New Zealand gold mines have been very rich. One quartz mine alone, the Caledonian, in the Thames district, yielded no less than £1,500,000 in gold, paying in one year £570,000 in dividends to its lucky shareholders. Of late years the production has been falling off. During 1887 the total value of all the gold yielded by the mines in the colony was £811,100, being a decrease of £92,000 on that of 1886.

The Bank of New Zealand, which is the chief consigner of the precious metals to foreign parts, has a most perfect and economical method of assaying and parting the metals, the secret of which, I am informed, is the property of the bank.

There being no mint in New Zealand, the bullion has to be sent to Melbourne, Sydney, or London for coinage.

8. *Other Metals.*

It is more difficult to name the metals that do *not* occur somewhere or other in this prolific metalliferous country than to enumerate in a brief space those that *are* found there.

Iron occurs in three forms: hæmatite, chrome iron ore, and iron-sand. For about 300 miles the beach of the west coast of the North Island, from Ahipara southwards to Egmont, is covered several inches deep with this very curious product, containing from sixty to seventy-two per cent. of metallic iron and titanium blended, the balance being pure silicious sand. Fiji produces iron-sand like it, but I am not aware of any other country south of the equator that contains a similar deposit. It presents great difficulties in working, but these have at last been overcome by 'Edison's magnetic separator' and by peculiarly constructed furnaces, so that the works at Onehunga, near Auckland, and at Taranaki (now united with the former), are beginning to manufacture good tough iron. There is a large and increasing demand in New Zealand for articles of iron and steel; and, after sinking thousands of pounds sterling in earnest experiments, the plucky Iron Works shareholders seem now to be in a fair way to commence supplying this demand within the colony.

The recent discovery of extensive petroleum springs at the Sugar-Loaves, and along the beach, at Taranaki, suggests a cheap and handy kind of fuel for the smelting processes.

Copper, cinnabar, tin—the last deposit having been found in the South (or Stewart's) Island; antimony, as stibnite; manganese as psilomelane; and lead as galena occur plentifully. D. Sutherland has discovered some rich mineral deposits in the West Coast Sounds, which in time will be worked. Many other minerals exist in the colony which I have not space to notice.

9. *Building Stone.*

Beautiful marble is found in Caswell Bay and other places; limestone in Otago and elsewhere; bluish-white granular freestone at Oamaru; roofing slate in the Kakanui Mountains; cement, kaolin, and granite have been discovered. Very good local cement is manufactured by Wilson Brothers, of Auckland, out of lime scoria and pebbles, which is becoming a favourite material for houses, water-channels, plinths of railings, and so on.

10. *Coal.*

Both lignite and coal are found in extensive deposits in New Zealand. Scientific men enumerate twenty-nine kinds of coal, but I can only mention the three chief varieties in use. The Taupiri (Waikato) is the favourite coal for household use, being a quick-burning coal with a dry light ash, and throwing out great heat. The Westport (Middle Island) and Bay of Islands (North Island) varieties are slow burning and leave much ash, but form good steaming coal: a good deal is now being exported to Australia for gas-making purposes. There are now in New Zealand 126 coal mines, employing 1499 men, and these mines are producing an increased quantity every year. In 1887 the entire output of coal amounted to 558,620 tons, of which 44,129 tons were exported.

11. *Miscellaneous Products.*

1. The native flax or hemp, *Phormium tenax*, a shrub belonging to the Liliaceæ, possesses a fibre which, when well soaked for a long time in water, and thus freed from most of the gum contained in it, is readily made into ropes, matting, cord, brushes, baskets, and other articles. By a new process wrapping paper is shortly to be made out of this useful fibre. As the shrub grows wild all over New Zealand one would expect it to have been a source of great profit by this adaptability; but the very great difficulty of entirely eradicating the gummy matter from the leaf and stalk has rendered useless, for real wear and tear, many articles which have been manufactured from it. In 1886, 1,112 tons of this flax fibre, valued at £15,922, were exported.

2. The fungus called *Hirneola polytricha*, which grows on decaying trees in Taranaki, at the East Cape, and elsewhere, is gathered for export by the Maoris, and by the children of settlers. The Maoris used to eat this fungus, but now prefer the better food provided for them. Dried and packed in bales the fungus is sent to China, where it is highly valued as a delicacy, and also as a medicinal blood-purifier. It brings $11\frac{1}{2}d$. per lb. in Hong Kong and $7\frac{1}{2}d$. per lb. in San Francisco. In 1886 the quantity amounting to 5627 cwt. of fungus, of the value of £11,047, was exported from New Zealand.

3. *Tanekaha* bark, derived from three species of the *Phyllocladus*, or celery-leaved pine, is one of the best vegetable dyes in the world for yellow, pink, and fawn colours. During the first six months of the year 1883, 375 tons of this bark were exported, valued at £3080.

The bark of the *Acacia mimosa*, or "wattle," is also used as a dye, and for tanning purposes. The manufacture of colonial leather is still increasing.

4. Most people outside New Zealand believe that the whaling industry round the coast is now extinct. But, though this business is certainly decreasing, it still exists, as is proved by the substantial fact that 25,571 gallons of sperm and black-fish oil, valued at £6105, were exported in 1886.

5. Petroleum springs have been discovered near Gisborne and at Taranaki (p. 188). The oil seems more adapted for lubricating purposes than for illumination.

12. *Minor Industries.*

Among these may be mentioned carriage-building—colonial buggies constructed after the American pattern, but more strongly built, being particularly good.

Furniture, besides all the moveable parts belonging to a wooden house, is now made in large quantities, both from the native woods mentioned on p. 185 and from imported wood. The *kauri, rimu, puriri,* and *rewarewa* woods are particularly well adapted for cabinet work. The industries of fruit-preserving—Nelson jam being especially good—of soap and candle making; sauce and pickles, tomato sauce being the favourite kind, because that valuable esculent grows to perfection in New Zealand; fish-curing and canning, (chiefly mullet and schnapper); biscuits and confectionery; the manufacture of tobacco, cigars, and cigarettes—all these and many others are in a more or less flourishing condition. There are also paper mills at Dunedin and Mataura; cast steel works at Green Island; glass works in two places in the colony, and gas is manufactured in all the towns of any importance.

No doubt a great impetus to local industries and manufactures was given by the influx of borrowed money and by the high protective tariff of the colony. The banks furnished capital freely so long as money was "easy" to start various enterprises. But when the loan expenditure came to an end many of these industries collapsed or changed hands. At times like these free traders look up and promulgate their views, but protectionists look down and are silent. But soon, in the rapid movement of colonial trade, capital flows in again to the colony, and the mills, factories, and workshops reopen on a basis of sounder experience. The resident in New Zealand finds at the present day that the price of some manufactured articles (imported)—clothes, for example—are reduced by over-stocking and keen competition, to almost English figures.

In 1881 the total number of works and manufactories in New Zealand was 1643; in 1886 the number had risen to 2263.

The Government have from time to time offered bonuses for the manufacture of raw materials found in the colony, and for the cultivation of new vegetable or animal products useful to the country. Between the years 1877 and 1885 payments of bonuses, varying from £150 to £1500, in all amounting to £5334, were made to manufacturers who had produced gunpowder, sulphuric acid, wrapping and grey paper, oil-cake, linseed oil, earthenware, cheese, and frozen meat. A bonus is still, I understand, being offered for the manufacture of a certain quantity of each of the following articles made in the colony:—kerosene, pig-iron, wrought-iron blooms, printing paper, silk (cocoons or eggs), and starch.

Several new cultivations of economic plants have been recently introduced experimentally, and bid fair to be successful. Among these are the sugar-beet (*Sorghum saccharatum*), banana, olive, raisin-grape, tea, coffee, cinchona, and white mulberry (*Morus alba*), for the silk culture. New Zealand wine has also been made, but has not yet attained, so far as regards the samples tested by the writer, to a palatable quality. It has been proved, however, that the climate of Whangarei, among other localities, is quite suitable for the culture of the French and German wine-grapes.

Whatever may be thought of the wisdom of the

"policy of bonuses," called by its free-trade enemies "pap-feeding," there can be no doubt that it *has* stimulated manufactures generally, and discoveries of useful indigenous material very greatly. Several household and educational articles have been creditably made at least twenty years before they would have been manufactured in the colony without such stimulus. On the whole the "bonus policy" is less objectionable than an Import Tariff so high as to be *really protective*. The annual industrial exhibitions held in each of the four capitals afford the best opportunities to the stranger to see for himself the great variety and excellent quality of New Zealand raw and manufactured productions. No visitor should miss them. In Christchurch I saw, at one of these industrial exhibitions, carpets, blankets, tweeds, soap, jams, and cabinet work of the exquisite native woods above mentioned (p. 185), which I had great difficulty in believing were not the work of first-class European makers. Both Scuffert and Norrie, of Auckland, astonished the world at the "Colinderies" by their inlaid cabinet ware, and the more these lovely natural products, their beauties being tastefully brought out by cutting and polishing, are known, the greater will be the demand for them by travellers and their friends. A table of inlaid woods presented to us by our good friends in Auckland is the central ornament of our drawing-room.

There is a free-trade party in the House of Representatives, headed by my friend Mr. E. Withy, member for Newton, Auckland, and though its numbers are small, the active *propaganda* it has recently carried on by lectures, speeches, and the distribution of the pamphlets of the Cobden Club is making converts to the doctrines of free trade in the House and among the public. But so long as the New Zealand manufacturers insist upon protection, and the working-men who have votes are firmly convinced that a high tariff means to them high wages and short hours of labour, there is no probability of any alterations in the fiscal policy of the colony during this generation. American ideas are gaining ground among the working-men of New Zealand, as is shown by the imposition of a tax of £10 upon every Chinaman entering the colony. In this "exclusion policy" New South Wales and Victoria preceded New Zealand.

The standard wages prevailing in the colony may be correctly judged of by the table I have drawn up in chapter i. They are always higher, and sometimes double the existing wages in England. In New Zealand even the boys in the fish canneries during the busy season can earn £1 per week. Lest employers should be discouraged, I may state that a New Zealand workman, mechanic, or artizan, fed upon an abundance of animal food (p. 204), can do more work in eight hours than a poorly fed Lancashire operative or a half-starved East Londoner. The Chartist rhyme—

> "Eight hours' work, eight hours' play,
> Eight hours' sleep and eight bob a day,"

has long been realized in this colony, often called "the paradise of the working-man." But employment is not constant, and house-rent is a heavy expense.

There seems to be a widespread belief in the colony among the *proletariat* that it is the duty of the Government in "slack times" to find or make work for the unemployed. This is quite a fallacy, for the Government of New Zealand never makes any such contract with the immigrant, and my working-men readers should clearly understand this. Just now only the classes of immigrants mentioned as being needed by the colony in my first chapter may expect to find immediate employment. High wages in a colony are often accompanied by irregularity or inconstancy of employment. Political economists, who are also practical men, tell us that these high wages cannot be long maintained in New Zealand even by the powerful trades unions. They say that New Zealand will lag behind the older Australasian colonies until wages are reduced (by immigration or other causes) to a point at which capital can make its favourite manufactures pay. A clever engineer and large employer of labour, Mr. W. N. Blair, dealt ably with this and other cognate questions affecting the industrial development of this colony in an address delivered to the Industrial Association of Canterbury at Christchurch, February 24, 1887. I quote the following passage, which would have been emphatically hooted by any colonial audience of working-men, but seems to have been approved by the Association: "In New Zealand we want, most of all, men, women, and children—'all sorts and conditions of men,' and of all 'kindreds and tongues,' to develop the varied resources of the colony. Anglo-Saxons to trade, grow corn, and drive engines, Italians to plant olives, Frenchmen to make wine, and Mongolians to grow tea and tobacco."

These ideas are good from one point of view, but it would be much more in accordance with the fitness of things and with Sir George Grey's oft-repeated patriotic wish, were the colony's need of population supplied solely from the overcrowded old country by harmonious co-operation between the Imperial and New Zealand Governments on the one hand, and between the Home Emigration Societies and colonial Chambers of Commerce on the other. These Chambers of Commerce are really representative practical associations, and are acquainted with the kinds of labour needed from time to time by the different districts of New Zealand. Settlers from European countries having *special knowledge of particular industries* (*e.g.* wine-making) should be welcomed to New Zealand, as indeed they are, but not in too large numbers. Having seen the detrimental effects upon the city of San Francisco of a large Mongolian element, I am opposed to the influx of any Asiatic nationality into this Anglo-Saxon colony.

Legislation regarding the employment of females and children in the various industries is both sensible and humane, and well enforced by the Government inspectors. I will give a few particulars. "No child under twelve may be employed in a factory. No female or child under fourteen may be employed at

night, or for more than eight hours a day; but a boy
or girl of fourteen may be employed for ten hours a
day for four days a week in fruit-preserving, fish-curing,
or newspaper printing." Proper ventilation in work-
rooms and factories, and an interval for meals every
four and a half hours, are also strictly enforced.
Thus the milliners, dressmakers, tailoresses, and boot-
sewers of this colony have a much happier time (when
employed) than their sisters in England.

The simple and inexpensive Patent Law of New
Zealand encourages the inventiveness of the New
Zealander to such an extent—co-operating, I suppose,
with the stimulating climate—that of late years there
have been produced more patents per head of the population than in the hitherto most inventive nation in
the world, the United States. But as comparison of this
kind to be effective must be made by a careful study of
trustworthy statistics extending over a long series of
years, I merely mention this fact as a singular one,
which the future may either make temporary or
permanent.

Certain it is, that in all branches of art and decorative
industry New Zealanders take precedence, despite
their small numbers, the youth of the colony, and the
absence of Art Schools, Museums of Design—in fact, of
all the finer developments of South Kensington training—of all the other Australasian Colonies. I could
enlarge on this subject for several pages, but will not
lest I weary the reader, and seem to "blow" about my
favourite colony.

It would be well for the exporter of English goods to
New Zealand, and for the emigrant, to make himself
accurately acquainted with the tariff in that colony,
the rates of which have been lately raised for revenue
purposes. Brett's Auckland Almanac, published
annually, generally towards the end of October,
contains the full, accurate, and revised duties, both
fixed and *ad valorem*, on every article that is liable to
pay, also the duty-free articles. The almanac for 1890
is published in New Zealand in October, 1889, reaching

this country in December, 1889. And at any time the tariff can be obtained from the Agent-general's office in London.

New Zealand is a country having all the natural resources in air, water, coal, iron, wool, sea-coast, and climate for manufactures; but its inhabitants must not be impatient in attempting to rival the mother country, or to become prematurely "self-contained." Rather should a genuine demand for an article of manufacture, when that need has for some time existed in their own colony, be gradually supplied. This will be a following out of the ordinary Law of Supply and Demand, instead of a "hot-house cultivation" of plants that shoot, indeed, quickly up, but are apt to fade and die. The recent want that has sprung up in the United States for "binder twine," made out of New Zealand hemp (*Phormium tenax*), is an example of the *natural demand and supply*. This fibre has proved such a failure in making cables for use at sea, on account of the swelling of the gum still remaining in it, that rope-makers have given it up in disgust, after losing heavily upon it.

On the other hand, the discovery by the coachmakers of New York and London of a gum that is equal in purity, lowness of melting-point, and hardness when dry to kauri gum (pp. 185, 186), and cheaper, has so lowered the price of the latter as to suggest to New Zealand that it ought to make its own coach-varnish out of this and other materials, which is now being done.

CHAPTER XI.

SOCIAL LIFE IN NEW ZEALAND.

Its heartiness and unconventionality—Tourists' mistakes and exaggerations—Ups and downs—Ruling forces in society—*Nouveaux riches*—The highest education and culture of England appreciated by colonial parents—Neighbourly kindness—Fire!—Hospitality—Effects of meat-eating on Character—The "larrikin"—How to cure "larrikinism"—Recreation out of doors—Cricket, football, tennis, cycling—Indoor amusements—Rinking—Lectures—Chess, Shakspeare, Dramatic clubs—Music, concerts, amateur singers—Professional teachers—A musical colony—Art, artists, and Art Exhibitions—Literature—Amateur science—Happy and unhappy Homes—Drinking customs—"Lambing down"—The slain by drink—Conclusion.

In New Zealand, the man who is adaptable to new conditions, and of a sympathetic nature, and who is not too old to learn, will find social life (as I have found it) very enjoyable, whether in town, or in the country. The reception given to such an one, whether man or woman, combines both English kindness, Australian heartiness, and the readiness to make a new neighbour feel "at home," that is characteristic of the Great Republic. Without disparagement to the United States, where I lived for nearly three years among many kind friends, nor to the dear Old Country, from which my heart has never been severed, I can truly say that my wife and I have formed the most genuine, helpful, and, we trust, lifelong friendships in the Colony of New Zealand. We felt, indeed, on quitting its shores for the old country that we were leaving home for a cold and strange foreign land! To the observant Englishman whose heart is not sterilized by the *morgue* so condemned by our French neighbours, nor by the lust for gold, the new life he leads in New Zealand derives a zest not only from its freedom, sincerity, and unconventionality, but from the many quaint and out-of-the-way characters he encounters, both in and out of "society." We must remember *en passant* that "Society" as well as society exists in New Zealand, though it is not quite as exclusive as in Belgravia. The passing-round-the-world traveller seldom sees actual New Zealand Society; and when he writes his inevitable book (of which crime I am also guilty, no doubt, but not of what follows) is prone to fill in his hasty sketches with the colouring of fancy. What vivid pictures of "life in New Zealand" we should obtain, for example, from Mr. W. J. Frater, as quoted in the *Otago Daily Times!* At Wellington he writes that *he saw* "a number of men *wearing red jackets* and *bound together by a long chain*, marching through the streets. They are guarded by several officials in uniform with rifles under their arms and revolvers by their side. This strange procession is the prisoners who have been at work on the roads, and are now returning home to dinner." The words I have italicized are embellishments of Mr. F.'s fancy, while the rest of the paragraph is accurate enough. At Waimate Mr. Frater visited "the humble abode of two wood-cutters," who were "cutting timber in the midst of bush containing *black men and wild animals.*" "Before retiring to rest," he continues, "a huge fire was lit outside the house. This precaution was *necessary in order to prevent wild animals* and other disagreeable creatures from approaching too near. *A sentry was on guard all night*, armed with a rifle and revolver." All this is highly dramatic, but as there are no wild animals in the colony, I suppose that Mr. Frater, who elsewhere states that "travel has increased his knowledge of the world and its inhabitants," felt bound to spice his *brochure* with some adventure, even if imaginary. "Minor inaccuracies, such as the statement that 'Port Chalmers is generally named the Bluff,' we may let pass, but we draw the line at wild animals," concludes the *Otago Times*.

It is only when one settles down in the colony for some years that one gets into touch with the residents, and enters fully into the thoughts, ways, and actions of colonial life. What a chapter I could write on the eccentrics I have met in New Zealand! What undeveloped geniuses, what utter bores, what strange and queer men and women, still, (so far as I know), outside the Whau (or, as it now is politely named, Avondale) Asylum! Perhaps some day I may give my reminiscences, but meantime forbear. That there is a distinction between life in Australia and life in New Zealand is sufficiently shown by the difference between the scenes, events, and characters in Mrs. Campbell Praed's successful romances (" Policy and Passion," for instance) and those two typical New Zealand books, Miss Clara Cheeseman's "A Rolling Stone," and Lady Barker's "Station Life in New Zealand." The former clever novel contains admirably drawn scenes and illustrations of genuine New Zealand life and character. Among others I can readily identify the "professor of music" and old Wasley, of Waitakerei, the lovely forest scenery so eloquently described by the authoress. In most parts of the book the scene is laid in towns, where, of course, the quaintest characters usually congregate. That too common event, a house on fire, is graphically described; and the wreck of a steamer on the coast (the ill-fated *Tararua*, evidently), is told with all the skill of a practised novelist, though I am informed that this is a "maiden work."

The latter book is a simple and graphic account of country life in New Zealand, in the Middle Island, which is made so attractive that it has induced many visitors to go out to the colony to try it. "Station life" has become more artificial and mechanical since Lady Barker's day. In a very democratic country such as New Zealand, where there is no aristocracy of birth or intellect to elevate society, where wealth, fluency of speech, and political influence seem to be the ruling forces in the community, the visitor might expect to find the entire social "tone" lower than at home. But my long experience of all *strata* of the mixed multitude has led me to the conclusion, different to that of some writers on the subject, that the average level of the intellectual and social life of New Zealand is not only higher than that of the other Australasian colonies, but that it is attaining, as time goes on, a still higher elevation. This high level is certainly not promoted by the so-called "society papers" of the colony, rather the reverse; the chief factors in this upward movement are the deepening and extending love of art, learning, literature, science, and the noble ambition, often fired by Sir George Grey's popular addresses, of founding a New Zealand nation upon the highest models of the age.

For, though the hardheaded, pushing, shrewd, money-making trader rather than the man of intellect and culture, acquires the reins of political and social power, yet education, culture, refinement, and learning *do* make their influence felt even in this utilitarian community. No one can doubt that not only natural gifts, but the high culture, dignity of manner, and the friendship with the "men of light and leading" of the day, possessed by Sir George Grey, have made him the orator of New Zealand, and given him the power to sway public opinion by his utterances. But in his rush through this colony, (or a *fringe* of it, so to speak,) the traveller is not usually fortunate enough to meet personally the real "makers of the country," but, coming across loud-voiced, coarse men, who "blow," as the colonial word is, only about themselves, *their* achievements, and *their* district or town—not the whole colony, else one might forgive them—he hastily and inaccurately puts these blatant *nouveaux riches* into his book (*libellus*, as Horace would term it) as representatives of New Zealand Society. One has to live there for years to understand the component parts and characteristics of "Society" and society. For my own part I do not attempt to analyze it in these pages of plain talk; it is kaleidoscopic to a degree; but of social life and the forces that sway it I can give an accurate idea. The same ups and downs that occur in older countries take place in

New Zealand more often, more rapidly, and are less noticed. In the course of nine years' residence I have witnessed six changes of Government, four changes of Native Lands Court policy; wholesale dismissals of Government officers; the civil service remodelled; and many unaccountable removals of head officials. In commercial life I have seen the Bank of New Zealand in great trouble; two suicides through losses in land; a tradesman become bankrupt three times; several merchants high in society move down from their grand mansions into cottages; and finally, some of them leave the colony at their friends' expense. I have seen fashionable ladies left destitute widows, and doctors apparently doing a large practice die, leaving their families nearly paupers. "Grass widows" and "grass widowers" abound in New Zealand; and deserted wives have a hard struggle. On the other hand I have seen a shabbily dressed mechanic who could not write his own name bequeath a large fortune to the most noble ends—the relief of the poor and the aged. Viewing society as a whole, in any of the larger cities of New Zealand, I regard its elements as almost as mixed and shifting as those of a Western city in America. If an "old identity," a self-made man, is genuine, honest, and kindhearted, one soon learns to overlook mere breaches of pronunciation, of dress, and of manners. The new-comer, whether old, young, or middle-aged, should always make the acquaintance, and if possible the friendship, of some of these colonists. One thing is much to be admired in these rough diamonds, namely, their desire to give their children the highest education attainable in the colony; and even in many cases to send their boys to an English university for a degree, and their girls to London for the season. Nothing could show more plainly than this custom of sending their children Home to finish their education, the parents' regard for the best interests of their family, and their deep appreciation of the value of that higher education which had been denied to them by the circumstances of their early life.

As regards getting into "Society," it is easier for a new comer in New Zealand than in the English provinces. To be able to play an instrument of music; to dance or to sing passably (especially a comic song); to live in good style, and to wear good clothes—these are the essentials for admission into "society." A newly arrived family occupying a good house will find many of the neighbours will call without any formal introduction. Such is the friendly colonial fashion. Neighbours in New Zealand are very kind and helpful in sickness, fire, accident, or any other domestic misfortune; therefore an English lady—though, if reserved and of retiring habits, she may be slightly startled at first at these colonial ways—would do well to return the calls, for she will thus acquire a large number of acquaintances, among whom in due time real friends may be found. In the freedom of selection thus gained, affinities seek each other, heart becomes linked to heart, and "home sickness," from which Englishwomen suffer more than Englishmen, gradually disappears. In all my "globe-trotting," I have nowhere seen such an amount of lovely self-sacrifice to others—to the lonely stranger just arrived, it may be, dying of consumption; or to the orphans and widows, many a time sent home by the subscriptions of those who could ill afford the money; or in starting again an honest man who has failed in business—as I have witnessed in New Zealand.

The Kauri pine being the favourite building material for houses, fire is much dreaded, especially as kerosene lamps constitute the favourite means of illumination in the poorer dwellings. Perhaps the commonest cause is the placing of Taupiri coal ashes in a wooden box at night, and leaving it against the wall of the house or next to a wooden fence. The heat is retained in the ashes for an extraordinary length of time, and, if a wind is blowing, the box may take fire, and from it the house. Such events are common in towns, and necessitate prompt action on the part of neighbours to save each other's property. Lives are seldom lost, because the majority of houses have only one storey. I remember one summer night a fine two-storey new house, standing opposite to mine in Symonds Street, being burnt to the ground in twenty minutes, the owner and his son barely escaping with their lives, the alarm not having been given promptly enough to the fire brigade, which is an excellent one. The next house, owned and occupied by a medical friend of mine, was badly scorched, and just escaped the same fate. We worked like Trojans, hauling out his pictures, furniture, &c., and two neighbours in *déshabille* kept their garden hose playing upon the walls and roof till the brigade appeared. Brick houses are thought to be damp in the winter, but a *well-dried* concrete house is both cool in summer, easily warmed up in winter, and proof against fire. In the matter of hospitality New Zealand scarcely displays that profuse open-handed treatment of visitors, whether provided with introductions or not, offered by Australia. As a rule, a New Zealander likes an introductory letter, wants to know something about the new-comer, and so on, as in England. But if he likes you at first sight—being a thorough believer in his own judgment—he will treat you handsomely even without introduction; and in the country districts especially you will find a hearty hospitality, such as one reads of in old-fashioned books. The old settler has witnessed the advent of so many "wastrels" and baneful adventurers under a respectable guise that he is, with reason, cautious in his reception of new-comers.

It has been observed that climate, scenery, and food have a powerful influence in modifying the character of a race of men imported into, and not indigenous to, a country. I consider that the characteristics of the New Zealander of British, not Maori blood, have been altered to some degree by his environment. It may be but a whimsical notion, but I have noticed, while studying the psychological features of New Zealand-born youths, that some of the Maori tendencies have been imparted to them. A certain stoicism and unimpressiveness are noticeable about native-born New Zealanders. For instance, in visiting London they never seem astonished at anything; nor can they "enthuse" over Westminster Abbey, St. Paul's, the Tower, Windsor Castle, or any of the "show places." I cannot explain this, except on the above theory, although well acquainted with all shades and grades of colonial character.

There may be nothing in the theory that an excessive meat diet conduces to hardness and even cruelty of disposition; but it is a fact that the flesh-eating and cannibalistic Maori of the recent past was conspicuously callous and cruel, quite unlike his *taro*-eating cousins, the Samoans and Hawaiians.

Now, it is a striking coincidence that the adult Anglo-Saxon in New Zealand consumes an average amount of 200 to 250 lbs. of meat in the course of a year, while the American is content with 120 lbs. and Briton with 110 lbs. The police-court records of New Zealand show the existence of a large and increasing class of evil-doers, termed "larrikins" or street-roughs, who are usually well fed—on meat chiefly. The "larrikin" is an unfeeling, callous, and cruel fellow, more ready to rob, knock down, and otherwise maltreat a feeble old woman, defenceless girl, or drunken man than to fight a policeman. Corrupted and incited to bad ways by a few rapscallions exported by their friends, or who had come as "shilling-a-month men" from London, New York, or San Francisco, these fellows are becoming a terror to all peaceful citizens. Yet there is in many of them a daring, an intelligence, and restless energy and ingenuity which might be turned to better ends. An excellent cure for "larrikinism" in the sea-port cities, might be found in the establishment of a training-ship like the *Conway* at Liverpool, for those who would take up the sea as a profession. Another "cure" would be the formation of a Cadet Corps of Volunteers in every town of a certain size, officered by educated men, kindly yet firm, who would drill them, enforce strict discipline; yet become personally interested in the rank and file; and give them all the recreation and freedom that is possible. I have seen several of these "larrikins," under the force of an awakened conscience and of kindness, reform, and become useful and honourable citizens. Certain it is, that unless the misdirected activity of these lads be guided into harmless or beneficial channels, their lawlessness will become a real danger to the colony.

I must now speak of the recreations which so diversify and brighten social life in this colony. Through its mild yet invigorating climate, its long summer, and the shortness of the customary hours of labour, New Zealand offers many facilities for open-air amusements. Therefore picnics, excursions, and riding-parties, drives, bowls, lawn-tennis, cricket, and football, are very much in vogue. In Auckland alone (with its suburbs) there were in 1888 no less than fifty clubs or associations for outdoor amusements—12 cricket-clubs, 22 football clubs, 10 yacht and boating clubs, and six bowling and tennis clubs. Some of these sports can be enjoyed all the year round in the North Island. Golfing is also played with great enthusiasm by the Scottish settlers in the Middle Island; and in some winters, with a harder frost than usual, curling and skating may be enjoyed there. So great is the interest exhibited by the populace of the cities in the visit of a cricket or football team, that the mayor is importuned to grant a public holiday or half-holiday on the day of the match. To the employer of labour this practice means the loss of a day's wages and a day's work, while to the employed it means an extra holiday on full pay. As the colonial, postal, and bank holidays are already more numerous in New Zealand than at home, these extra holidays, sometimes falling upon mail-day, are not a little inconvenient to business men, who often protest against this growing custom. But the *employés* always carry the day, for the mayor is elected, as in the United States, by the general body of townspeople, and he seldom cares to risk unpopularity by refusing the holiday.

Gymnasia are not numerous in the colony, but those that exist are of first-class quality and seem to be well patronised.

Volunteering is decidedly popular in the colony, although one sees complaints in the newspapers of the parsimony of the Government as to grants for outfit, capitation fees, and so forth. Now and then there is a little disturbance in a Corps, because there are more candidates for officers' commissions than can possibly be appointed. As the Royal holidays (Queen's Birthday, &c.) and Easter week all fall in the warm season of the year, the volunteer corps have many opportunities of camp-training. Their *physique* is noticeably superior to that of the average British volunteer. Their numbers fluctuate considerably, because of the frequent removal of the privates from one part of the colony to another, to fulfil the requirements of business. The official return of the number of volunteers of all ranks on March 31, 1888, was as follows:—

North Island—3632 effectives, including cavalry, artillery, engineers, naval artillery, mounted infantry, and riflemen. Middle Island—4432 effectives, comprising the same division as those of the North Island, with the addition of 69 honorary reserve men. Total for the whole colony, 8064 effective volunteers. There were also at this date 2773 cadets enrolled.

As there is a law of compulsory service in the militia, in case of invasion in the colony, these volunteers would in such event prove most useful *cadres* for the undrilled recruits.

The last two winters I spent in New Zealand were characterized by a mania for Rinking. Rinks were opened in every town and in every suburb. Despite bruises, fractures, dislocations, sprains, and the doubtful acquaintances made in these halls by young ladies, there seemed to be a fascination about the tedious circling round a floor on imitation skates, to the music of a noisy band, amidst dust of a pine-splintery nature, and in the heat of a crowded gas-lit room, against which no other amusement could compete. I once went into the Choral Hall, Auckland (used one evening a week for rinking) and the scene reminded me of Leland's humorous lines upon cycling:—

> "The dimes that Breitmann doomble
>   In learning for to ride,
> Vas oftener as de sand grains
>   Dat rollen in der tide."

The tumbling, indeed, at the rink seemed part of the fun, but it generally turned out no joke to the rinker who was undermost in the heap of sprawling, entangled humanity. The glamour of the roller-skate was that of the bicycle:—

> ". . . The best of it, you bet,
>   Vas that man could go so nicely
> Pefore he got oopset."

In winter the indoor amusements of the New Zealanders are as varied as they are in England. Clubs for chess, whist, Shakspeare reading, amateur acting, and opera flourish. Choral and orchestral societies give their performances, and dinners, dances, evening parties, church socials, and entertainments of all kinds are numerous. At dinner parties there is less formal stiffness than in England; men reveal their ideas more frankly and genially, and do not assume an unnatural frigidity, or a professional *raconteur* style along with their evening dress. After dinner there is always plenty of good music and singing in the drawing-room. Speaking of dinners, I may mention that there are excellent clubs in every large New Zealand town, where visitors may be entered as honorary members for one month. The *cuisine* of the very best New Zealand clubs stands well the closest criticism of a London gastronome, particularly when its best efforts are displayed on the occasion of a banquet to some distinguished visitor, or to a popular member who is leaving the city.

There is nothing corresponding to the "London season" in New Zealand, unless it be that pale imitation of it called "The Wellington season"—from April or May, till the end of July—when the colonial Parliament is in session. At that time an unusual bustle and gaiety prevail in the breezy city. "There is a sound of revelry by night;" the theatre is open every night with something attractive, the ministers give dinners, balls, and evening parties, and the Governor holds his *levées*.

There is no particular time of the year which may be called the "lecture season," as with us in England. Professional lecturers take New Zealand in the course of their Antipodean tour, as it suits them. Occasionally an eminent man, like Joseph Cook, of Boston, delivers a lecture while the mail steamer stays in port; and we are very glad to obtain a glimpse and a hearing of one whose works had stirred our hearts and intellects. But systematic lecture courses, well advertised and "paragraphed" in the newspapers, are usually successful at any time of the year. To really ensure large audiences night after night, lectures must be bright, terse, not too heavy in facts and figures, and relieved by music or lantern illustrations. I remember that R. A. Proctor, Archibald Forbes, G. A. Sala, and Major Dane achieved a complete success in New Zealand, the four large cities vying with each other to give the lecturer the largest audience. In the country districts settlers will strain their slender exchequer and ride long distances in stormy weather in order to hear some favourite preacher or lecturer; and woe to him who gives them chaff for wheat!

Having occasionally lectured on scientific and literary subjects—"Plant Life," "Shakspeare and Euphuism," "Esoteric Buddhism," "Longfellow," "Tennyson's Lyrics," "The Sphygmograph," and others—the writer can testify how intelligent and appreciative New Zealand audiences are. In five or ten minutes the speaker feels thoroughly *en rapport* with those he is addressing.

Throughout New Zealand, especially in the North Island, excursions and picnics by sea and land are rendered easy and delightful by the great advantages of a long steady summer, good springs, and streams of pure water everywhere, and the plentiful choice of picturesque spots of country, absolutely free from snakes, "wild animals," or poisonous insects (except the very rare *Katipo*, a small black spider marked by a red spot); from malaria; and from shrubs which exhale poisonous emanations, like the *Rhus diversiloba* of California. Merry parties of young people are very seldom broken up by a thunderstorm, hail, or rain, as in Britain; and the proximity of good excursion places to the towns in New Zealand does away with the necessity of a dull tiring journey home by rail, 'bus, or cab, which at Home often neutralises or mars the enjoyment of "a day in the country," or a "sniff of the briny."

Many a time and oft have I longed to transport to dear old cloudy England—year by year becoming more of a vast city—some lovely bit of forest scenery—the sky above of the purest blue, the "bush" below rich in evergreen trees and shrubs, interlaced with creeping and climbing plants, and carpeted with flowers—in the centre a ferny dell, with a waterfall whose soothing music blends with the strange notes of the native birds—the loud clear "ping" of the parson-bird (*tui*), the *staccato* cries of the tree-parrot (*kaka*) and the delicious three-note-chime of the bell-bird (*korimako*). Scenes like these give inspiration to the local artists and form the chief charm and attraction of the local Art Exhibitions in the chief cities of the colony. But nature cannot be perfectly reproduced on canvas; and I have enjoyed scenery in this colony which transcends in weird beauty anything that has come within my experience in England, America, and Australia.

The enjoyment of the country is enhanced, let me assure the reader who may think of visiting New Zealand, by some knowledge of the art of photography. Nearly all the year round it is easy to obtain in that clear atmosphere well-defined photographs. I advise tourists to bring a camera of the latest type, and to take views as they pass along, which may be developed and printed by the photographers of the towns in which they make a stay. Thus a permanent and most interesting record of their New Zealand tour may be brought home. From experience I can state that there is a great fascination about amateur photography, especially about one's failures!

In the social life of the people of New Zealand, art and music are becoming important elements; and this is one of the good omens for the future of the nation. Excellent exhibitions of paintings are held annually in each of the four centres, Auckland, Wellington, Christchurch, and Dunedin. In Auckland, where the Society of Arts (of which I was one of the original committee) manage the annual exhibition, there are never less than from 250 to 300 original oil or water-colour pictures presented for public inspection. Some, in each year, are of great merit, and the sales are very satisfactory, in good times. Landscape, still life, and flowers are the predominant subjects, drawing from the live model having only very recently been introduced into the art school. The majority of the pictures are by "amateur" artists, many of whom add to their income by the sale of their works; and even of the "professional" artists in Auckland, most are self-educated men whose innate genius and perseverance in the lines of study (nature chiefly) accessible to them have triumphed over deficiencies in their Art-training. Take, for example, not invidiously to other artists however, Mr. Charles Blomfield, who was originally a carpenter. He has created for himself a world-wide fame as *the* painter of the Pink and White sinter Terraces, which were destroyed, to our grief and dismay, in the terrible event described in chapter vii. The peculiarly intense blue of the water in the basins of both Terraces, and the roseate pink shading, like the hues of dawn, of the steps of the Pink Terrace have been caught by him in a marvellously accurate manner. The figure-drawing, too, for which he used to be so sharply criticized, has greatly improved, and the introduction of life into his landscapes adds just the feature that was wanting. Space forbids mention of Ball, Drummond, Sturtevant, and others whose artistic development has been most creditable. It is pleasant to see how cordially both professionals and amateurs work upon the committees of these art societies, and to see pictures by both classes of artists hung impartially, according to their merits.

Much encouragement of late has been given in Auckland by the Society of Arts to Decorative Household Art, with the result of educing much latent talent and taste, and of brightening the colonial home by beautifying its interior. The number and variety of the native woods, so exquisite when inlaid and polished, further the latter desirable result. One family I knew intimately, whose home I never visited without finding some new object of art, the work of the young ladies of the house; some painted panel or plaque; some embroidered bird or flower; some hand-painted mirror or card; exemplifying not only the taste but the originality of its artist. All the young people of this family could sing at sight, and each could play some instrument—the violin being the favourite. No one becoming well acquainted with such Auckland homes could truthfully call the modern New Zealander a "Philistine."

A sincere love for music is diffused throughout New Zealand. At the risk of being condemned by the Wellingtonians, Christchurchmen, and Dunedinites as a fanatical Aucklander, I have clearly pointed out in chapter iv. the pre-eminence of that city in the development of the divine art. What is needed now for its further culture is a complete Academy of Music in one of the large cities, and a musical festival (without prizes for brass-bands, and all that nonsense) to be held triennially in each of the four local capitals in rotation, managed by a standing committee of really musical amateurs, carefully selected from these cities. Nothing would give a greater impetus to choral and instrumental music than this move, which I commend to the present Governor of New Zealand, and to those in high places there, who love the "Art Divine" for its own sake.

Singing from musical notation being now made a compulsory subject in the primary schools of the colony, the ear of a child is trained from an early age. The boy or girl who is really musical carries on the singing, first of Sankey's Hymns, and Christy's songs, and then by joining a choral society, where "singing at sight" is usually required, becomes familiarized with high-class modern music. Almost every cottage in New Zealand contains a piano or American organ. The choirs of churches and the organ-playing have received favourable notice from most travellers. It has come to pass that amateur vocalists, *soprani* and *bassi* being more numerous than *alti* and *tenori*, are so numerous and of such good quality that a concert is looked upon as the readiest means of raising funds for religious or benevolent purposes. But this "readiness to oblige" has another side. The services of amateur singers being always *gratis*, it is difficult for a resident professional vocalist to make a living in the same city. If he relies on teaching, there is not much encouragement in the fact brought to my knowledge by a music teacher in 1888, namely, that qualified professors of music were giving shilling lessons! Probably terms may have improved, *pari passu* with the improvement in the times, since that date. The reader can thus understand that it is not difficult for the artizan in full work, who receives 8s. to 10s. a day, to be able to give at least one of his family a musical education. The tenor of the day becomes soon a spoiled favourite, so greatly is he sought after; but I was amused to see that when he begins to put a price upon his voice his public engagements cease—at least in Auckland.

Elocution is not so much studied in New Zealand as music and painting; but now and then a young man shows conspicuous talent as a reciter, and is then as much in request as the tenor above mentioned.

Poetry (or rhyming) is much cultivated in New Zealand, the Auckland and Wellington newspapers generally overflowing with it. Sometimes a really poetic insight and power of expression is revealed. I wish that I had space to quote some of my clerical friend E. H. G.'s verses. His poetic genius must have slumbered until Auckland scenery and climate, and perhaps "the storms of fate" also awoke it. Passing to another subject—amateur science as a recreation—the collections of coins, minerals, insects, shells, and so forth, amassed by diligent workers in science in the colony are astonishingly numerous and good. Captain Broun, of Howick near Auckland, has made the most complete collection of the *Coleoptera* in Australasia. The formation in 1887 of the Australian Association for the Advancement of Science gives just the impulse that is needed to unite these scattered students of science in one society, and thus utilize their detached researches for the good of the whole scientific world.

The average New Zealand settler is very glad to avail himself of the facilities near him in the shape of Free Libraries, Mechanics' Institutes, Athenæums, and similar institutions (of which there are three hundred in the colony), in order to supply the deficiencies of his early education and to keep his reading well up to date. Each monthly mail brings its shoal of English and American books and magazines, and the bookseller who is late or incorrect in delivering them to customers is much berated. Having in a humble way striven to promote the intellectual culture of Auckland by founding Magazine Clubs, an Essay and Debating Club (the " Kiwis ") and in conjunction with others the Athenæum of Auckland, I am in a position to state that there is a real and increasing love for good literature, permanent and serial, and a desire for the full and free discussion of all questions of the day. Henry George's " Progress and Poverty " aroused public attention in New Zealand months before England was stirred up by its startling problems. I congratulate the reading public of the colonies in general, and of New Zealand in particular, that two eminent London publishers (Macmillan and Kegan Paul, Trench, & Co.) have brought out recently special colonial editions of their publications, so that good reading is brought within the reach of the many who cannot afford the English prices, and have no circulating library accessible.

There exists out at the Antipodes a vigour of untrammelled thought and a receptiveness of mind which, while tending on the one hand to lead some men into unsettlement of religious faith, and into injurious practices, such as spiritualism, or wild mystic theories like Theosophy or Esoteric Buddhism, on the other hand encourages many weaker intellects to emerge from traditional grooves of thought into new truths, moral, mental, and spiritual, which they might never have found out in conventional England. There are also unconventional methods of preaching Christian truth, such as tent-missions, Salvation Army work, home Bible-readings, which are doing a grand work in New Zealand by counteracting the evil forces that exist in new countries where high wages, plenty of play-time, parental laxity, an independent spirit in children, free social intercourse among young people, and a stimulating climate, powerfully influence the social life of the community.

Domestic life in New Zealand does not greatly differ from that in England, except that, good servants being scarce, and dear, the wife has to do more actual household work than in the old country. Notwithstanding what I have to say later on regarding the drink question, I believe that, class for class, there is a smaller proportion of drunken husbands in the colony than in Great Britain. Very seldom do the newspapers report cases brought before the police courts of such brutal assaults on wives and children made by men under the influence of drink as one reads of every day in the English newspapers.

Miss E. Katharine Bates, an observant traveller (whom I met in Auckland), goes so far as to assert in her book "Kaleidoscope, or Scenes from East to West," that nowhere in her travels had she "seen so many married couples who were happy as in this colony." Contrast this with E. W. Payton's impression: "The normal condition of all housewives below that of the upper middle class is that of overworked house drudges. One result of this a sad breaking-down of character. Women drink a good deal on the quiet and this reacts on their temper, &c."

Mr. Payton must have derived his impressions from some pessimist. I, who in the course of my professional duties have gone into all classes of homes at all hours, have seen neither evidences of secret drinking nor of temper produced thereby. Probably the truth lies between these two extremely opposite impressions.

This quotation leads me to point out plainly, but yet in all kindness, what are the conspicuous blemishes in the social life of New Zealand. I mean the prevalence of gambling, immoderate drinking, and excessive smoking. The totalisator, a betting machine highly favoured all over the colonies, is the cause of ruin of thousands of young men. By purchasing a ticket for five or ten shillings each "subscriber" stands a chance of winning a prize of from ten pounds to five hundred pounds. It is a bad thing to waste money in buying tickets which only draw blanks, but it is a worse thing to win a prize, for then the gambling spirit is thoroughly stimulated. I knew one fine young fellow who won the large prize of a certain totalisator (£400 I think it was). He never did any good in the world afterwards. I believe the New Zealand Government charge the proprietor of such an instrument a fee for permission to use it in public. If this be true it is a disgrace to the Government; for the law of the colony against gambling is so strict now, that even a clergyman who gets up a bazaar or fancy fair has to ask the Colonial Secretary for special permission to hold either a "raffle" or an "Art Union." I hope I am inaccurately informed; for this is indeed "straining at a gnat and swallowing a camel."

No Government can put down verbal betting, of course, but it seems to me the bounden duty of the New Zealand Government to enact a law to make the totalisator or any similar machine as illegal as *roulette* and *rouge-et-noir* are already. It is a pity to see such innocent, healthful games, such as cricket, football, and tennis, made the occasion for betting, as they are made in the colonies. Naturally the horse-races, so beloved by the mass of the colonists, are not free from the "speelers" and other blacklegs who in England haunt these scenes and demoralise the old English sport.

The pernicious and increasing habit of young lads beginning to smoke from the ages of nine or ten, is a vice which is destroying the health of hundreds. It cannot be met by prohibitive legislation, as a certain Legislative Councillor, now deceased, wished to meet it. Parents who themselves smoke should give it up as an example to their boys, and should sternly discourage any smoking by a boy until he is at least twenty years old. The crude and strong tobacco leaf now grown and manufactured in New Zealand is deleterious to young smokers because it is so rich in nicotine. I shall give in chapter xii. definite reasons for these strong opinions.

Unnecessary and immoderate drinking of liquor, chiefly in the form of "nipping," has grown into a serious social evil, nursed by the injurious colonial habit of treating friends and acquaintances to a drink at any hour of the day they may chance to meet. Standing treat all round goes by the singular term of "shouting" in Australasia. *Punch* satirized this habit in 1886, the Indian and Colonial Exhibition year, when he had a cartoon representing Britannia bidding "adieu to her Australian son, and his inexhaustible bottle."

The waste of time, health, and money, in the colony caused by this custom is deplorable. Let me describe the usual incident. A. meets B. whom he has not seen for some days, perhaps. After the "How d'ye do?" A. says, "Have a drink, old fellow?" "Don't care if I do," says B. All drinks being sixpence each, down goes a shilling. Then B. treats A.—two shillings. C. comes in: "Hallo! How d'ye do? Will you join us?" "Thanks, I don't mind." Drinks all round; three-and-sixpence gone. Lastly C. "shouts" in return, perhaps even B. also, and all retire. Thus five or seven shillings, and perhaps three quarters of an hour of the best business time in the day, have been consumed; and none of the three men's heads are as clear for thought and calculation as they had been before the "shouting." I am glad to learn that this custom is on the decline among educated people; and that another baneful habit, that of sealing orders given to commercial travellers by a drink, is also going out of fashion. There are other good signs of the spread of total abstinence. There is an agitation in the School Boards for the adoption of Dr. B. W. Richardson's Temperance Lesson Book in the primary schools; the granting by law of Local Option over the whole colony; the general substitution of tea and coffee for wine at afternoon calls and at evening parties; and the interesting fact observed by ministers and clergymen that most of the *native-born youth* (European race) are either abstemious or total abstainers.

Among the degrading elements of social life in the colony are those poor fellows who are kept in New Zealand by money remitted by their friends in England once a month, either direct to them or through trustees. They are called "remittance men," and are a source of trouble to everyone acquainted with them. Usually they drink away the money within a few days of its receipt and then go about borrowing until the next mail comes in. They "shout" for other drinkers of a lower grade who hang round the post-office, with that object in view.

Among bushmen, shepherds, shearers, and others in the country the cashing of the half-yearly cheque for wages is made the occasion of a long drinking spree. When the poor wretch comes to his senses he generally finds himself lying on the road, robbed of everything except his clothes. This little process by which the publican is fattened and the bushman skinned is facetiously called "lambing down." The victim walks back to his employer's station, begging his meals on the way and a shakedown in a stable at night: to repeat the same folly at the end of another half-year. "Many a man," says E. W. Payton, "who can earn £3 and live comfortably upon £1 per week will drink away £2 and run into debt besides."

It is calculated by some profound temperance mathematician that New Zealanders spend no less than three millions per annum upon drink! I can scarcely credit this, but have not the figures by me to check it. There must, however, be some connection between an inordinate expenditure in alcohol and the comparatively large number of lunatics in New Zealand, for the records of the Asylums, which contained in 1886 over 1600 lunatics, show that alcoholism is the prevailing cause of mental disease.

Sir Wm. Fox, K.C.M.G., the eloquent and energetic President of the United Kingdom Alliance in New Zealand, has remarked that while people are horrified at the appalling description of 10,000 corpses that were found heaped up in one place in the Johnstown, U.S., disaster, they are never shocked at the thought of the awful spectacle that would be presented were it possible to bring together the scattered bodies of the thousands slain by drink in a single year. He states further that 1500 deaths every year—one for each public-house in the colony—are distinctly caused by drink in New Zealand. But after all the "Britain of the South" is a more sober country than its northern prototype and parent.

In conclusion, I may sum up my impressions of social life in New Zealand by saying that it is freer, fuller, more friendly, more democratic, and more original in development, than it is at Home. Though the influence of the nearer United States is distinctly felt the New Zealanders are yet thoroughly English, with much of the Australian heartiness about them. Any honest, industrious, self-respecting man or woman can form a pleasant home among them, with facilities for cultivating the mind and the taste, and for acquiring a host of congenial friends.

CHAPTER XII.

PROFESSIONAL EXPERIENCES.

Openings for Practice, and prospects of new comers—Age at which to emigrate — Outfit — Registration—Fees — Clubs—Working Expenses of Practice—Diseases prevalent among the Maoris—Native remedies—Singular mode of reviving the apparently drowned—Decrease of the natives still going on—Letter from a missionary—Diseases of the colonists—Typhoid fever, its cause, prevention, and death-rate — The Exanthemata — Diphtheria maligna—Poisoning from tinned meat and from Ptomaines—Phthisis pulmonalis—Cases arrested by climate of New Zealand —Phthisis laryngea—Bronchitis and Cynanche benefitted by Auckland climate—Entozoa common—Caries of teeth—No Ague in the colony—Katipo-bite—Diseases arising from Abuse of Alcohol and Tobacco—Lunacy in New Zealand—Vital statistics.

IN view of the numerous letters I have received since my return to England from medical men, both those who are seeking openings for practice in the colonies, and those who want to know all about New Zealand as a Health Resort, I have thought it well to add this chapter in order to supply the definite information required.

The non-medical reader will understand, therefore, that this chapter is written for the medical profession alone.

First, let me inform my medical brethren that there are openings occurring from time to time in New Zealand.

Second, that there are not now any "fortunes" to be made in practice as seems to have been the case twenty years since.

Third, that even now, a thorough knowledge of one's profession, especially of surgery, steady hard work, and a little more "push" than is advisable in the old country will meet with success.

Of late years, so many medical men have settled in New Zealand for the sake of their own or their family's health, and so many young surgeons go out there with emigrant ships and on steamers, that our profession is becoming almost as overstocked there as it is at home, in proportion to the general population. In chapter i. I quoted the exact number (495) on the New Zealand register in 1887, but by the time this book reaches the reader the number will have increased to at least 530; besides a large number of unregistered practitioners who obtain a fair amount of support from the New Zealand public. A Medical Registration Act is now being promoted by the New Zealand Medical Association to extinguish unlicensed practice.

There are usually more ready openings for new comers in the country districts of New Zealand than in the towns, where medical men are apt to linger, like the artizan-emigrants, in the hope of obtaining immediate and lucrative employment.

In the leading newspapers one finds now and then an advertisement for a fully qualified doctor, at a fixed salary, or a *guaranteed minimum* income, capable of being improved and extended. Very often the house-surgeon of a District Hospital is allowed private practice, so long as his routine duties are not interfered with. If the salary offered is under £300 per annum the probability is that he will be allowed private practice; if it is £300 or over, he will be debarred from it. Mining companies unite in employing a surgeon; the salaries given varying from £300 to £500 per annum. The work is hard, and the exposure to weather and to risk of accident great, but a young, strong, energetic man, firm in the saddle and of steady nerve, will do well in such a position.

In the towns the usual mode of starting in practice is to occupy the consulting-room generally attached to the shop of a chemist who is doing a large business, during certain hours of the day. The chemist has a telephone, and the doctor's residence may be connected therewith; the expense to the latter not exceeding £10 per year. In consideration of the prescriptions made up for patients, the chemist makes no charge for the use of his room. This system resembles the American "office-hour" custom, and it enables a medical man to live in one of the healthiest suburbs of the town, while still all the time accessible to messages. After some years, having become fully established in the confidence of the citizens, he can retire from the chemist's rooms—where his place will be promptly taken by a fresh arrival—and conduct his practice entirely at his own house. Were I again starting practice in any of the towns I know in New Zealand, I should rent consulting rooms in the main street; have a man or boy there all day; a telephone; and live where I liked, but not too far for patients to walk from office to house, or *vice versâ*. I should carefully select my consulting-hours to suit the habits of the locality, and should keep them punctually. Always make the fee for seeing you at the house or rooms *less* than for a visit. There is a difference in the elements of immediate success in a colonial and in a British community. The dull steady-plodding doctor in the former case does not get on so well as one with "dash and volubility." The doctors I knew who succeeded most rapidly in building up large practices were young men of pleasing manners, fluent talk, and social accomplishments, who married soon after their arrival into some well-known, perhaps wealthy local family, and became thoroughly identified with the place. They became almost at once colonials in freedom of manner and unconventionality of dress. On my return Home everything and everybody in the profession seemed formal and stiff in dress, etiquette, and behaviour.

The proper age at which our colleagues may emigrate with the best chance of success I should place at from twenty-four to fifty. From the study of the careers of the twenty-four colleagues who settled in or near Auckland after my arrival there in 1879, and from personal knowledge of many others, I am of opinion that, whether married or unmarried, a medical man after the age of fifty cannot adapt himself to colonial ways. There may be exceptions. If a doctor breaks down in health, yet not so much as to debar him from work, and needs the change to any particular colony, if his wife is healthy, adaptable, and *hopeful*—it is the women who suffer most from nostalgia—and if his family consists chiefly of strong healthy boys, then he may emigrate even after that age. But in New Zealand I have generally seen, in the competition of practice, that "the race is to the swift and the battle to the strong."

Buying a practice, as is done in England, is almost unknown in New Zealand; even purchasing a medical partnership is an uncertain speculation, for the "goodwill" of a colonial practice cannot be purchased. Patients are generally "independent," as they call it, roaming from one doctor to another, believing devoutly in specialties, and regarding the newest arrival from the old country as the incarnation of all the learning and wisdom of medicine. Thus a New Zealand doctor always has patients leaving him, just as he has always patients coming to him—a constant influx and efflux, without that strong "back-bone" to his practice, which the affection and respect of his *clientèle*, won by long years of toil for them, and by clinical triumphs, secures for him in the Old Country.

One of the best openings I have seen in good city practice is when a colonial practitioner is desirous of taking a six or twelve months' holiday in England. Then some new arrival takes his entire practice as *locum tenens*, with permission to remain in the same locality on the return of the owner; and the loss of patients, if any, is chiefly on the latter's side. Colonial patients like their favourite doctors to visit the old country every few years, and acquire the newest ideas and inventions.

The outfit for a medical emigrant should comprise a very complete set of surgical instruments, duplicates being taken of the more commonly used, a good library of standard professional works; a first-class microscope; a few of the more costly drugs; and large coloured diagrams of the body for "Medical Talks," which are much in request. A hammock for hot nights, and a strong tent for "camping-out" will be found useful. A powerful telescope is also an enjoyable companion in the clear atmosphere of New Zealand. When I left the colony there was no duty either upon surgical instruments or upon philosophical apparatus.

Having selected his place of work, the new doctor must comply with the registration law of New Zealand, which commands him to show his diplomas to the Registrar-general, or the Provincial Registrar; to pay a fee of £2; and to advertise in a daily newspaper his declaration of intention to practise, setting forth his full titles and qualifications. No title or qualification is registrable in New Zealand which is not recognized by the General Council of Medical Education and Registration of Great Britain.

The average fees of a respectable practitioner in New Zealand city practice are equal to the best scale of those paid to the general practitioner of London, and are much better than those realised by our provincial colleagues. But, even for important operations, the Auckland fees were not equal, as they ought to be, to those paid to London surgeons. At the time I left, the fees seemed to be declining, in consequence of the commercial depression, and the unfair competition started by a doctor, who advertised "Advice and medicine at English rates," which meant giving for 2s. 6d. what all of us, correctly, charged five shillings for. One is always exposed to this sort of thing in the colonies. There is less booking, and a larger proportion of ready-money payments, than in England.

Clubs pay the doctor on a higher scale than at home —£1 per head per annum, or 15s. being a common rate. Even with the increased cost of drugs, caused by the heavy tariff, and the greater expense of surgical appliances, which are all imported, these payments remunerate the club doctor better than the pittance of four or five shillings he receives in England. I steadily refused clubs because I did not need them, but they are useful appointments to begin with.

In estimating the working expenses of a New Zealand practice, one must take into account the hilly nature of the country, the long distance, and the badly kept roads. A riding hack must be kept for even a small practice, and an American or colonial buggy for a fair-sized area of work. In Auckland and its vicinity, walking for some hours as we sometimes do in an English town practice at the beginning, is not possible in summer; cabs are twice as expensive as at home; and omnibuses are neither cheap, comfortable, nor frequent enough to be useful to a doctor. A good buggy with hood, lamps, and all appurtenances costs £45 to £60; a good horse (ride or drive) varies from £16 to £30; harness about £8, and a coachman's wages average 30s. a week and all found; or £2 5s. a week, if he finds his own board and lodging. The livery "jobbing" system, so much in vogue here, does not pay the doctor in New Zealand. Horse-feed is cheaper than in England, but carriage repairs are extravagantly dear. Collisions and runaways are more frequent—speaking of the city where I practised—than with us, from reckless driving by small boys in charge of horses they were powerless to check or guide, by drunken carters, and from the evasion of the city bye-law respecting carrying lamps after dark.

To set up in good style, a new-comer must take a neat house in a first-class street, paying £80 to £100 rent; keep two servants; have a carriage, and a coachman who will also keep his garden trim; have his own stable; a telephone, and consulting-rooms "down town," either at a chemist's, or separately. "Self-supporting" dispensaries do not pay. The poorest working-man will pay his fee of 2s. 6d. or 3s. 6d. cheerfully, and is too proud to accept any of that pauperising in medical charity that we observe in England. On the whole a new doctor obtains a practice more quickly in the colonies than in the old country, but there is not the same stability about it, nor is there anything of the warm personal attachment to the family doctor, as to a family friend, that exists at Home.

Diseases Prevalent among the Maoris.

Although the natives in New Zealand do not trouble the *pakeha* doctor very much, yet my colleagues will, I am sure, not consider space wasted if I mention some professionally interesting details concerning them.

In the years intervening between 1847 and 1853, Surgeon A. S. Thompson, of the 58th Foot Regiment, then serving in New Zealand, made copious notes of the diseases he observed and heard of as existing among the Maoris. His valuable records were given to the medical world in the *British and Foreign Medico-Chirurgical Review;* and as much of the information he gives us holds true of the Maori of to-day, I condense the most important of his observations, adding my own experience, and what I learned from other medical men who have had more to do with the "noble savage" than I have.

There was a greater variety and a larger amount of imported and endemic disease among the natives then than there is now; though even now, as I shall show later on, there is a great deal that is quite preventible. Fevers were then common, of a continued, not intermittent type, constituting seventy-four cases in every 1000 cases of disease. Scarlet fever entered New Zealand in 1848, but did not spread. The natives have been always apt to catch infectious or contagious diseases, so this was a fortunate circumstance.

Phthisis pulmonalis, following prolonged influenza, was not uncommon, the disease carrying off persons at all ages.

Diseases of the skin, especially scabies, ringworm, and psoriasis, were then and are still common; hence the discovery of one of the many healing powers of the Rotorua hot springs. Scrofula was and is the bane of the whole race, though not now so universal, thanks to better food, as in the early days. It was caused by breathing impure air in crowded huts; by indolent uncleanly habits; by bad food; and by intermarriage with near and scrofulous relations.

In those days cases of elephantiasis, or Lepra gangrænosa, a true kind of leprosy, were sometimes seen. It was caused, Dr. Thompson thought, by the habit of eating putrid maize and half-rotten potatoes. Diseases of the liver are now more common among the natives than they were forty years since, because of the alcoholic drinks consumed. I once treated the famous chief Wahanui, of Otorohanga, Waikato, a faithful ally of ours, for a disease of this kind, in the cause of which an excessive use of animal food, blended with a too great indulgence in alcohol, in producing, in addition to the liver derangement, an inordinate obesity. He was the finest specimen of a warrior chief I have seen.

The diseases epilepsy, apoplexy, chorea, cancer, and ague were unknown.

Wounds used to heal quickly: the natives used various vegetable or earthy applications, the favourite being an ointment of red ochre. Parturition was easy and rapid.

Rheumatism was and is very common, caused by the utter recklessness of the Maoris about the situation of their dwellings, drying their wet clothes or mats, and so on. Very early in the history of the Maoris the curative powers of the hot baths and springs in this disease were discovered. Syphilis exists, but not of a virulent type, in both sexes. Its local manifestations are removed sooner by the hot mud-baths than by medicinal treatment.

Melancholia, with a tendency to suicide, from the superstition of being bewitched, was common, and even now exists, though much more rarely, owing to the general spread of Christianity through the whole nation.

The custom of *tapu* (chapter iii., p. 48) had certainly its sanitary uses, which unfortunately have not been replaced, now that *tapu* is out of fashion, by that "cleanliness which is next unto godliness" which should be characteristic of a Christianized nation.

The Maori of old time, believing that all sickness was caused by an *atua* or evil spirit entering the body, used to employ all kinds of violent measures to the sick man, in order to drive it out, such as rolling him for hours on the ground, placing baskets of stones on his abdomen, and so forth; these well-meant exertions more often killing than curing the patient.

But their mode of shampooing—the same as the *lomi-lomi* of the Hawaiian, (the basis of modern massage); their artificial steam-baths; and their extraordinary but successful method of resuscitating an apparently drowned person by holding him head downwards over the smoke of a fire, and then pouring hot water down his throat as soon as he could swallow—all these were useful in disease. Being intelligent observers of the properties of native plants, the Maoris used various parts of the following shrubs in diseases and injuries: these may give some hints to those who are continually seeking additions to the Materia Medica.

Mesembryanthemum (Ficoideæ) was used as a poultice for boils.

Phormium tenax, the native flax, or more properly hemp (see p. 189), nat. ord. Liliaceæ. The leaf was used for bandaging wounds; the root and the gummy exudation for disorders of menstruation.

Podocarpus, or *Kahikatea*, the white Pine (Coniferæ), a decoction of the leaves for urinary complaints.

Piper excelsus, or *Kawakawa* (Piperaceæ)—for cuts, wounds, skin diseases, gonorrhœa, and in the hot steam baths.

Dysoxylum spectabile, or *Kohekohe* (Meliaceæ)—an infusion of the leaves to stop the secretion of milk in the breasts.

Veronica, or *Koromiko* (Scrophulariaceæ)—bruised leaves as poultice for ulcers.

Cyathea, or tree-fern (Filicineæ)—the bruised pith as a poultice for swollen feet and for sore eyes.

Sophora tetraptera, or *Kowhai* (Leguminosæ)—the inner bark in Scabies.

Dacrydium cupressinum, or *Rimu* (Coniferæ)—infusion of the bark for ulcers and wounds,

Coriaria, or *Tutu* (Coriariæ)—leaves which are poisonous to cattle, and the leaves and twigs of the Leptospermum ericoides, or *Manuka* (Myrtaceæ), are used effectually to cure dysentery.

Some of these therapeutic applications of native plants have been tried and confirmed by local practitioners. The Veronica seems scarcely ever to fail in relieving dysentery and diarrhœa. Another plant, the Brachyglottis repens, or *Puka-puka*, of the Nat. Ord. Compositæ, has been found useful in Bright's disease of the kidneys and in "neuralgic" rheumatism.

A curious kind of slow poisoning among the Maori old men and women by the *Karaka* berry is sometimes found. Its characteristic feature is a spastic contraction of the flexor muscles of the arms and legs, *not* of the trunk muscles. There are no twitches or spasms. This phenomenon is produced by the imperfect cooking of the bean or berry whose dark inner skin (next to the albumen of the seed) contains a toxic alkaloid named *karakine*. If this skin is perfectly removed by long maceration in water, the berry is not only harmless but forms a nutritious food.

I have not heard of any disease arising from the habit of the Maoris of eating fern-root, the pith of the *Nikau*, or cabbage palm, or the fungus, *Hirneola*. Poisoning by the bite of the *Katipo*, a small black spider marked by a red cross on its back, which haunts the clumps of grass near the sea, is more common among and more dreaded by the Maoris than by the white people. One case of chronic blood-poisoning by the bite of this insect—the only venomous one with the exception of the centipede, in New Zealand—came under my observation. A half-caste woman, aged about thirty-eight, consulted me for disease of the cartilaginous *septum narium*. She stated that two years before her visit to me a *Katipo* had bitten her hand; the usual acute inflammation followed, and after the hand had completely healed, the mucous lining of the nostrils became ulcerated. This process went on deeper and deeper until the bones began to slough away. There being no history or visible trace of syphilis, I concluded that this sequela of *Katipo* bite, quite a rare one, was probably due to a metastasis of the blood-poison to the nose, acting virulently upon a scrofulous constitution. The immunity enjoyed by these islands from snakes and all kinds of poisonous insects except the *Katipo* and centipede is remarkable when we consider their proximity to Tasmania, Australia, and New Guinea, which are all characterized by these plagues.

The children of half-castes frequently die of tubercular diseases. Dr. Thompson gives in his articles an interesting table comparing the mortality in various diseases among the Maoris of his day with the death-rate in Sheffield (as a specimen of a large densely populated English town), taking as a standard of comparison the register of the Sheffield General Infirmary for twenty-two years previous to 1852. We can thus perceive that in five classes of disease the death-rate among the Maoris was much heavier than that of one of the most unhealthy and crowded towns in our country.

In one thousand deaths from all causes there were—

	Sheffield.	Maoris of New Zealand.
From Scrofula	59	82
,, Rheumatism	119	191
,, Diseases of the Skin	45	70
,, ,, ,, Lungs	109	169
,, ,, ,, Stomach and Bowels . .	71	119

In chapter iii. I have summarized the Registrar-general's report on the causes of the decrease of the native race. Since that was written I have received an interesting letter from my friend who, though a settler up in the north, has become a volunteer missionary among the Maoris of the Pakanae district, which gives valuable information on this point, which I will condense for the reader. Mr. Fell says that one prominent cause of the decline of the race is traceable to too early marriages, which are generally barren. He mentions one instance of a Maori bride of twelve and a bridegroom of twenty. In readjusting the ownership of a block of ground at Pakanae, formerly held by a *hapu* of 1000 adults, only fifty adult Maori owners could be found, and of these a large number were childless. "One principal reason," writes Mr. Fell, "of the very great mortality is from their sleeping on the ground all the year round. All whom we have met with, except the very young children, suffer from asthma, and the men especially seem to suffer from chest complaints and die young. We have one [Maori] now felling the bush for us; he has pitched the tent we have lent him on the flat, and he sleeps on green ti-tree. . . . They never change their wet clothes." Contemporary evidence thus proves that the habits of the Maoris of old are continued to the present day, and are conducing to the extinction of the race.

Diseases Prevalent among the Colonists.

1. Acute Diseases.—Of these the most common is enteric or typhoid fever, arising from the insanitary state of most of the New Zealand cities and towns. Settlers build where and how they like, up and down the hills and along the valleys, which often constitute the natural features of a town site. The owner of an allotment may pack as many houses as he chooses upon it provided he makes what is euphemistically called "an earth closet" for each building. The lower classes of inhabitants are not very particular as to where the gleanings of the kitchen are deposited.

During the long hot summer of North New Zealand the decomposition of this refuse goes on, and when the first rains of winter fall there is some years an outbreak of typhoid fever lasting several months. It seems as if the *bacteria* (or other *materies morbi*) were liberated from their *nidus* by the rain, and washed into the drinking water, or, in some way, found access into the bodies of their numerous victims, generally the young and apparently strong, of from fifteen to forty years of age. As a typhoid endemic has a knack of seizing now and then upon well-known families of good position, this plague, so preventible by proper drainage and good sanitation, every year excites much public outcry. But somehow corporations look more to the amount of their rates than to the health of the citizens, and little is done *effectually* to stop this drawback to life and health. In 1887 my friend, Dr. G. Toussaint Girdler, in an able paper read before the Athenæum Society of Auckland on the Sanitary Condition of that City proved that out of six thousand inhabited houses within the city limits only six hundred were provided with water-closets, the rest having merely the "earth-closets,"—so called because the contractor who cleaned them out was supposed to supply fresh dry earth each time—but did not! He showed that if even the existing Municipal Regulations were made compulsory, and not merely permissive, many of the nuisances which generated diseases would be prevented, much sickness and many valuable lives saved. The reading of this Paper excited much attention, more especially as during the very time that typhoid fever was prevalent the city council of Auckland had, under the pretext of economy, reduced their sanitary staff, which was already too small in number. More efficient modes of collecting the refuse and of disposing of the sewage were earnestly discussed at a second meeting of the Athenæum; and the Mayor (A. E. T. Devore, Esq.) expressed himself in favour of a kiln, such as is used with excellent results in Manchester and Salford, where all the garbage is burnt up, and the products utilized. There has been a permanent improvement in the sanitary condition of Auckland since, and a lessening of the number of cases of typhoid.

The flatness of some cities, such as Christchurch, does not admit of a perfect system of underground drainage, but Auckland is eminently adapted for it. There seems to me no reason why both typhoid fever and diphtheria should not, by efficient sanitation, (which demands, unfortunately for the colony's position, a large expenditure), be banished from New Zealand. Although the highest mortality from typhoid fever in Auckland, where during the last two "seasons" it has averaged fifteen to twenty-two per cent., is much lower than the ordinary mortality from that disease in Melbourne and Sydney, the death-rate was far from encouraging. During five years of my practice I treated forty cases of typhoid fever, of which I lost only one—a boy who died of a cerebral complication five days after I was called in. There are few private nurses in the New Zealand towns who are properly trained to nurse fever patients, and this is a great difficulty in the way of clinical success.

I have never seen a case of *true typhus* fever in New Zealand, a fact which thus far corroborates the theory that typhus is the product of starvation, want of pure air, and overcrowding.

No case of Asiatic cholera has been reported so far as my research extends in New Zealand, though cases of European cholera occur every summer, when the heat is unusually high and prolonged.

The infectious Exanthemata are of a mild type in New Zealand. Although the compulsory clauses of the New Zealand Vaccination Act seem to be a dead letter, Small-pox has been so well excluded from the islands that it does not appear at all as a cause of death in the mortality records of the quinquennial period, 1881–1886. The genial climate permits of more complete ventilation of the sick-room during a much greater portion of the year than is possible in England, and this advantage limits the risk of contagion or infection; otherwise the wooden houses are certainly not so easily well disinfected as our brick and stone houses here.

Many children grow up to adult age without ever having caught any of the Exanthemata. Once during my residence there was a tremendous "scare" about small-pox, a steamer having a case on board brought from San Francisco, if I remember aright. All the passengers for Auckland were landed at Motuihi, the island where the quarantine station, a Government building, was situated. A rush to the doctors for vaccination took place. Having secured some pure and fresh calf lymph through the praiseworthy exertions of my energetic chemist, I vaccinated about sixty-six cases during that year with perfect satisfaction to the parents, some of whom held anti-vaccination opinions, and to the adults, whose constitutions all showed the need of re-vaccination by the vigorous way in which they "took." The gratifying results of the fright were, (1) that no case of small-pox occurred on shore; (2) that the Motuihi station, then dirty and dilapidated, because so long unused, was cleaned, repaired, and made fairly decent for human beings.

Croup and Diphtheria are deplorably common in the towns of the colony; the former from the storms, rain, and high winds that occur, and the latter from miasmatic emanations from the animal and vegetable refuse heaps above described (p. 231). I remember one very sad instance of how diphtheria may be contracted from noxious emanations without any contact with previous cases of the disease. A fine little girl who, with her brother, had been playing about a certain street in the west of Auckland, and hovering about a ditch which had been cut into the clay subsoil for the purpose of laying gas-pipes, succumbed in a few days to malignant diphtheria. A few days after her death the brother showed this disease in the same intensity, and died after all that medical skill and attention could do for him, thus leaving the parents childless. That heaps of decomposing garbage will generate this disease I had a most painful experience in my own family when my son was very nearly carried off by this fell destroyer. I had no control whatever over the use of the vacant unfenced allotment next to my house where the miasma had been generated.

I am not able to obtain comparative statistics of Diphtheria in the other colonies; but it is a fact that during the five years preceding the census of 1886, the rate of mortality in New Zealand proceeding from specific febrile, and zymotic diseases was considerably less than in England and in the Australian colonies.

Cases of irritant poisoning, sometimes fatal, caused by eating canned meat, half-decomposed or contaminated by solder, are not uncommon. A sad case of poisoning by the formation of *ptomaines* in twice-cooked canned meat occurred in Parnell. Three lives of Maori clergymen were lost, and three white people made dangerously ill.

Acute rheumatism, pneumonia, and pleurisy seldom reach the same intensity or duration that they exhibit in Britain.

2. Chronic Diseases.—The most important class of chronic diseases of which I must write are Pulmonary diseases, for the relief of which so many invalids come out from England to this colony. In chapters ii., iv., and v. I have given useful suggestions as to the suitability or unsuitability of certain Climatic Zones and localities for various certain chest complaints, and these may now be supplemented by some general observations deduced from experience on the subject. A study of those three chapters, of the maps accompanying this volume, and of the temperatures I have quoted in the text, will enable consulting physicians to indicate to their chest patients what part of New Zealand they should try on arrival, and what parts they should avoid. In general terms the north of Auckland district, and a few spots on the highest ranges of the hills near Auckland city, offer in winter the best climate in New Zealand for real tubercular consumption

of the lungs or larynx, and for that very large class of cases which are chronic pneumonias in tuberculous or strumous constitutions, of which most of those cases benefitted or cured by sea voyages, or changes of climate, consist.

If a *poitrinaire*, in whom phthisis pulmonalis has not advanced far into the second stage, will go out by the Cape to New Zealand, so as to arrive there in October or November, he will enjoy the glorious summer weather, and improve steadily, if he conducts himself carefully, until the middle of April of the next year, when the rains will have begun. He will be able to remain in Auckland, Taranaki, or Napier later in April or even into May than he would in other cities further south. In April or May he can sail away to Norfolk Island or to the Fijis, where he may bask in genial sunshine until summer once more returns to New Zealand.

I knew a clergyman in Auckland who was in good health, fulfilling the duties of an important parish, married, with three healthy children, who owes his life to the local climate, having landed there fourteen years since with a cavity in one of his lungs.

Another favourable case was that of a bank manager who came out from England about ten years since with phthisis pulmonalis in both lungs and frequent hæmoptysis. He steadily improved in Auckland, and became stout and strong. For five years he remained in good health, but the bank's arrangements compelling him to move off to Christchurch, the extremes of that climate disagreed with him; his old disease broke out again, and he was a dead man in less than two years (I believe) from the time he left the northern city. None of his friends, myself included, doubted that he would have survived many years had he been able to remain in Auckland or North of it.

A third case in which I felt much interest, though I had very little to do with its treatment, was that of a clergyman who came out to get a cure of a "weak throat"—in fact, "*Dysphonia Clericorum*." At first the voice improved in a locality near Auckland, but after two winters, during which he felt obliged to do clerical duty, the constant use of his voice and the colds he occasionally took developed that terrible disease, real phthisis laryngea. Although the ravages of this disease in the larynx may be delayed by a pure, dry, warm air such as that of Egypt or Western Australia, I have never yet known a case recover. One patient I knew was kept alive for four years by the dry climate of California, but eventually he succumbed.

Very often it has been noticed by medical men that the consumptive patient who does not improve under treatment in a certain part of the city, will begin to improve if he moves his residence on to a different subsoil—say, from off *clay* to *scoria* ground. I may mention one homely matter which is often neglected. A chest invalid should always bring flannel under-clothing of two thicknesses, one for the winter and one for the summer, so that wool may be next the skin all the year round. Even the hottest days in the northern summer of New Zealand are followed by cool evenings, which visitors enjoy seated under the verandahs outside the house, when frequently chills are contracted by sensitive and too thinly clad invalids.

Most practitioners of long experience in New Zealand have noticed the singular fact that, though phthisical sufferers from colder climates derive much benefit, even sometimes a cure, from that genial air, yet when this disease arises in a native-born New Zealander, it generally carries the victim off in a short time. I know one case in which only six months elapsed from the first manifestations of the disease (true phthisis) until death.

In such cases the best change of climate is to the Darling Downs of Queensland, the nearest approach to Davos or St. Moritz that exists in Australasia. This health resort is also beneficial to "clerical sore throat."

In estimating the mortality from phthisis pulmonalis in the records of the New Zealand Registrar-general, one must remember that the death-rate is largely increased by the number of persons who arrive in the colony far advanced in the disease—sometimes even in the third stage; or with a very strong predisposition to consumption. In 1886, out of the total deaths from phthisis in New Zealand eleven per cent. were persons who had not resided three years in the colony. Yet with even the addition from this source, the death-rate from phthisis among the colonists in New Zealand is much less than in England, or than in any of the Australian colonies, except Western Australia.

Invalids suffering from recurrent attacks of bronchitis, chronic enlargement of the tonsils, and ordinary follicular sore-throat improve very much in the North Island.

On the other hand, very few cases of asthma seem to do well in New Zealand. Apparently the all-pervading marine dampness of the atmosphere is the cause of this unsuitability. Bronchial asthma, however, I have known to be very much benefited by residence near the sea.

Diseases caused by Entozoa, especially among young children, are much more common in New Zealand than at home. Tænia solium, Ascaris lumbricoides, and Ascaris vermicularis are found in both adults and children. Even infants at the breast have been known to pass Ascarides.

Hydatids of the liver, caused by the *echinococcus* of the sheep passing into the human body, is a common disease in Australia, but rare in New Zealand. Sometimes, however, cases are reported from the Middle Island, arising from the careless use of unwholesome mutton as food. The risk of acquiring this parasitic disease is the greater from the constant use of mutton alone for "the hands" at the sheep stations for many months consecutively.

The frequent decay of teeth in adults, young children, and even in infants cutting their milk set, in Auckland arrests the attention of newly arrived medical men. This premature decay is due to the too complete absence of lime from the water supply. The rain water percolates through scoria and clay (chiefly the former) down to the springs from which the city water is taken, thus reaching the consumer in an almost too pure condition. The deeper springs which assist in the water supply are also almost chemically free from calcareous salts, therefore there is not *pabulum* enough supplied to the human frame for the efficient growth of the teeth and bones before the age at which animal food can be consumed and assimilated. Even the nursing mother's breast-milk is thus rendered deficient in this important ingredient. The only remedy is to give lime-water to the children, or to place a small lump of unslaked lime in the cistern or family filter. The latter is too rarely used in colonial households. There is a good opening in business for a *cheap* and good domestic filter in New Zealand, if the sale were briskly pushed. The plague of entozoa would be thereby much diminished.

There are no malarial fevers in the colony; hydrophobia is unknown; calculus and sunstroke are rare.

3. Diseases arising directly or indirectly from the *abuse* (not the moderate use) of alcoholic liquors and tobacco deserve notice here. Although the city wherein I practised is *not* more intemperate than the other cities and towns of New Zealand, nor is the colony *less* sober, as a whole, than any or all of the other Australasian colonies, yet in a work designed to advance the best interests of the country I feel bound to raise a warning voice against these vices of habit, which engender disease.

The habit of "nipping," upon which I have already adversely commented, is proved by statistics collected by Dr. George Hurley, in an able paper written for the *Provincial Medical Journal*, to largely increase the mortality from liver diseases (and from other diseases) among the classes of men most exposed to this temptation in the old country. Among brewers, publicans, vintners, commercial travellers, barmen, and waiters, the death-rate from liver diseases is *six times greater* than it is among those not so apt to "nip;" for example, maltsters, farmers, drapers, printers, and gardeners. I regret that I have not space for his full table of death-rates: it is novel and instructive. It tallies with my colonial experience; and I can further add that among merchants, tradesmen, lawyers' clerks, and warehousemen there is a terrible amount of liver disease in the colony, quite preventible if this injurious habit were dropped. Open drunkenness seldom overtakes the victims of "nipping," but I have, alas! seen many of them, often good and useful citizens of Auckland, die from cirrhosis of the liver, Bright's disease, or congestion of the brain, before they had lived out their regular "expectation of life."

The sudden deaths by accident and suicide which seem so common in New Zealand are often cases in which an intoxicated man attempts to drive or ride along a precipitous road; to cross a swollen river; or to enter or leave a train while in motion; or some rash action of that kind; while suicides are frequently the result of the awful depression following a prolonged drinking bout. One must, in permitting, advising, or refusing alchoholic stimulants to patients, take into account the *difference in the climatic zones* of New Zealand. The only districts of New Zealand where I conceive whisky—the newest Scotch is the favourite brand—to be harmless are Otago, Southland, and Westland, all in the Middle Island. But in the more northern districts of the Middle and in the whole of the warmer North Island, brandy and whisky (however permissible in cases of illness) should be avoided in health. Of the two kinds of spirits, pure French brandy, *if you can get it*, is the less injurious. It is to be regretted that the very high duty upon Australian light wines, lager beer, and claret so enhances their cost as to place them beyond the means of any but the well-to-do. If ever North New Zealand becomes a wine-drinking country, after producing and maturing wholesome wine, which could be done, drunkenness will almost disappear, and the diseases I have mentioned will no longer form part of the Registrar's returns.

I have never attended a native-born colonist for Delirium Tremens, a fact corroborative of the statement made on p. 217 (chapter xi.). My medical readers may note that I found it possible to bring through successfully many cases of typhoid fever without alcoholic stimulants, and, when these are absolutely necessary, it was found sufficient to give half the quantity usually ordered in similar cases in England. And so in the case of most acute diseases. When a man is thirsty in the summer, iced "lemon squash" or Zoedone will satisfy the craving.

The abuse of tobacco by adults and the premature indulgence in smoking by young lads bring on or aggravate a number of diseases and derangements, which I must here touch upon, in order to explain my strong condemnation of these habits in the previous chapter. To some persons of a lymphatic temperament tobacco may really be a sedative, but to most people it is an excitant at first and a depressant afterwards. In the clear stimulating air of New Zealand no artificial stimulus to the nervous system is necessary. In summer smoking is apt to excite a thirst which water alone does not slake. My professional *confrères* know as well as I do, that premature or immoderate smoking produces the following derangements of the human economy:—

1st. Impairment of the primary digestion, caused by the excessive flow of saliva induced.

2nd. A chronic nervousness and irritability, with irregular action of the heart, often accompanied with insomnia, or with a minor degree of amaurosis.

3rd. Anæmia, with cardiac palpitation, due to the power nicotine possesses of preventing the transformation of the pale into the red corpuscles of the blood.

4th. An insidious disease of the kidneys, with albuminuria, often undetected until far advanced, or ascribed to other causes.

But I do not condemn the moderate use of tobacco in the winters of New Zealand. It is indeed a "solace" to the solitary miner, to the shepherd and to the bushman. In the North Island smokers would do well to use the lightest "twist" or "returns;" to smoke only after a meal; and where possible in the open air.

Having alluded to the large amount of lunacy in New Zealand in chapter xi. I will now complete my reference to the subject by giving a comparative table of statistics, which, so far as the year 1885 is concerned, places New Zealand in her right place as regards the prevalence of Mental Disease, as compared with other countries. I quote this table because an erroneous notion is abroad that there is more Mental Disease in this colony than in any other south of the line.

It must be borne in mind, that in the official returns for New Zealand are, every year, included several persons who have been shipped off from England to the colony by their relatives, in order to get rid of them, and so throw the burden of their support upon the colony. Most of these lunatics improve during the sea voyage, but become more insane than ever after a month or two in the exciting or stimulating air of New Zealand. They are then taken charge of by the Government, and so troublesome had this practice become that some years since the Colonial Government got an Act passed through Parliament designed to put a stop to it.

At the close of 1885:—

Victoria	had one	lunatic	for	297	of the general population.			
England and Wales	,,	,,	,,	339	,,	,,	,,	,,
New South Wales	,,	,,	,,	374	,,	,,	,,	,,
New Zealand	,,	,,	,,	401	,,	,,	,,	,,
Queensland	,,	,,	,,	416	,,	,,	,,	,,
South Australia	,,	,,	,,	439	,,	,,	,,	,,

We thus perceive that New Zealand, dead-weighted as it is by the unfair English practice mentioned above, stands only fourth on the list, ranking below Victoria, England and Wales, and New South Wales as to the number of lunatics in proportion to the general mass of the people. I do not consider that the *climate* of New Zealand in any way conduces to the *development* of latent mental disease; but if that disease is already manifested, it may become aggravated there. Did space permit of its insertion in this already too lengthy section, I could show, by a comparative table of the vital statistics of all the Australasian colonies, that New Zealand is favoured with the highest birth-rate and the lowest death-rate—taking a long series of years —of them all.

But, failing this, by merely quoting the Vital Statistics of the sixteen largest New Zealand towns, for the few scattered months, which happen to be at hand, I can easily demonstrate that the *natural increase*, without any accretion from surplus of immigrants over emigrants, is remarkable. The viability of children born in New Zealand is greater than of those born in the more tropical Australian colonies.

The sixteen large towns from which these figures are summarised are—Auckland, Wellington, Christchurch, Dunedin, Thames, New Plymouth, Napier, Wanganui, Nelson, Sydenham, Lyttelton, Timaru, Oamaru, Hokitika, Caversham, and Invercargill.

In these towns there were registered the following number of births and deaths, a monthly record being furnished by the Registrar-general:—

	Births.	Deaths.	Natural Increase.
In October, 1883	562	200	362
„ November, 1883	468	135	333
„ July, 1884	506	177	329
„ August, 1884	511	201	310
„ November, 1884	467	128	339
„ December, 1884	465	165	300
„ January, 1885	501	189	312
„ December, 1885	420	188	232
	3900	1383	2517

The natural net increase in these sixteen towns for the eight scattered months quoted amounts to 2517, being some compensation for the falling-off in immigration during 1884 and 1885.

There is no reason why an emigrant, when he settles in New Zealand should not live to a green old age, if he avoids steadily the injurious habits I have pointed out as the source of acquired disease, and lives on wholesome properly cooked food and purified water. In my experience New Zealand is far beyond California for health and enjoyment—which is saying a good deal, for the latter is one of the most delightful countries in the world for travel or residence. I trust that both my medical and non-medical readers will agree with me that there is no place like

NEW ZEALAND FOR THE EMIGRANT, INVALID, AND TOURIST.

TABLE OF DISTANCES
In nautical miles.

Ocean Distances: — Miles.

Plymouth to Lyttelton	11,740
„ „ Port Chalmers	11,930
„ „ Wellington	11,915
„ „ Auckland	12,479
Liverpool to Auckland *viâ* United States	12,210
„ „ „ „ Suez	12,706
„ „ „ „ Cape of Good Hope	14,073
San Francisco to Auckland	5,910
New York to Auckland *viâ* Cape Horn	11,860
„ „ „ „ „ Panama Canal	8,940

Inter-Colonial:

Melbourne to the Bluff Harbour	1,200
„ „ Wellington	1,479
Sydney to Wellington	1,239
„ „ Auckland	1,281
Fiji to Auckland	1,172
Samoa to Auckland	1,950

New Zealand:

Auckland to Russell	128
„ Gisborne	301
„ Wellington	564
Gisborne to Napier	86
Napier to Wellington	203
Wellington to Lyttelton	175
„ Port Chalmers	332
„ Picton	53
„ Nelson	101
„ New Plymouth	172
Port Chalmers to the Bluff	132
Onehanga to New Plymouth	135
New Plymouth to Nelson	148
Nelson to Picton	85
„ Westport	160
Westport to Greymouth	63
Greymouth to Hokitika	20
Hokitika to Milford	190
Milford Sound to the Bluff	210

INDEX.

ABERDEEN, Earl, and Countess of, 66
Acclimatization in N.Z., 71, 72
Academy of Music, An, 211
Acheron Passage, 113, 114
Advice to Emigrants, 6-10, 12, 148
Agricultural Land, 144
Agriculture, School of, 162
Akaroa, 33
Akiteo Spring, 77
Albertland Settlement, 155
Alcoholic Liquors, Abuse of, 216, 238-240
Alderton, George E., 21
Aldis, Professor, 161
Alpine Plateau, The, 20, 37, 38
Amateur Photography, 209
    ,, Science, 213
    ,, Vocalists, 212
Amberley, 77
American Organs, 212
Amuri, 78
Analyses of Springs, 78, 81, 82, 87, 88, 90, 91, 92, 93
Analysis of Volcanic Ash, 128
Anglo-American Unions, 3
Anglo-Saxon Race, The, 1, 3, 56
Aorangi, (Mt. Cook), 33
Apero, Capt., 103, 108
Arawa Tribe, The, 125
Arthur River, 118
Art Exhibitions, Local, 209
Arts, Society of, 68, 210, 211
Asbestos, Discovery of, 113
Asthmatic Complaints, 37, 86, 237
Aspiring Mount, 100, 117
Assignees in Bankruptcy, 175
Asylums, Benevolent, 166
    ,, Lunatic, 167, 218

Atoamuri, 134
Athenæum, The Auckland, 68, 73, 231
Athletic Club Grounds, 69
Atkinson, Sir Harry, 143, 151
Atua, The, 46, 227
Auckland, City of, 57-73
    ,, Beauty of, 59, 62, 73
    ,, Caricatured, 164, 165
    ,, Choral Society, 66
    ,, Climate, 23, 24, 235
    ,, Grammar School, 71
    ,, Free Library, 63, 65
    ,, Geographical Position, 57, 58
    ,, Harbour, 61, 63
    ,, Institute and Museum, 68
    ,, City Institutions, 63-73
    ,, Music in, 67, 68
    ,, Newspapers, 67
    ,, Population, 58, 59
    ,, Port of, 61, 62
    ,, Savings Bank, 66
    ,, Schools, 71
    ,, Seat of the Government, 59, 138
    ,, Shipping, 61, 62
    ,, Theatre, 69
    ,, University College, 68, 71, 161
    ,, Y.M.C.A., 65, 66
    ,, Y.W.C.A., 66
    ,, Province, 20-23
    ,, Acclimatization in, 71
    ,, *Avifauna* of, 23
    ,, Climate of, 24, 25
    ,, *Flora* of, 22
    ,, Vital Statistics, 57
Aurora Australis, 86
Australian *v.* New Zealand Climates, 15

Australasian Science Association, 213

BAINBRIDGE, Edwin A., 125, 130–132
Balclutha Schoolboy, A, 70
Barker, Lady, 199
Bates, E. Katherine, 214
Bay of Islands, 77
  ,, Plenty, 82, 85
Bealey, 33
Benefit Societies, 13, 223
Bible-Reading in Schools, 158
  ,, Translated into Maori, 45
Binder twine, 196
Birkenhead (Auckland), 63
Black, Professor, 162
Blair, W. N., 194
Blenheim, 31
Blomfield, Charles, 210
Blueskin (Dunedin), 34
Bonuses offered by Government, 191
Bourne, C. F., 159
Bowen Falls, The, 116
Breaksea Sound, 114
Breakwaters (Napier, New Plymouth and Timaru), 27, 171
Brett's Almanac, 61, 195
'Britain of the South,' 8
Bronchitis, 25, 29, 237
Brown, Capt., 213
Brown, Professor F. D., 161, 162
Bryce, the Hon. John, 49
Building Societies, 13, 176
  ,, Stone, 188
'Bush,' beauty of the, 99, 102, 209
Buying a Practice, 222

Cabinet Ministers, trials of, 143, 144
Cadets, Volunteer, 204, 206
"Cæsar," 118
Calliope Dock, 61, 171
Campbell, Dr., 63
  ,, the Poet, 9
Cameron, Capt., 111
  ,, General, 55
Cameron's Bath, 89
Canterbury College, 162
  ,, Plains, 32
Caswell Bay, Marble, 115, 188
Caswell Sound, 114
Cathedral City, the, 32

Centralization, tendency to, 132
Centrifugal Law of Migration, 3
Centripetal Law of Migration, 3
Chalybeate Springs, 77
Chambers of Commerce, 194
Cheeseman, Clara, 199
  ,, T. F., 68
Chinese in N.Z., 6, 193
Choice of N.Z. Climates, 5, 19
Cholera, Asiatic and European, 232
Christchurch, City, 32, 194
  ,, Cathedral, 32
  ,, Children in, 32
  ,, Climate, 32, 33
  ,, Industrial Exhibition, 192
  ,, Population, 32, 58
Climate of N. Zealand, 16–19
Climate Zones of N.Z., 19–38, 239
Clubs, *Cuisine* of, &c., 207
  ,, Sick and Benefit, 223
Coach Varnish, 186, 196
Coal, varieties of, 188
Coleoptera, 213
Coode, Sir John, 27
Cook's Strait, 16, 29
Cook, Captain, 111
Cook, Mount, 33
Cook, Joseph, of Boston, 66, 208
Copper, 188
Corduroy Roads, 98
Coromandel, 186
Costley, the late Edward, 63, 64
  ,, Industrial Home, 65
  ,, Legacy, the, 64, 65
Cows, average yearly value of, 183
Cowie, Bishop, 156
Craters Extinct, 63, 124
Criminal Class, the, 169
Crisp, Miss (Mrs. Bond), 167
Croup, 233
Crown Lands ready for occupation, 144
  ,, ,, Classified, 144
  ,, ,, Offices, 145
  ,, ,, Terms of Lease or Purchase, 145–149
Crow's Nest, Wairakei, 134
Cuttle Cove, 111

Dairy Produce, 183
Daldy, Captain, 65
Dane, Major, 66

Darling Downs (Queensland), 15, 236
Death by Accident, 239
Decay of Teeth, Premature, 237
     ,,   Remedy for, 238
Decorative Industry, 195
Deferred Payment System, 146
Delaware's Crew Rescued, 55
Dentists in N.Z., 7
Devil's Blow Hole, 106
Devonport, 24, 60, 62, 79
Diphtheria, 233, 234
Direct Mail Steamers, 10, 61, 182
Diseases curable by Hot Springs, 94
Diseases unsuited to Hot Springs, 95
Dobie, T., 21
Doherty, T., 113
Domain, the (Auckland), 60
Domett, Alfred, 51, 101, 143.
Drought, unknown in N.Z., 17
Dunedin City, 34
    ,,   Buildings, 34
    ,,   Children in, 35
    ,,   Climate of, 34
    ,,   Club of, 35
    ,,   Population, 34
    ,,   Prevalent Complaints, 35
    ,,   Prices in, 13, 35
    ,,   Rainfall, 17, 35
    ,,   Scenery of, 34
    ,,   Temperature, 34
    ,,   Town Belt, 35
Dusky Sound, 113

EARNSLAW Mount, 36, 109
Economical Government, An, 141
Economic Plants, Culture of, 21, 191
Eccentric Characters, 199
Eden, Mount, 58, 59, 122
    ,,   ,,   View from, 59
Edison's Magnetic Separator, 187
Education System, 156-165
    ,,   Boards, 157
    ,,   Primary, 157, **158**
    ,,   Secondary, 159
    ,,   Technical, 162
    ,,   University, 159-163
Edwin, Captain, 17
Effect of Climate on Character, 203
Effect of Climate on the Voice, 25

Egmont, Mount, 18, 25, 135
    ,,   Ascent of, 26
Emigration Societies, 5
Employment of Children and Females, 194, 195
Enamel-lined Butter-boxes, **183**
Entozoa, 237
Eocene Period in N.Z., 123
Equal Electoral Districts, 144
Eruption of Tarawera,
    ,,   Earthquakes, 126
    ,,   Explosions, 127
    ,,   Height of Dust Column, 127
    ,,   Loss of Life, 130-132
    ,,   Results of, 128-130
"Evening Star," the, 58, 67
Exanthemata, the, 232, 233

FACTS showing return of prosperity, 152, 153
Fares to N Z., 11
    ,,   Railway in N.Z., 170
Fast Mail route to N.Z., 11, 61
Fell, Henry Ellcray, 230
Fiji Islands, 235
Finances of N.Z., 141, 151-3
Fires, Causes of, &c. 202, 203
First Offenders' Probation Act, 169
Fissure, the Great, 123, 128
Fish, Acclimatized 71, 72
    ,,   Native, 71, 111
Fitzroy, Captain, 138, 141
Flax (*Phormium tenax*), 46, 189, 196, 227
Folgefond Glacier (Norway), 117
Food, Prices of, 13, 71
Forbes, Archibald, 208
Fornander, Dr., 48
Foreign Workmen in Britain, 4
Fox, Sir William, 70, 143, 218
Free Trade Party, the, 192
Free Libraries, 31, 65, 163, 164
Friendly Societies, 176
French Pass, the, 31
Froude, J. A., 19, 58
Fruit-Preserving, 29, **190**
Fungus (*Hirneola*), 189, **228**
Furniture, 10, 190, 192
Furnishing, Expense of, 13

GAMBLING Spirit, the, 215
Gaols, 168, 169

Gardens, Auckland, 24
George, Henry, 213
George Sound, 115
Germany's need of Colonies, 3
Geysers, 75, 105, 129, 133
Ginders, Dr. A., 75, 85, 87, 96
Girdler, Dr. G. T., 231
Gisborne, 27, 57, 145
Glass-Works, 190
Glenorchy, 36
"Globe-Trotter," 2, 198, 202
Gold Mines, 186, 187
„ Tax upon, 186
Gordon, Sir Arthur, 141
Gout, Thermal treatment of, 95
Government Life Insurance, 174, 175
Government, Responsible, granted, 139
Governors of New Zealand, 141
Graham, The late Robert, 45, 54, 79
Graham, Miss, 79
"Grass" Widows and Widowers, 201
Great Britain, Annual Increase of, 4
Greater Britain, Pref., 1, 4
Grazing Runs, 148
Green, Rev. W. Spottiswoode, 33
Grey, Sir George, K.C.B., 51, 54, 63, 141, 143, 144, 194, 200
Grey, collection of MSS., 64
„ Maori Legends, 51
Griffin, Consul G. W., 62, 73
Gymnasia, 65, 205

Hæmatite, Iron-Ore, 187
Haka (the Maori dance), 51
Hall, Sir John, 143
Hamner Plains Springs, 78
Hapus (tribes), 40, 45, 49, 137
Hare, system of voting, 144
Haszard, the late C. A., 103, 130
Hastings (Napier), 27
Haultain, Col., 65
Havelock, 27
Hawaiian Dialect, 41, 42
Hawkes Bay, 26, 48
Hector, Sir James, 82, 115, 163
Hill, Rev. J. S., 65
Hobson, Captain, First Governor of New Zealand, 136, 138
Hochstetter, Dr. F. von, 63, 122

Hokitika, 17, 18, 33, 37
"Home," used for Britain, 3, 4, &c.
Home, a happy, in N.Z., 3, 8, 218
Homestead system, the, 147
Honey, exported, 183
Hongi (rubbing noses), 52
Hospitals of New Zealand, 165-167
Hospital, the Auckland, 62, 65, 167
„ „ Dunedin, 163
Hospital and Charitable Aid Boards, 166
Howick, 25, 155
Humour of W. J. Frater, 198
„ „ D. Sutherland, 118
Hururunui River, 27, 31
Hydatids of the Liver, 237
Hymn, Maori version of a, 44

Incubator, the, 70
Immigrants wanted in N.Z., 6, 8, 9
„ not wanted in N.Z., 7, 8
"Indian summer," of Rotorua, 86
Industrial exhibitions, 192
Inlaid Cabinet Ware, 192
Insomnia, 24
Inspectors of Sheep and Rabbits, 176
Institute, the New Zealand, 163
Institutes, Local Scientific, 163
Inventiveness of the Colonists, 195
Invercargill, 36, 37, 145
„ Climate of, 37
Iodine, Springs containing, 77
Ironsand Deposits, 187
Iron works, 187

Jackson, Samuel, Senr., 98
Jervois, Sir W. F. D., G.C.M.G., C.B., &c., 61, 141, 172
"Joshua's," Taupe, 38

Kainga (village), 48, 50, 135
Kaingaroa Plains, 133
Kaiwaka Creek, 104, 107, 129
Kaka, 23, 99, 209
Kakapo, 23, 99
Kakaramea Mt., 133
Kamo, 22, 77
Karaka, 99, 228
„ Poisonous effects of, 228
Karakine (the alkaloid), 228
Karakia (a spell), 48, 132

INDEX. 249

Kahikatea (White Pine), 185
Katipo Spider, and effects of its bite, 209, 228, 229
Kate and Sophia, guides, 102, 108
Kauri, the, 18, 185, 202
" Gum, 185, 196
Kauwhanga Spring, 89
Kawau I, 69
Kimberley Mount, 116
"King Country," the, 27, 38, 45
Kinloch, Lake Wakatipu, 36
Kiwi, the, 23
Kohekohe, 227
Korero, 50, 51
Korimako (Bell Bird) 23, 210
" Maori Journal, 44
Koromiko, 53, 71, 227
Korohotis, 92, 93
Koura, 53, 71
Krakatoa, Eruption, the, 121
Kuirau Spring, 76
Kuripapanga (Napier), 27

LAKES of Otago, Fish in the, 71
Lake Ada, 116, 118
" Manapouri, 109
" Ngahewa, 133
" Rotokakahi, 102, 104, 125
" Rotokawau, 94
" Rotomahana, 102–108, 129
" Rotomakiriri, 104
" Rotorua, 83–96, 100
" Takapuna, 62
" Tarawera, 103, 104
" Taupo, 27, 77, 84, 133, 134
" Te Anau, 109
" Tikitapu, 102
" Wakatipu, 36, 42, 115, 119
Land Tenure in N.Z., 144, 145
Larrikinism, Causes and Cure, 204, 205
Laughing-Gas Bath, 89
Lectures, successful in N.Z., 208
Ledum palustre, 119
Leprosy, 95, 226
Lewis, Dr. T. H., 85, 87, 96
Lithia in Springs, 82, 89, 90, 93
Little Barrier Island, 23, 59
Literature in N.Z., love of, 213
Lithographic Stone (Dusky Sound), 113
Living, cost of, 12, 13
Local Option, 169
Lomond Ben, 36

Lomi-lomi, of Hawaii, 99, 257
Long Sound, 112
Loyalty of the Colonists, 140, 165
Lunacy in N.Z., 168, 218, 241
Lyttelton Port, 32

MACKELVIE, the late J. T., 63, 66
Macrae's Hotel, Wairoa, 102, 103, 131.
"Madame Rachel" Bath, 88, 95
Maire, black and white, 185
Mana, 53, 54
Manawatu Gorge, 27
Maning, Judge, 45, 52, 98, 100, 108
Manuka or *Ti-tree*, 60, 98, 104, 228
Manukau Harbour, 25, 58
Mauna Loa, 122
Maungongaonga Mount, 133
Maunsell, Archdeacon, 45
Maoris, The, 39–56
" their appearance, 40
" character, 41, 45, 54
" customs, 48–54
" decline, 47, 230
" Missions among the, 42, 44, 45, 55, 56
" Origin of, 39
Marlborough Province, 31
Martin, Lady, 55
Mean Annual Rainfall, 17
" " Temperature, 16
" Daily Range of do, 17
Meat, Frozen, 182
" Tinned, Cured, Salted, 182, 234
Mechanics' Institutes, 213
Medical Men, Number of, 7
" " Prospects of, 7, 219–225
Melancholia among Natives, 226
Mercury (Cinnabar), 77, 188
Mere (of Jade), 51, 54
Meteorological Department, 17
Midland Railway of N.Z., 33
Militia Law, the, 206
Milford Sound, 115–119
Mills, James, 110
Minett, T., 131
Ministry, Frequent Changes of, 142, 201
Minor Industries, 190
Mitre Peak, 116, 117

Moa, the (Dinornis), 23
Mohi (Moses), 55
Mount Eden, 59, 63
Moretou, S. H., 117
Morriusville, 81
Motuihi, 59, 233
Motutapu, 59, 69
"Muggy" Weather, 18, 24
Müller, George, 66
Muru, 48, 49
Music in Auckland, 68
   ,,   ,, New Zealand 7, 211
Musical Festival, A, 211
Mutton Delicious, 182

NAPA, Soda Spring, 77
Napier, Agricultural Show at, 27
   ,,   Climate of, 26
   ,,   Population, 26
   ,,   Port of, "The Spit," 26
   ,,   Public Buildings, 27
   ,,   Subsoil of, 26
Native Birds of N Z., 23, 209
   ,,   Lands Act, 145
   ,,   ,,   Court, 47, 137
   ,,   Remedies, 227, 228
Necessity of Emigration for England, 4, 5
Nelson, City, 29
   ,,   Climate of, 29, 30
   ,,   Export of Gold, 30
   ,,   ,,   hops, 30
   ,,   ,,   jam, 29
   ,,   Population of, 30
New Grand Tour, the, 134, 135
New Plymouth, 25, 26
New Zealand, Area of, 16
   ,,   Birth-rate of, 6
   ,,   Climate, 16-19
   ,,   Colonization of, 138, 139, 155
   ,,   for the Europeans, 9, 194
   ,,   Population of, 7
   ,,   Public Debt, 141
   ,,   *Herald*, the, 67, 165
   ,,   Natural Resources of, 196
   ,,   Society, 198, 199
   ,,   Shipping Co., 10
   ,,   University, 7, 159, 160
Ngaruawahia, 42
Ngauruhoe Volcano, 78, 121, 133

Ngongotaha, Mt., 84
Nikau Palm, 99, 228
Niuafu Volcano, 122
Norsewood, 139, 147
North Island Trunk Railway, 58, 135, 164
Norwegian Immigrants, 139
Normauby, Marquis of, 141

OAMARU, 33, 188
Oats, New Zealand, 184
Obsidian, 103
Ocean Beach (Dunedin), 31
Ohaeawai, 77
Ohinemutu, 91, 99, 100
Oil Bath, the, 92, 93
Onehunga, 58, 181, 187
Onetapu Spring, 76, 78
Onslow, Lord, 144
Orange Culture, 21, 22
Oruawhata Spring, 89
Ostrich Farm (Auckland), 70
   ,,   Schoolboy's Essay on the, 70
Otago Daily Times, 198
   ,,   Climate of, 34-36
   ,,   University, 159, 162, 163
Otorohanga, 226
Otumahike Spring, 76
Outdoor Sports, 69, 205
Outfit for the Emigrant, 9, 10
   ,,   Medical man, 222, 223
Oxford, 85

PAHUA Spring, 77, 78
"Painkiller" Spring, the, 89, 90
Pakeha, 45
Pakeha-Maori, 45
Palmerston North, 27, 28
   ,,   Climate of, 28
   ,,   Boating at, 28
Panama Canal, 58
Paper Mills, (Dunedin, Mataura) 190
Parihaka, 49
Parnell Orphan Asylum, 64
Pastoral Runs, 148
Patent Laws of N.Z., 195
Payton, E. W., 214, 215, 217
Pembroke Glacier, the, 117
Petroleum Springs, 188, 190
Phthisis Laryngea, 236
   ,,   pulmonalis, 225, 236, 237
   ,,   ,,   cases of, 235
   ,,   ,,   mortality, 237

INDEX.   251

Phthisis pulmonalis, localities suitable for, 20, 22, 26, 29, 234
Phthisis pulmonalis, localities unsuitable for, 35, 37, 38
Pianos everywhere, 212
Picton, climate of, 31
" Herrings, 30
Pink Cauldron of Waiotapu, 133
" Terrace, the, 107, 129, 210
Poetry in N.Z., 212
Police, the, 169
Pohutakawa, 99
Port Chalmers, 111, 177
Posnett, Professor, 161
Post Office, 184
Postage, rates of, 172
Potatoes, 184
Poverty Bay, 48
Praed, Mrs. Campbell, 199
Preservation Inlet, 111, 112
Priest's Bath, the, 87, 88
Proctor, the late R. A., 208
Protective Tariff, the, 192, 195
Proude, Robert, 98
Psoriasis, Thermal Treatment of, 95, 96
Public Works Policy, 150
Puhoi (Waiwera), 139
Puka-puka, 99, 228
Pumice, deposit of Taupo Zone, 123
" passing into Obsidian, 123
Puriri Spring, 77
Puriri tree, 99, 185, 190

Quarantine station, 233
Queen's assent to Colonial Acts, 140
Queen's disallowance of Colonial Acts, 141
Queen Charlotte's Sound, 30
Queenstown, 35
" Climate of, 36
" Earthquake at, 36
" Scenery around, 36
Queen Street, Auckland, 59, 63

Railways of N.Z.
Ralph, Dr. T. S., 125
Rangi (First Maori Convert), 45
Rangitoto Mt., 62
Raratongan Dialect, 41
Rata, the, 112, 185
Reductions in Government Expenditure, 141, 142

Registrar-General's report, 47, 154, 169
Registration, Medical, 223
Religion, (of all Denominations), 139, 153-156
Reischek, A., 118
Remittance men, 62, 217
Remueta, 59, 62
Resemblance of N.Z. to Italy, 16, 123
Resuscitation of apparently drowned, by the natives, 227
Revenue, Surplus over Expenditure, 153
Rewa-rewa, 99, 185, 190
Rheumatism, Thermal Treatment of, 80, 94, 95, 96
Richardson, Dr. B. W., 217
Richmond, Hon. J. C., 36
Rimutaka Pass, the, 170
Rimu, 99, 112, 190, 228
Rinking, 206, 207
Rock of the *Taipo*, 104
Rotomahana, Great Crater of, 128
Robinson, Sir Hercules, 141
Rotorua District, 84
" "Season" 86, 87
" Township, 83-87
Routes to New Zealand, 10, 11
Ruapehu, Mount, 28, 76, 78, 82

Sailors' Rests, 177
Sailors' Homes, 65, 177
Sala, G. A., 208
Salutation, the Native, 43
Samoan Dialect, 41
Sandflies and their bite, 119
Scarlet Fever, 225
Schmitt, Herr Carl, 68
Schools, Native, 48
School of Applied Science, 162
" Forestry, 22
Sects, Harmony among the, 155
Self-Help Emigration Societies, 5
Selwyn, Bishop, G. A., 54, 155
Sequence of Volcanic Events (1883-6) preceding Tarawera, 122
Settlement of the Chief Towns, 139
Seventy-Mile-Bush, 27
Sewell, Hon. Henry, 143
" Shilling-a-Month Men," 204
Shortland, Lieut.-Col. 138
Sibilants in Maori, Absence of, 41

Silver, Export of, 186
Sinclair, Captain, 110, 115
Skey, F. C., Analyst, 76, 86]
Skins and Hides, Export of, 122, 183
Skin Diseases, Cured by the Springs, 94, 95
"Slain by Drink," 218
Smallpox in N.Z., 233
Shaw, Saville, and Albion Co., 10
Smith, S. Percy, F.R.G.S., 123, 128
Social Life, Refinement of, 205
Socialistic Revolution, Danger of, 4
Sounds, West Coast. The, 109–119
Southern Alps, 18, 32
Southland, Province, 36, 37
Spectral Canoe, Story, 125
Spinach, Discovery of, 113
Spout Bath, the, 92
Stafford, Sir Edward, 143
State-Regulated Emigration, 5
Stout, Sir Robert, 143
Stonewall Jackson Bath, 90
Sub-Tropical Fruits, 21
Sunday Closing of Public-houses, 70
Supreme Court, the, 168
Sutherland Fall, the, 116
Svartisen Glacier (Norway), 117
Synod of the Church of England in New Zealand, 156

TABLE of Distances, 244
Taj-Mahal of Agra, 106
Tamati-Waka-Nene, 136
Tanekaha Bark (*Phyllodadus*), 189
Tangi, 48, 52, 53
Tapu, 40, 48, 226
Taranaki, Climate of, 17, 25, 26, 37
Tarawera Mountain, 63, 124
  „   River, 104, 129
  „   Spring, 77
  „   Steamer, 109–118
Tatooing, 41
Tauhara Mt., 133
Taupo Volcanic Zone, 20, 37, 38, 123
Tauranga, 85, 94, 96, 108, 126
Tawhiao, "King," 49, 50
Tawhai, the late Graham, 55
Technical Education, 162
Te Ariki, 104, 126, 130
  „ Aroha, 81, 82
  „ Aute, 27
  „ Heu-Heu, 135

Te Ika o Maui, 51, 123
  „ Kute Spring, 93
  „ Moura, 130
  „ Ngae, 52, 108
  „ Reinga, 53
  „ Tapui, 92
  „ Tarata, 104
  „ Whiti, 49
Telegrams "Delayed," 173
Telephones, 67, 173, 221
Temperance Societies, 169
Terraces Destroyed, the, 129
Thames Gold Mines, 186, 187
Thermal Springs District Act, 84
Thomas, Professor A. P. W., 161
Thompson, Surgeon A. S., 225, 229
Thunderstorms, 37
Tikitere, 93–95
Timaru, 33
Tin, 188
Tiri-Tiri, 59
Tobacco, Abuse of, 216, 240
Tohunga, 48, 132
Tongariro, Mount, 16, 82, 133, 135
Totara, 99, 185
Totalisator, Evil of the, 215
Tourists' Tales, 198
Towsey, A. J., 111, 114
Trust Office, Public, 175
Tuhoto, the *Tohunga*, 48, 132
Tuhourangi Tribe, the, 108, 124
Tui (Parson Bird), 23, 99, 209
Tupakihi, 99
Turikore Spring, 92
Tweeds, New Zealand, 181
Typhoid Fever, 230–232
Tylor, Dr. E. B., 48

UNION S.S. Co., 61, 110, 149
United Kingdom Alliance, 218
United States, the, 196, 197, 218
'Ups and Downs' of Colonial Life, 201
Utu, 48, 49

VACCINATION, 232, 233
  „   with Calf Lymph, 233
Vancouver, 113
Village Settlement, 147
Viniculture, 21, 191, 194, 239
Vital Statistics, 57, 58, 241, 242
Vogel, Sir Julius, 142, 143, 150
Volcanic Eruption of Tarawera, 126–128

Volcanic Extinct Craters, 63, 124
„ Ash, Dust, and Mud, 127-129
Volcanoes of the Pacific, 120, 121
Volunteers, 206

WAGES in New Zealand, 12, 193
Wage-earning Students, 160
Wahanui (Maori Chief), 226
Wahi-tapu, 48
Waiheke I., 62
Waihou River, 81
Waihunuhunukuri Spring, 91
Waikato, 71, 98
Waikite, 91
Waimarino, 135
Waiorongomai, 81
Wai-o-tapu Valley, 108, 133
„ Pink Cauldron, 133
„ White Terrace, 133
Waipu Caves, the, 22
Wairakei, 134
Waiarapa, 71
Wairoa (Tarawera), 102, 126, 129, 130
Waitakerei, 197
Waitaki, S.S., 98
Waitangi, Treaty of, 136, 137
Waitemata, 58, 59, 63
Waiwera, 78-81
Wangaehu, River, 78
Wanganui, 28
„ Falls, 135
„ River, 27, 135
Wasley of Waitakerei, 199
Watchman, the, 63
Waterhouse, Hon. G. M., 143
Weather Stations, 17
Weld, Sir Frederick A., 28, 59, 143
Wellington, 28
„ Climate, 28
„ Earthquakes, 28, 164
„ Harbour, 29
„ Legislature at, 207
„ Population, 29
„ Rainfall, 17, 28
„ "Season," the, 207
West Coast Sounds, 108-119
„ „ „ Fishes, 111
„ „ „ Flora, 112
Westland, Climate of, 33
Westport Coal, 188

Wet Jacket Arm, 114
Whaling Industry, 190
Whakarewarewa, 86, 92, 93, 130
Whangapipiro Spring, 88
Whangarei, 21, 22
Whangaroa, 21
Whare (hut), 43, 47, 92, 94, 101
Whare-kura (temple), 40
Whare-puni (council-room), 50
Wheat, Exported, 184
„ land sown in, 183
„ yield per acre, 184
Whitaker, Sir Frederick, 143, 144
Whitebait in the Rivers, 71
White Island (*solfatara*), 121, 122
White Terrace, the, 104-108, 129
Williams, Rev. Henry, 136
Withy, Edward, M. H. R., 192
Wonderland of North Island, 98-108
„ „ Middle Island,108-109
„ „ the NEW, 132-135
Woods, Ornamental Native, 185, 192
Woodville, 27
„ Climate, 28
Wool, Export of, 180, 181
„ favourite staples of, 180
Woollen Goods of N.Z., 181
„ Mills of N.Z., 181
Works and Manufactories (1881-6), 191
Worthington, Henry, 114
Wounds, how treated by natives, 226
Wright, Dr. A., 82

YOUNG Men's Christian Association of Auckland, 65, 66
Young Women's Christian Association, 66
Young New Zealand—
Artistic Taste of, 210, 211
Inventiveness of, 195
Sobriety of, 217, 240
Stoicism of, 203, 204

ZONES OF CLIMATE, 19, 20
Zone No I., 20-27
„ No. II., 27-31
„ No. III., 31-37
„ No. IV., 20, 37, 38

LONDON:
PRINTED BY WILLIAM CLOWES AND SONS, LIMITED,
STAMFORD STREET AND CHARING CROSS.

A Catalogue of American and Foreign Books Published or Imported by MESSRS. SAMPSON LOW & CO. *can be had on application.*

St. Dunstan's House, Fetter Lane, Fleet Street, London,
October, 1890.

A Selection from the List of Books
PUBLISHED BY
SAMPSON LOW, MARSTON, SEARLE, & RIVINGTON,
LIMITED.

Low's Standard Novels, page 17.
Low's Standard Books for Boys, page 19.
Low's Standard Series, page 20.
Sea Stories, by W. CLARK RUSSELL, page 26.

ALPHABETICAL LIST.

ABNEY (W. de W.) and Cunningham. Pioneers of the Alps. With photogravure portraits of guides. Small 4to, gilt top, 21s.

Adam and Wetherald. An Algonquin Maiden. Cr. 8vo, 5s.

Alcott. Works of the late Miss Louisa May Alcott:—
Aunt Jo's Scrap-bag. Cloth, 2s.; gilt, 2s. 6d.
Eight Cousins. Illustrated, 2s.; cloth gilt, 3s. 6d.
Jack and Jill. Illustrated, 2s.; cloth gilt, 3s. 6d.
Jo's Boys. 5s.
Jimmy's Cruise in the Pinafore, &c. Illustrated, cloth, 2s.; gilt edges, 3s. 6d.
Little Men. Double vol., 2s.; cloth, gilt edges, 3s. 6d.
Little Women. 1s. } 1 vol., cloth, 2s.; larger ed., gilt
Little Women Wedded. 1s. } edges, 3s. 6d.
Old-fashioned Girl. 2s.; cloth, gilt edges, 3s. 6d.
Rose in Bloom. 2s.; cloth gilt, 3s. 6d.
Shawl Straps. Cloth, 2s.
Silver Pitchers. Cloth, gilt edges, 3s. 6d.
Under the Lilacs. Illustrated, 2s.; cloth gilt, 5s.
Work: a Story of Experience 1s. } 1 vol., cloth, gilt
—— Its Sequel, "Beginning Again." 1s. } edges, 3s. 6d.

Alcott. Life, Letters and Journals of Louisa May Alcott. By EDNAH D. CHENEY. Cr. 8vo, 6s.

—— *Recollections of My Childhood's Days.* Crown 8vo, 3s. 6d.

—— See also LOW'S STANDARD SERIES.

Alden (W. L.) Adventures of Jimmy Brown. Ill. Sm. 8vo, 3s. 6d.

—— *Trying to find Europe.* Illus., crown 8vo, 2s. 6d.

A

Alger (J. G.) Englishmen in the French Revolution, cr. 8vo, 7s. 6d.
Amateur Angler's Days in Dove Dale: Three Weeks' Holiday in 1884. By E. M. 1s. 6d.; boards, 1s.; large paper, 5s.
Andersen. Fairy Tales. An entirely new Translation. With over 500 Illustrations by Scandinavian Artists. Small 4to, 6s.
Angling. See Amateur, "Cutcliffe," "Fennell," "Halford," "Hamilton," "Martin," "Orvis," "Pennell," "Pritt," "Senior," "Stevens," "Theakston," "Walton," "Wells," and "Willis-Bund."
Arnold (R.) Ammonia and Ammonium Compounds. Ill. Cr. 8vo, 5s.
Art Education. See "Biographies," "D'Anvers," "Illustrated Text Books," "Mollett's Dictionary."
Artistic Japan. Illustrated with Coloured Plates. Monthly. Royal 4to, 2s.; vols. I. to IV., roy. 4to, extra emblematic binding, Japanese silk, 15s. each.
Ashe (Robert P.) Uganda, England's Latest Charge. Cr. 8vo, stiff cover, 1s.
—— *Two Kings of Uganda.* New Ed. Cr. 8vo, 3s. 6d.

BALDWIN (James) Story of Siegfried. 6s.

—— *Story of the Golden Age.* Illust. by HOWARD PYLE. Cr. 8vo, 6s.
—— *Story of Roland.* Crown 8vo, 6s.
Barlow (Alfred) Weaving by Hand and by Power. With several hundred Illustrations. Third Edition, royal 8vo, £1 5s.
Barnum (P. T.) Dollars and Sense. 8vo.
Bassett (F. S.) Legends and Superstitions of the Sea. 7s. 6d.

THE BAYARD SERIES.

Edited by the late J. HAIN FRISWELL.

Pleasure Books of Literature produced in the Choicest Style.

"We can hardly imagine better books for boys to read or for men to ponder over."—*Times*.

Price 2s. 6d. each Volume, complete in itself, flexible cloth extra, gilt edges, with silk Headbands and Registers.

The Story of the **Chevalier** Bayard.
Joinville's St. **Louis** of France.
The Essays of **Abraham** Cowley.
Abdallah. By Edouard Laboullaye.
Napoleon, Table-Talk and Opinions.
Words of Wellington.
Johnson's Rasselas. With Notes.
Hazlitt's Round Table.
The Religio Medici, Hydriotaphia, &c. By Sir Thomas Browne, Knt.

Coleridge's Christabel, &c. With Preface by Algernon C. Swinburne.
Ballad Poetry of the Affections. By Robert Buchanan.
Lord Chesterfield's Letters, Sentences, and Maxims. With Essay by Sainte-Beuve.
The King and the Commons. Cavalier and Puritan Songs.
Vathek. By William Beckford.

The Bayard Series (continued.)

Essays in Mosaic. By Ballantyne.
My Uncle Toby; his Story and his Friends. By P. Fitzgerald.
Reflections of Rochefoucauld.
Socrates: Memoirs for English Readers from Xenophon's Memorabilia. By Edw. Levien.
Prince Albert's Golden Precepts.

A Case containing 12 Volumes, price 31s. 6d.; or the Case separately, price 3s. 6d.

Beaconsfield. See HITCHMAN.

Beaugrand (C.) Walks Abroad of Two Young Naturalists. By D. SHARP. Illust., 8vo, 7s. 6d.

Beecher (H. W.) Authentic Biography, and Diary. Ill. 8vo, 21s.

—— *Norwood; Village Life in New England.* Crown 8vo, 6s.

Beer Manufacture. See THAUSING.

Behnke and Browne. Child's Voice: its Treatment with regard to After Development. Small 8vo, 3s. 6d.

—— See also BROWNE.

Bell (H. H. J.) Obeah: Negro Witchcraft in the West Indies. Crown 8vo, 2s. 6d.

Beyschlag. Female Costume Figures of various Centuries. 12 reproductions of pastel designs in portfolio, imperial. 21s.

Bickersteth (Bishop E. H.) Clergyman in his Home. 1s.

—— *From Year to Year: Original Poetical Pieces.* Small post 8vo, 3s. 6d.; roan, 6s. and 5s.; calf or morocco, 10s. 6d.

—— *The Master's Home-Call.* N. ed. 32mo, cloth gilt, 1s.

—— *The Master's Will.* Funeral Sermon. 1s., sewed, 6d.

—— *The Reef, and other Parables.* Crown 8vo, 2s. 6d.

—— *Shadow of the Rock.* Select Religious Poetry. 2s. 6d.

—— *Shadowed Home and the Light Beyond.* 5s.

—— See also "Hymnal Companion."

Billroth (Th.) Care of the Sick, at Home and in the Hospital. Illustrated, crown 8vo, 6s.

Biographies of the Great Artists (Illustrated). Crown 8vo, emblematical binding, 3s. 6d. per volume, except where the price is given.

Barbizon School. I. Millet, &c. } 2 in 1, 7/6
—— II. Corot, &c. }
Claude le Lorrain, by Owen J. Dullea.
Correggio, by M. E. Heaton. 2s. 6d.
Cox (David) and De Wint.
George Cruikshank, Life and Works.
Della Robbia and Cellini. 2s. 6d.
Albrecht Dürer, by R. F. Heath.
Figure Painters of Holland.
Fra Angelico, Masaccio, and Botticelli.
Fra Bartolommeo, Albertinelli, and Andrea del Sarto.
Gainsborough and Constable.
Ghiberti and Donatello. 2s. 6d.
Giotto, by Harry Quilter.
Hans Holbein, by Joseph Cundall.
Hogarth, by Austin Dobson.
Landseer, by F. G. Stevens.
Lawrence and Romney, by Lord Ronald Gower. 2s. 6d.
Leonardo da Vinci.
Little Masters of Germany, by W. B. Scott.
Mantegna and Francia.
Meissonier, by J. W. Mollett. 2s. 6d.

Biographies of the Great Artists (continued.)

Michelangelo Buonarotti, by Clément.
Mulready Memorials, by Stephens.
Murillo, by Ellen E. Minor. 2s. 6d.
Overbeck, by J. B. Atkinson.
Raphael, by N. D'Anvers.
Rembrandt, by J. W. Mollett.
Reynolds, by F. S. Pulling.
Rubens, by C. W. Kett.
Tintoretto, by W. R. Osler.
Titian, by R. F. Heath.
Turner, by Cosmo Monkhouse.
Vandyck and Hals, by Head.
Van de Velde and the Dutch Painters.
Van Eyck, Memlinc, Matsys.
Velasquez, by E. Stowe.
Vernet and Delaroche, by J. Rees.
Watteau, by J. W. Mollett. 2s. 6d.
Wilkie, by J. W. Mollett.

IN PREPARATION.
Miniature Painters of Eng. School.

Bird (F. J.) American Practical Dyer's Companion. 8vo, 42s.
———— *(H. E.) Chess Practice.* 8vo, 2s. 6d.
Bishop (E. S.) Lectures to Nurses on Antiseptics. With diagrams, crown 8vo, 2s.
Black (Robert) Horse Racing in France: a History. 8vo, 14s.
Black (W.) Standfast Craig Royston. 3 vols., cr. 8vo, 31s. 6d.
———— See also LOW'S STANDARD NOVELS.
Blackburn (Charles F.) Hints on Catalogue Titles and Index Entries, with a Vocabulary of Terms and Abbreviations, chiefly from Foreign Catalogues. Royal 8vo, 14s.
Blackburn (Henry) Art in the Mountains, the Oberammergau Passion Play. New ed., corrected to 1890, 8vo, 5s.
———— *Breton Folk.* With 171 Illust. by RANDOLPH CALDECOTT. Imperial 8vo, gilt edges, 21s.; plainer binding, 10s. 6d.
———— *Pyrenees.* Illustrated by GUSTAVE DORÉ, corrected to 1881. Crown 8vo, 7s. 6d. See also CALDECOTT.
Blackmore (R. D.) Kit and Kitty. A novel. 3 vols., crown 8vo. 31s. 6d.
———— *Lorna Doone. Édition de luxe.* Crown 4to, very numerous Illustrations, cloth, gilt edges, 31s. 6d.; parchment, uncut, top gilt, 35s.; new issue, plainer, 21s.
———— *Novels.* See also LOW'S STANDARD NOVELS.
———— *Springhaven.* Illust. by PARSONS and BARNARD. Sq. 8vo, 12s.; new edition, 7s. 6d.
Blaikie (William) How to get Strong and how to Stay so. Rational, Physical, Gymnastic, &c., Exercises. Illust., sm. post 8vo, 5s.
———— *Sound Bodies for our Boys and Girls.* 16mo, 2s. 6d.
Bodleian. See HISTORIC BINDINGS.
Bonwick. British Colonies. Asia, 1s.; Africa, 1s.; America, 1s.; Australasia, 1s. One vol., cloth, 5s.
Bosanquet (Rev. C.) Blossoms from the King's Garden: Sermons for Children. 2nd Edition, small post 8vo, cloth extra, 6s.
———— *Jehoshaphat; or, Sunlight and Clouds.* 1s.

Bower (G. S.) and Webb, Law of Electric Lighting. New edition, crown 8vo, 12s. 6d.
Boy's Froissart. King Arthur. Knightly Legends of Wales. Percy. See LANIER.
Bradshaw (J.) New Zealand as it is. 8vo, 12s. 6d.
—— *New Zealand of To-day*, 1884-87. 8vo, 14s.
Brannt (W. T.) Animal and Vegetable Fats and Oils. Illust., 8vo, 35s.
—— *Manufacture of Soap and Candles.* Illust., 8vo. 35s.
—— *Metallic Alloys. After Krupp and Wildberger.* Cr. 8vo, 12s. 6d.
—— *Vinegar, Cider, and Fruit Wines.* Illust., 8vo., 25s.
Bright (John) Public Letters. Crown 8vo, 7s. 6d.
Brisse (Baron) Ménus. In French and English, for every day in the Year. 7th Edition, with 1200 recipes. Crown 8vo, 5s.
Brittany. See BLACKBURN.
Brown (A. J.) Rejected of Men, and Other Poems. Fcp. 8vo, 3s. 6d.
—— *(A. S.) Madeira and Canary Islands for Invalids*, Maps, crown 8vo, sewed, 2s. 6d.
—— *(Robert) Jack Abbott's Log.* 2 vols., cr. 8vo, 21s.
Browne (G. Lennox) Voice Use and Stimulants. Sm. 8vo, 3s. 6d.
—— *and Behnke, Voice, Song, and Speech.* 15s.; new ed., 5s.
Bryant (W. C.) and Gay (S. H.) History of the United States. Profusely Illustrated, 4 vols., royal 8vo, 60s.
Bryce (Rev. Professor) Manitoba. Illust. Crown 8vo, 7s. 6d.
—— *Short History of the Canadian People.* 7s. 6d.
Burnaby (Mrs F.) High Alps in Winter; or, Mountaineering in Search of Health. With Illustrations, &c., 14s. See also MAIN.
Burnley (J.) History of Wool and Woolcombing. Illust. 8vo, 21s.
Burton (Sir R. F.) Early, Public, and Private Life. Edited by F. HITCHMAN. 2 vols., 8vo, 36s.
Butler (Sir W. F.) Campaign of the Cataracts. Illust., 8vo, 18s.
—— *Invasion of England, told twenty years after.* 2s. 6d.
—— *Red Cloud; or, the Solitary Sioux.* Imperial 16mo, numerous illustrations, gilt edges, 3s. 6d.; plainer binding, 2s. 6d.
—— *The Great Lone Land; Red River Expedition.* 7s. 6d.
—— *The Wild North Land; the Story of a Winter Journey* with Dogs across Northern North America. 8vo, 18s. Cr. 8vo, 7s. 6d.
Bynner (E. L.) See LOW'S STANDARD NOVELS.

CABLE (G. W.) See LOW'S STANDARD NOVELS.
Cadogan (Lady Adelaide) Drawing-room Plays. 10s. 6d.; acting edition, 6d. each.

Cadogan (Lady Adelaide) Illustrated Games of Patience. Twenty-four Diagrams in Colours, with Text. Fcap. 4to, 12s. 6d.
────── *New Games of Patience.* Coloured Diagrams, 4to, 12s. 6d.
Caldecott (Randolph) Memoir. By HENRY BLACKBURN. With 170 Examples of the Artist's Work. 14s.; new edit., 7s. 6d.
────── *Sketches.* With an Introduction by H. BLACKBURN. 4to, picture boards, 2s. 6d.
California. See NORDHOFF.
Callan (H.) Wanderings on Wheel in Europe. Cr. 8vo, 1s. 6d.
Campbell (Lady Colin) Book of the Running Brook. 5s.
Carleton, City Legends. Special Edition, illus., royal 8vo, 12s. 6d.; ordinary edition, crown 8vo, 1s.
────── *City Ballads.* Illustrated, 12s. 6d. New Ed. (Rose Library), 16mo, 1s.
────── *City Ballads and City Legends.* In one vol., 2s. 6d.
────── *Farm Ballads, Farm Festivals, and Farm Legends.* Paper boards, 1s. each; 1 vol., small post 8vo, 3s. 6d.
Carnegie (A.) American Four-in-Hand in Britain. Small 4to, Illustrated, 10s. 6d. Popular Edition, paper, 1s.
────── *Round the World.* 8vo, 10s. 6d.
────── *Triumphant Democracy.* 6s.; also 1s. 6d. and 1s.
Chairman's Handbook. By R. F. D. PALGRAVE. 5th Edit., 2s.
Changed Cross, &c. Religious Poems. 16mo, 2s. 6d.; calf, 6s.
Chapin (F. H.) Mountaineering in Colorado, Peaks about Estes Park, Illus., 10s. 6d.
Chess. See BIRD (H. E.).
Choice Editions of Choice Books. (2s. 6d. each.) Illustrated by C. W. COPE, R.A., T. CRESWICK, R.A., E. DUNCAN, BIRKET FOSTER, J. C. HORSLEY, A.R.A., G. HICKS, R. REDGRAVE, R.A., C. STONEHOUSE, F. TAYLER, G. THOMAS, H. J. TOWNSHEND, E. H. WEHNERT, HARRISON WEIR, &c. New issue, 1s. per vol.

Bloomfield's Farmer's Boy.	Milton's L'Allegro.
Campbell's Pleasures of Hope.	Poetry of Nature. Harrison Weir.
Coleridge's Ancient Mariner.	Rogers' (Sam.) Pleasures of Memory.
Goldsmith's Deserted Village.	Shakespeare's Songs and Sonnets.
Goldsmith's Vicar of Wakefield.	Tennyson's May Queen.
Gray's Elegy in a Churchyard.	Elizabethan Poets.
Keats' Eve of St. Agnes.	Wordsworth's Pastoral Poems.

"Such works are a glorious beatification for a poet."—*Athenæum.*

(Extra Volume) Bunyan's Pilgrim's Progress. Illustrated, 2s.

Christ in Song. By PHILIP SCHAFF. New Ed., gilt edges, 6s.
Clark (Mrs. K. M.) Southern Cross Fairy Tale. Ill. 4to, 5s.
Clarke (P.) Three Diggers: a Tale of the Australian Fifties. Crown 8vo, 6s.

Collingwood (*Harry*)   See LOW'S STANDARD BOOKS.
Collinson (*Sir R. ; Adm.*) *H.M.S.* "*Enterprise*" *in search of Sir*
   J. Franklin.   8vo, 14s.
Colonial Year-book.   By A. J. R. TRENDELL.   Crown
   8vo, 6s.   Annually.
Cook (*Dutton*) *Book of the Play.*   New Edition.   1 vol., 3s. 6d.
—— *On the Stage: Studies.*   2 vols., 8vo, cloth, 24s.
Craddock (*C. E.*) *Despot of Broomsedge Cove.*   Crown 8vo, 6s.
Crew (*B. J.*) *Practical Treatise on Petroleum.*   Illust., 8vo, 28s.
Crouch (*A.P.*) *Glimpses of Feverland : West African Waters*
   6s.
—— *On a Surf-bound Coast.*   Cr. 8vo, 7s. 6d. ; new ed. 5s.
Cumberland(*Stuart*)*Thought Reader's Thoughts.*   Cr. 8vo., 10s.6d.
—— *Queen's Highway from Ocean to Ocean : Canadian*
   Pacific Railway.   Ill., 8vo, 18s. ; new ed., 7s. 6d.
—— See also LOW'S STANDARD NOVELS.
Cundall (*Joseph*).   See "Remarkable Bindings."
Curtin (*J.*) *Myths and Folk Lore of Ireland.*   Cr. 8vo, 9s.
Cushing (*William*) *Anonyms, Dictionary of* **Revealed Author-**
   ship.   2 vols., large 8vo, gilt top, 52s. 6d.
—— *Initials and Pseudonyms.*   25s. ; second series, 21s.
Cutcliffe (*H. C.*) *Trout Fishing in Rapid Streams.*   Cr. 8vo, 3s. 6d.

*D*ALY (*Mrs. D.*) *Digging, Squatting,* **and** *Pioneering in*
   Northern South Australia.   8vo, 12s.
Dana (*J. D.*) *Characteristics of Volcanoes, Hawaiian Islands,*
   &c.   Illus., 18s.
D'Anvers. Elementary History of Art.   New ed., 360 illus.,
   2 vols., cr. 8vo.   I. Architecture, &c., 5s. ; II. Painting, 6s. ; 1 vol.,
   10s. 6d. ; also 12s.
—— *Elementary History of Music.*   Crown 8vo, 2s. 6d.
Daudet (*A.*) *Port Tarascon,* **Tartarin's** *Last Adventures ; By*
   H. JAMES.   Illus., crown 8vo.
Davis (*Clement*) *Modern Whist.*   4s.
—— (*C. T.*) *Bricks, Tiles, Terra-Cotta, &c.*   N. ed.   8vo, 25s.
—— *Manufacture of Leather.*   With many Illustrations.   52s.6d.
—— *Manufacture of Paper.*   28s.
—— (*G. B.*) *Outlines of International Law.*   8vo.   10s. 6d.
Dawidowsky. Glue, Gelatine, Isinglass, Cements, &c.   8vo, 12s.6d.
Day of My Life at Eton.   By an ETON BOY.   New ed.   16mo, 1s.
De Leon (*E.*) *Under the Stars and under the Crescent.*   N. ed., 6s.
Dictionary.   See TOLHAUSEN, "Technological."

Diggle (J. W.) Lancashire Life of Bishop Fraser. With portraits; new ed., 8vo, 12s. 6d.

Donkin (J. G.) Trooper and Redskin: N.W. Mounted Police, Canada. Crown 8vo, 8s. 6d.

Donnelly (Ignatius) Atlantis; or, the Antediluvian World. 7th Edition, crown 8vo, 12s. 6d.

—— *Great Cryptogram: Francis Bacon's Cipher in the* so-called Shakspere Plays. With facsimiles. 2 vols., 30s.

—— *Ragnarok: Age of Fire and Gravel.* Illus., cr. 8vo, 12s. 6d.

Dougall (James Dalziel) Shooting. New Edition. Crown 8vo, 7s. 6d.
"The book is admirable in every way. . . . . We wish it every success."—*Globe.*
"A very complete treatise. . . . . Likely to take high rank as an authority on shooting."—*Daily News.*

Doughty (H.M.) Friesland Meres, and through the Netherlands. Illustrated, new edition, enlarged, crown 8vo, 8s. 6d.

Dunstan Standard Readers. See LOW'S READERS.

EBERS (G.) Joshua, Story of Biblical Life, Translated by CLARA BELL. 2 vols., 18mo, 4s.

Edmonds (C.) Poetry of the Anti-Jacobin. With Additional matter. New ed. Illust., crown 8vo, 7s. 6d.; large paper, 21s.

Educational List and Directory for 1887-88. 5s.

Educational Works published in Great Britain. A Classified Catalogue. Third Edition, 8vo, cloth extra, 6s.

Edwards (E.) American Steam Engineer. Illust., 12mo, 12s. 6d.

Emerson (Dr. P. H.) English Idylls. Small post 8vo, 2s.

—— *Pictures of East Anglian Life.* Ordinary edit., 105s.; édit. de luxe, 17 × 13½, vellum, morocco back, 147s.

—— *Naturalistic Photography for Art Students.* Illustrated. New edit. 5s.

—— *and Goodall. Life and Landscape on the Norfolk Broads.* Plates 12 × 8 inches, 126s.; large paper, 210s.

—— *Wild Life on a Tidal Water.* Copper plates, ord. edit., 25s.; édit de luxe, 63s.

—— *in Concord.* By Edward Waldo Emerson. 8vo, 7s. 6d.

Emin Pasha. See JEPHSON AND STANLEY.

English Catalogue of Books. Vol. III., 1872—1880. Royal 8vo, half-morocco, 42s. See also "Index."

—— *Etchings.* Published Quarterly. 3s. 6d. Vol. VI., 25s.

—— *Philosophers.* Edited by E. B. IVAN MÜLLER, M.A. Crown 8vo volumes of 180 or 200 pp., price 3s. 6d. each.

Francis Bacon, by Thomas Fowler.	Shaftesbury and Hutcheson.
Hamilton, by W. H. S. Monck.	Adam Smith, by J. A. Farrer.
Hartley and James Mill.	

Esler (E. Rentoul) Way of Transgressors. 3 vols., cr. 8vo, 31s. 6d.
Esmarch (F.) Handbook of Surgery. New Edition, 8vo, leather, 24s.
Eton. About some Fellows. New Edition, 1s. See also "Day."
Evelyn. Life of Mrs. Godolphin. By W. HARCOURT, 7s. 6d.
Eves (C. W.) West Indies. Crown 8vo, 7s. 6d.

FARM BALLADS, Festivals, and Legends. See CARLETON.

Fenn (G. Manville). See LOW'S STANDARD BOOKS.
Fennell (Greville) Book of the Roach. New Edition, 12mo, 2s.
Ferns. See HEATH.
Fforde (Brownlow) Subaltern, Policeman, and the Little Girl. Illust., 8vo, sd., 1s.
—————— *The Trotter, A Poona Mystery.* Illust. 8vo, sewed, 1s.
Field (Prof.) Travel Talk in Italy. 16mo, limp, 2s.
Fiske (Amos K.) Midnight Talks at the Club Reported. 12mo, gilt top, 6s.
Fitzgerald (P.) Book Fancier. Cr. 8vo. 5s.; large pap. 12s. 6d.
Fleming (Sandford) England and Canada: a Tour. Cr. 8vo, 6s.
Folkard (R., Jun.) Plant Lore, Legends, and Lyrics. 8vo, 16s.
Forbes (H. O.) Naturalist in the Eastern Archipelago. 8vo. 21s.
Foreign Countries and British Colonies. Cr. 8vo, 3s. 6d. each.

Australia, by J. F. Vesey Fitzgerald.	Japan, by S. Mossman.
Austria, by D. Kay, F.R.G.S.	Peru, by Clements R. Markham.
Denmark and Iceland, by E. C. Otté.	Russia, by W. R. Morfill, M.A.
Egypt, by S. Lane Poole, B.A.	Spain, by Rev. Wentworth Webster.
France, by Miss M. Roberts.	Sweden and Norway, by Woods.
Germany, by S. Baring-Gould.	West Indies, by C. H. Eden, F.R.G.S.
Greece, by L. Sergeant, B.A.	

Foster (Birket) Some Places of Note in England.
Franc (Maud Jeanne). Small post 8vo, uniform, gilt edges:—

Emily's Choice. 5s.	Vermont Vale. 5s.
Hall's Vineyard. 4s.	Minnie's Mission. 4s.
John's Wife: A Story of Life in South Australia. 4s.	Little Mercy. 4s.
	Beatrice Melton's Discipline. 4s.
Marian; or, The Light of Some One's Home. 5s.	No Longer a Child. 4s.
	Golden Gifts. 4s.
Silken Cords and Iron Fetters. 4s.	Two Sides to Every Question. 4s.
Into the Light. 4s.	Master of Ralston. 4s.

*** There is also a re-issue in cheaper form at 2s. 6d. per vol.

Frank's Ranche; or, My Holiday in the Rockies. A Contribution to the Inquiry into What we are to Do with our Boys. 5s.

Fraser (Bishop). See DIGGLE.
French and English Birthday Book. By K. D. CLARK. Imp. 16mo, illust., 7s. 6d.
French. See JULIEN and PORCHER.
Fresh Woods and Pastures New. By the Author of "An Amateur Angler's Days." 1s. 6d.; large paper, 5s. ; new ed., 1s.
Froissart. See LANIER.

GASPARIN (Countess) Sunny Fields and Shady Woods. 6s.
Gavarni (Sulpice Paul; Chevalier) Memoirs. By FRANK MARZIALS. Illust., crown 8vo.
Geary (Grattan) Burma after the Conquest. 7s. 6d.
Geffcken (F. H.) British Empire. Translated by S. J. MACMULLAN. Crown 8vo, 7s. 6d.
General Directory of Johannesberg for 1890. 8vo, 15s.
Gentle Life (Queen Edition). 2 vols. in 1, small 4to, 6s.

THE GENTLE LIFE SERIES.

Price 6s. each ; or in calf extra, price 10s. 6d. ; Smaller Edition, cloth extra, 2s. 6d., except where price is named.

The Gentle Life. Essays in aid of the Formation of Character.
About in the World. Essays by Author of "The Gentle Life."
Like unto Christ. New Translation of Thomas à Kempis.
Familiar Words. A Quotation Handbook. 6s.; n. ed. 3s.6d.
Essays by Montaigne. Edited by the Author of "The Gentle Life."
The Gentle Life. 2nd Series.
The Silent Hour: Essays, Original and Selected.
Half-Length Portraits. Short Studies of Notable Persons. By J. HAIN FRISWELL.
Essays on English Writers, for Students in English Literature.
Other People's Windows. By J. HAIN FRISWELL. 6s.; new ed., 3s. 6d.
A Man's Thoughts. By J. HAIN FRISWELL.
Countess of Pembroke's Arcadia. By Sir P. SIDNEY. 6s.; new ed., 3s. 6d.

Germany. By S. BARING-GOULD. Crown 8vo, 3s. 6d.
Giles (E.) Australia twice Traversed : five Expeditions, 1872-76. With Maps and Illust. 2 vols, 8vo, 30s.
Gill (F.) See LOW'S READERS.

Gillespie (W. M.) Surveying. New ed., by CADEY STALEY. 8vo, 21*s.*

Glances at Great and Little Men. By PALADIN. Cr. 8vo, 6*s.*

Goldsmith. She Stoops to Conquer. Introduction by AUSTIN DOBSON; the designs by E. A. ABBEY. Imperial 4to, 42*s.*

Gooch (Fanny C.) Face to Face with the Mexicans. Ill. roy. 8vo, 16*s*

Gordon (J. E. H., B.A. Cantab.) Electric Lighting. Ill. 8vo, 18*s.*

—— *Physical Treatise on Electricity and Magnetism.* 2nd Edition, enlarged, with coloured, full-page, &c., Illust. 2 vols., 8vo, 42*s.*

—— *Electricity for Schools.* Illustrated. Crown 8vo, 5*s.*

Gouffé (Jules) Royal Cookery Book. New Edition, with plates in colours, Woodcuts, &c., 8vo, gilt edges, 42*s.*

—— Domestic Edition, half-bound, 10*s.* 6*d.*

Gounod (C.) Life and Works. By MARIE ANNE BOVET. Portrait and Facsimiles, 8vo, 10*s.* 6*d.*

Grant (General, U.S.) Personal Memoirs. With Illustrations, Maps, &c. 2 vols., 8vo, 28*s.*

Great Artists. See "Biographies."

Great Musicians. Edited by F. HUEFFER. A Series of Biographies, crown 8vo, 3*s.* each :—

Bach.	Handel.	Rossini.
Beethoven.	Haydn.	Schubert.
Berlioz.	Mendelssohn.	Schumann.
Cherubini.	Mozart.	Richard Wagner.
Church Composers.	Purcell.	Weber.

Groves (J. Percy) Charmouth Grange. 2*s.* 6*d.*; gilt, 3*s.* 6*d.*

Guizot's History of France. Translated by ROBERT BLACK. 8 vols., super-royal 8vo, cloth extra, gilt, each 24*s.* In cheaper binding, 8 vols., at 10*s.* 6*d.* each.

"It supplies a want which has long been felt, and ought to be in the hands of all students of history."—*Times.*

———————— *Masson's School Edition.* Abridged from the Translation by Robert Black, with Chronological Index, Historical and Genealogical Tables, &c. By Professor GUSTAVE MASSON, B.A. With Portraits, Illustrations, &c. 1 vol., 8vo, 600 pp., 5*s.*

Guyon (Mde.) Life. By UPHAM. 6th Edition, crown 8vo, 6*s.*

HALFORD *(F. M.) Floating Flies, and how to Dress them.* New edit., with Coloured plates. 8vo, 15*s.*

—— *Dry Fly-Fishing, Theory and Practice.* Col. Plates, 25*s.*

Hall (W. W.) How to Live Long; or, 1408 *Maxims.* 2*s.*

Halsey (Frederick A.) Slide Valve Gears. With diagrams, crown 8vo, 8*s.* 6*d.*

Hamilton (E.) Fly-fishing for Salmon, Trout, and Grayling; their Habits, Haunts, and History. Illust., 6*s.*; large paper, 10*s.* 6*d.*

—— *Riverside Naturalist.* Illust. 8vo.

Hands (*T.*) *Numerical Exercises in Chemistry.* Cr. 8vo, 2s. 6d.
and 2s.; Answers separately, 6d.

Handy Guide to Dry-fly Fishing. By COTSWOLD ISYS, M.A.
Crown 8vo, limp, 1s.

────── *Guide Book to Japanese Islands.* With Folding Outline
Map, crown 8vo, 6s. 6d.

Hanoverian Kings. See SKOTTOWE.

Hardy (*A. S.*) *Passe-rose: a Romance.* Crown 8vo, 6s.

────── (*Thomas*). See LOW'S STANDARD NOVELS.

Hare (*J. L. Clark*) *American Constitutional Law.* 2 vls., 8vo, 63s.

Harkut (*F.*) *Conspirator; A Romance of Real Life.* By
PAUL P. 8vo, 6s.

Harper's Young People. Vols. I.-VI., profusely Illustrated
with woodcuts and coloured plates. Royal 4to, extra binding, each
7s. 6d.; gilt edges, 8s. Published Weekly, in wrapper, 1d.; Annual
Subscription, post free, 6s. 6d.; Monthly, in wrapper, with coloured
plate, 6d.; Annual Subscription, post free, 7s. 6d.

Harris (*W.B.*) *Land of an African Sultan: Travels in Morocco.*
Illust., crown 8vo, 10s. 6d.; large paper, 31s. 6d.

Harrison (*Mary*) *Complete Cookery Guide.* Crown 8vo, 6s.

────── *Skilful Cook.* New edition, crown 8vo, 5s.

Harrison (*W.*) *Memorable London Houses: a Guide.* Illust.
New edition, 18mo, 1s. 6d.; new ed., enlarged, 2s. 6d.

Hatton (*Joseph*) *Journalistic London: with Engravings and
Portraits* of Distinguished Writers of the Day. Fcap. 4to, 12s. 6d.

────── See also LOW'S STANDARD NOVELS.

Haweis (*H. R.*) *Broad Church, What is Coming.* Cr. 8vo.

────── *Poets in the Pulpit.* New edition. Crown 8vo, 3s. 6d.

────── (*Mrs.*) *Art of Housekeeping: a Bridal Garland.* 2s. 6d.

Hawthorne (*Nathaniel*) *Life.* By JOHN R. LOWELL.

Hearn (*L.*) *Youma, History of a West Indian Slave.* Crown
8vo, 5s.

Heath (*F. G.*) *Fern World.* With coloured plates, new ed.
Crown 8vo, 6s.

Heldmann (*B.*) See LOW'S STANDARD BOOKS.

Henty (*G. A.*) See LOW'S STANDARD BOOKS.

────── (*Richmond*) *Australiana: My Early Life.* 5s.

Herbert (*T.*) *Salads and Sandwiches.* Cr. 8vo, boards, 1s.

Herrick (*Robert*) *Poetry.* Preface by AUSTIN DOBSON. With
numerous Illustrations by E. A. ABBEY. 4to, gilt edges, 42s.

Hetley (*Mrs. E.*) *Native Flowers of New Zealand.* Chromos
from Drawings. Three Parts, 63s.; extra binding, 73s. 6d.

Hicks (*E. S.*) *Our Boys: How to Enter the Merchant Service.* 5s.

────── *Yachts, Boats and Canoes.* Illustrated. 8vo, 10s. 6d.

Hill (G. B.) Footsteps of Dr. Johnson. Ordinary ed., half-morocco, gilt top, 63s.; *édit de luxe*, on Japanese vellum, 147s.
Hints on Wills. See WILLS.
Historic Bindings in the Bodleian Library. 24 plates, 4to, 42s.; half-morocco, 52s. 6d. Coloured, 84s.; half-morocco, 94s. 6d.
Hitchman. Public Life of the Earl of Beaconsfield. 3s. 6d.
Hoey (Mrs. Cashel) See LOW'S STANDARD NOVELS.
Holder (C. F.) Marvels of Animal Life. Illustrated. 8s. 6d.
────── *Ivory King: Elephant and Allies.* Illustrated. 8s. 6d.
────── *Living Lights: Phosphorescent Animals and Vegetables.* Illustrated. 8vo, 8s. 6d.
Holmes (O. W.) Before the Curfew, &c. Occasional Poems. 5s.
────── *Last Leaf: a Holiday Volume.* 42s.
────── *Mortal Antipathy,* 8s. 6d.; also 2s.; paper, 1s.
────── *Our Hundred Days in Europe.* 6s. Large Paper, 15s.
────── *Over the Tea Cups, Reminiscences and Reflections.* Crown 8vo, 6s.
────── *Poems: a new volume.*
────── *Poetical Works.* 2 vols., 18mo, gilt tops, 10s. 6d.
────── See also ROSE LIBRARY.
Howard (Blanche Willis) Open Door. Crown 8vo, 6s.
Howorth (H. H.) Mammoth and the Flood. 8vo, 18s.
Hundred Greatest Men (The). 8 portfolios, 21s. each, or 4 **vols.**, half-morocco, gilt edges, 10 guineas. New Ed., 1 vol., royal 8vo, 21s.
Hymnal Companion to the Book of Common Prayer. By BISHOP BICKERSTETH. In various styles and bindings from 1d. to 31s. 6d. *Price List and Prospectus will be forwarded on application.*
  *** Also a new and revised edition, 1890, distinct from the preceding. Detailed list of 16 pages, post free.

ILLUSTRATED Text-Books of Art-Education. Edited by EDWARD J. POYNTER, R.A. Illustrated, and strongly bound, 5s. Now ready:—

PAINTING.
Classic and Italian. By HEAD. | **French and Spanish.**
German, Flemish, and Dutch. | **English and American.**

ARCHITECTURE.
Classic and Early Christian.
Gothic and Renaissance. By T. ROGER SMITH.

SCULPTURE.
Antique: Egyptian and Greek.
Renaissance and Modern. By LEADER SCOTT.

Inderwick (F. A.; Q.C.) Interregnum; Studies of the Common-wealth. Legislative, Social, and Legal. 8vo, 10s. 6d.
────── *Side Lights on the Stuarts.* New edition, 7s. 6d.

Index to the English Catalogue, Jan., 1874, *to Dec.*, 1880.
Royal 8vo, half-morocco, 18*s.*

Inglis (*Hon. James;* "*Maori*") *Tent Life in Tiger Land.*
Col. plates, roy. 8vo, 18*s.*

Irving (*Washington*). Library Edition of his Works in 27 vols., Copyright, with the Author's Latest Revisions. "Geoffrey Crayon" Edition, large square 8vo. 12*s.* 6*d.* per vol. *See also* "Little Britain."

JACKSON (*J.*) *New Style Vertical Writing Copy-Books.*
Series I, Nos. I.—XII., 2*d.* and 1*d.* each.

——— *St. Dunstan's Series*, 8 Nos., 1*d.* each.

——— *New Series of Vertical Writing Copy-books*, specially adapted for the seven standards. 22 Nos., 2*d.* each.

——— *Shorthand of Arithmetic.* Crown 8vo, 1*s.* 6*d.*

——— (*L.*) *Ten Centuries of European Progress.* With maps, crown 8vo, 12*s.* 6*d.*

James (*Henry*). See DAUDET (A.)

Janvier (*T. A.*), *Aztec Treasure House: Romance of Contemporaneous Antiquity.* Illustrated. Crown 8vo, 7*s.* 6*d.*

Japan. See "Artistic," also MORSE.

Jefferies (*Richard*) *Amaryllis at the Fair.* N. ed., cr. 8vo, 7*s.* 6*d.*

——— *Bevis: The Story of a Boy.* New ed., crown 8vo, 5*s.*

Jephson (*A. J. Mounteney*) *Emin Pasha and the Rebellion at the Equator.* Illust. 21*s.*

Jerdon (*Gertrude*). See LOW'S STANDARD SERIES.

Johnson (*Samuel*) See HILL.

Johnston (*H. H.*) *River Congo.* New Edition, 8vo, 21*s.*

Johnstone (*D. L.*) *Land of the Mountain Kingdom.* Illus. 2*s.* 6*d.*

Julien (*F.*) *English Student's French Examiner.* 16mo, 2*s.*

——— *Conversational French Reader.* 16mo, cloth, 2*s.* 6*d.*

———*French at Home and at School.* Book I., Accidence. 2*s.*

——— *First Lessons in Conversational French Grammar.* 1*s.*

——— *Petites Leçons de Conversation et de Grammaire.* 3*s.*

——— *Phrases of Daily Use.* 6*d.* *Leçons and Phrases*, 1 vol., 3*s.* 6*d.*

KEATS. Endymion. Illust. by W. ST. JOHN HARPER.
Imp. 4to, gilt top, 42*s.*

Kempis (*Thomas à*) *Daily Text-Book.* Square 16mo, 2*s.* 6*d.*; interleaved as a Birthday Book, 3*s.* 6*d.*

Kennedy (*E. B.*) *Blacks and Bushrangers.* New ed., Illust., crown 8vo, 5*s.*

Kent's Commentaries: an Abridgment for Students of American Law. By EDEN F. THOMPSON. 10*s.* 6*d.*

*Kershaw (S. W.) Protestants from France in their English
    Home.* Crown 8vo, 6s.
*Kingsley (Rose) Children of Westminster Abbey: Studies in
    English History.* 5s.
Kingston (W. H. G.) Works. Illustrated, 16mo, gilt edges,
    3s. 6d.; plainer binding, plain edges, 2s. 6d. each.

Ben Burton.
Captain Mugford, or, Our Salt
 and Fresh Water Tutors.
Dick Cheveley.
Heir of Kilfinnan.
Snow-Shoes and **Canoes.**
Two Supercargoes.
With Axe and Rifle.

Kipling (Rudyard) Soldiers Three. New edition, 8vo, sewed, 1s.
—— *Story of the Gadsbys.* New edition, 8vo, sewed, 1s.
—— *In Black and White.* New edition, 8vo, sewed, 1s.
    The three foregoing bound in one volume, cloth, 3s. 6d.
—— *Wee Willie Winkie, &c., Stories.* 8vo, sewed, 1s.
—— *Under the Deodars.* 8vo, sewed, 1s.
—— *The Phantom Rickshaw.* 8vo, sewed, 1s.
Knight (E. J.) Cruise of the "Falcon." New Ed. Illus. Cr. 8vo,
    7s. 6d. Original edition with all the illustrations; 2 vols., 24s.
Knox (Col.) Boy Travellers on the Congo. Illus. Cr. 8vo, 7s. 6d.
Kunhardt (C. B.) Small Yachts: Design and Construction. 35s.
—— *Steam Yachts and Launches.* Illustrated. 4to, 16s.

LANIER'S Works. Illustrated, crown 8vo, gilt edges, 7s. 6d.
    each.

Boy's King Arthur.
Boy's Froissart.
Boy's Knightly Legends of Wales.
Boy's Percy: Ballads of Love and
 Adventure, selected from **the**
 "Reliques."

Lansdell (H.) Through Siberia. 2 vols., 8vo, 30s.; 1 vol., 10s. 6d.
—— *Russia in Central Asia.* Illustrated. 2 vols., 42s.
—— *Through Central Asia; Russo-Afghan Frontier.* 12s.
Larden (W.) School Course on Heat. Third Ed., Illust. 5s.
Laurie (A.) Conquest of the Moon: a Story of the Bayouda.
    Illust., crown 8vo, 2s. 6d.; gilt edges, 3s. 6d.
—— *New York to Brest in Seven Hours.* Illust., cr.
    8vo, 7s. 6d.
Leffingwell (W. Bruce; "Horace") Shooting on Upland, Marsh
    and Stream. Illust. 8vo, 18s.
Lemon (M.) Small House over the Water, and Stories. Illust.
    by Cruikshank, &c. Crown 8vo, 6s.
Leo XIII.: Life. By O'REILLY. Large 8vo, 18s.; *édit.
    de luxe*, 63s.
Leonardo da Vinci's Literary Works. Edited by Dr. JEAN
    PAUL RICHTER. Containing his Writings on Painting, Sculpture,
    and Architecture, his Philosophical Maxims, Humorous Writings, and
    Miscellaneous Notes on Personal Events, on his Contemporaries, on

Literature, &c.; published from Manuscripts. 2 vols., imperial 8vo, containing about 200 Drawings in Autotype Reproductions, and numerous other Illustrations. Twelve Guineas.

Library of Religious Poetry. Best Poems of all Ages. Edited by SCHAFF and GILMAN. Royal 8vo. 21s.; cheaper binding, 10s. 6d.

Lindsay (W. S.) History of Merchant Shipping. With 150 Illustrations, Maps, and Charts. 4 vols., 8vo, cloth extra. Vols. 1 and 2, 11s. each; vols. 3 and 4, 14s. each. 4 vols., 50s.

Little (Archibald J.) Through the Yang-tse Gorges. N. Ed. 10s. 6d.

Little Britain, The Spectre Bridegroom, and *Legend of Sleepy Hollow.* By WASHINGTON IRVING. Édition de luxe. Illus. Designed by Mr. CHARLES O. MURRAY. Re-issue, square crown 8vo, cloth, 6s.

Lodge (Henry Cabot) George Washington. 2 vols., 12s.

Longfellow. Maidenhood. With Coloured Plates. Oblong 4to, 2s. 6d.; gilt edges, 3s. 6d.

—— *Courtship of Miles Standish.* Illust. by BROUGHTON, &c. Imp. 4to, 21s.

—— *Nuremberg.* Illum. by M. and A. COMEGYS. 4to, 31s. 6d.

—— *Song of Hiawatha.* Illust. from drawings by F. REMINGTON. 8vo, 21s.

Lorne (Marquis of) Viscount Palmerston (Prime Ministers). Crown 8vo.

Lowell (J. R.) Vision of Sir Launfal. Illustrated, royal 4to, 63s.

—— *Life of Nathaniel Hawthorne.* Sm. post 8vo. [*In prep.*

Low's Readers. Specially prepared for the Code of 1890. Edited by JOHN GILL, of Cheltenham. Strongly bound, being sewn on tapes.

NOW READY.

FIRST READER, for STANDARD I. Every Lesson Illustrated. Price 9d.
SECOND READER, for STANDARD II. Every Lesson Illustrated. Price 10d.
THIRD READER, for STANDARD III. Every Lesson Illustrated. Price 1s.
FOURTH READER, for STANDARD IV. Every Lesson Illustrated. Price 1s. 3d.
FIFTH READER, for STANDARD V. Every Lesson Illustrated. Price 1s. 4d.
SIXTH READER, for STANDARDS VI. and VII. Every Lesson Illustrated. Price 1s. 6d.

Already adopted by the School Board for London; by the Edinburgh, Nottingham, Aston, Birmingham and other School Boards.

In the Press, INFANT PRIMERS, In two Parts. PART I., Illustrated, price 3d. PART II., Illustrated, price 6d.

Low's Standard Library of Travel and Adventure. Crown 8vo, uniform in cloth extra, 7s. 6d., except where price is given.

 1. **The Great Lone Land.** By Major W. F. BUTLER, C.B.

Low's Standard Library, &c.—continued.
2. **The Wild North Land.** By Major W. F. BUTLER, C.B.
3. **How I found Livingstone.** By H. M. STANLEY, 3s. 6d.
4. **Through the Dark Continent.** By STANLEY. 12s. 6d. & 3s. 6d.
5. **The Threshold of the Unknown Region.** By C. R. MARKHAM. (4th Edition, with Additional Chapters, 10s. 6d.)
6. **Cruise of the Challenger.** By W. J. J. SPRY, R.N.
7. **Burnaby's On Horseback through Asia Minor.** 10s. 6d.
8. **Schweinfurth's Heart of Africa.** 2 vols., 3s. 6d. each.
9. **Through America.** By W. G. MARSHALL.
10. **Through Siberia.** Il. and unabridged, 10s.6d. By H. LANSDELL.
11. **From Home to Home.** By STAVELEY HILL.
12. **Cruise of the Falcon.** By E. J. KNIGHT.
13. **Through Masai Land.** By JOSEPH THOMSON.
14. **To the Central African Lakes.** By JOSEPH THOMSON.
15. **Queen's Highway.** By STUART CUMBERLAND.
16. **Two Kings of Uganda.** By ASHE. 3s. 6d.

Low's Standard Novels. Small post 8vo, cloth extra, 6s. each, unless otherwise stated.

JAMES BAKER. John Westacott.

WILLIAM BLACK.
A Daughter of Heth.—House-Boat.—In Far Lochaber.—In Silk Attire.—Kilmeny.—Lady Silverdale's Sweetheart.—Penance of John Logan.—Sunrise.—Three Feathers.—New Prince Fortunatus.

R. D. BLACKMORE.
Alice Lorraine.—Christowell, a Dartmoor Tale.—Clara Vaughan.—Cradock Nowell.—Cripps the Carrier.—Erema.—Kit and Kitty.—Lorna Doone.—Mary Anerley.—Springhaven.—Tommy Upmore.

E. L. BYNNER. Agnes Surriage.—Begum's Daughter.

G. W. CABLE. Bonaventure. 5s.

Miss COLERIDGE. An English Squire.

C. E. CRADDOCK. Despot of Broomsedge Cove.

Mrs. B. M. CROKER. Some One Else.

STUART CUMBERLAND. Vasty Deep.

E. DE LEON. Under the Stars and Crescent.

Miss BETHAM-EDWARDS. Halfway.

Rev. E. GILLIAT, M.A. Story of the Dragonnades.

THOMAS HARDY.
A Laodicean.—Far from the Madding Crowd.—Mayor of Casterbridge.—Pair of Blue Eyes.—Return of the Native.—Hand of Ethelberta.—Trumpet Major.—Two on a Tower.

FRANK HARKUT. Conspirator.

JOSEPH HATTON. Old House at Sandwich.—Three Recruits.

Mrs. CASHEL HOEY.
A Golden Sorrow.—A Stern Chase.—Out of Court.

BLANCHE WILLIS HOWARD. Open Door.

JEAN INGELOW.
Don John.—John Jerome (5s.).—Sarah de Berenger.

GEORGE MAC DONALD.
Adela Cathcart.—Guild Court.—Mary Marston.—Stephen

Low's Standard Novels—continued.
>Archer. — The Vicar's Daughter. — Orts. — Weighed and Wanting.

Mrs. MACQUOID. Diane.—Elinor Dryden.
DUFFIELD OSBORNE. Spell of Ashtaroth (5s.)
Mrs. J. H. RIDDELL.
>Alaric Spenceley.—Daisies and Buttercups.—The Senior Partner.—A Struggle for Fame.

W. CLARK RUSSELL.
>Betwixt the Forelands.—Frozen Pirate.—Jack's Courtship.—John Holdsworth.—Ocean Free Lance.—A Sailor's Sweetheart.—Sea Queen.—Watch Below.—Strange Voyage.—Wreck of the Grosvenor.—The Lady Maud.—Little Loo.

FRANK R. STOCKTON.
>Ardis Claverden.—Bee-man of Orn.—The Late Mrs. Null.—Hundredth Man.

MRS. HARRIET B. STOWE.
>My Wife and I.—Old Town Folk.—We and our Neighbours.—Poganuc People, their Loves and Lives.

JOSEPH THOMSON. Ulu: an African Romance.
TYTLER. Duchess Frances.
LEW WALLACE. Ben Hur: a Tale of the Christ.
C. D. WARNER. Little Journey in the World.—Jupiter Lights.
CONSTANCE FENIMORE WOOLSON.
>Anne.—East Angels.—For the Major (5s.).
>French Heiress in her own Chateau.

Low's Standard Novels. NEW ISSUE at short intervals. Cr. 8vo, 2s. 6d.; fancy boards 2s.

BLACKMORE.
>Clara Vaughan.—Cripps the Carrier.—Lorna Doone.—Mary Anerley.—Alice Lorraine.—Tommy Upmore.

CABLE. Bonaventure.
CROKER. Some One Else.
DE LEON. Under the Stars.
EDWARDS. Half-Way.
HARDY.
>Madding Crowd.—Mayor of Casterbridge.—Trumpet-Major.—Hand of Ethelberta.—Pair of Blue Eyes.—Return of the Native.—Two on a Tower.—Laodicean.

HATTON. Three Recruits.—Old House at Sandwich.
HOEY. Golden Sorrow.—Out of Court.—Stern Chase.
HOLMES. Guardian Angel.
INGELOW. John Jerome.—Sarah de Berenger.
MAC DONALD.
>Adela Cathcart.—Guild Court.—Vicar's Daughter.—Stephen Archer.

OLIPHANT. Innocent.
RIDDELL. Daisies and Buttercups.—Senior Partner.
STOCKTON. Casting Away of Mrs. Lecks.—Bee-Man of Orn.
STOWE. Dred.—Old Town Folk.—Poganuc People.
THOMSON. Ulu.
WALFORD. Her Great Idea

Low's Standard Books for Boys. With numerous Illustrations, 2s. 6d.; gilt edges, 3s. 6d. each.

Dick Cheveley. By W. H. KINGSTON.
Heir of Kilfinnan. By W. H. KINGSTON.
Off to the Wilds. By G. MANVILLE FENN.
The Two Supercargoes. By W. G. KINGSTON.
The Silver Cañon. By G. MANVILLE FENN.
Under the Meteor Flag. By HARRY COLLINGWOOD.
Jack Archer: A Tale of the Crimea. By G. A. HENTY.
The Mutiny on Board the Ship Leander. By B. HELDMANN.
With Axe and Rifle on the Western Prairies. By W. H. G. KINGSTON.
Red Cloud, the Solitary Sioux: a Tale of the Great Prairie. By Col. Sir WM. BUTLER, K.C.B.
The Voyage of the Aurora. By HARRY COLLINGWOOD.
Charmouth Grange: a Tale of the 17th Century. By J. PERCY GROVES.
Snowshoes and Canoes. By W. H. G. KINGSTON.
The Son of the Constable of France. By LOUIS ROUSSELET.
Captain Mugford; or, Our Salt and Fresh Water Tutors. Edited by W. H. G. KINGSTON.
The Cornet of Horse, a Tale of Marlborough's Wars. By G. A. HENTY.
The Adventures of Captain Mago. By LEON CAHUN.
Noble Words and Noble Needs.
The King of the Tigers. By ROUSSELET.
Hans Brinker; or, The Silver Skates. By Mrs. DODGE.
The Drummer-Boy, a Story of the time of Washington. By ROUSSELET.
Adventures in New Guinea: The Narrative of Louis Tregance.
The Crusoes of Guiana. By BOUSSENARD.
The Gold Seekers. A Sequel to the Above. By BOUSSENARD.
Winning His Spurs, a Tale of the Crusades. By G. A. HENTY.
The Blue Banner. By LEON CAHUN.
Startling Exploits of the Doctor. CÉLIÈRE.
Brothers Rantzau. ERCKMANN-CHATRIAN.
Adventures of a Young Naturalist. BIART.
Ben Burton; or, Born and Bred at Sea. KINGSTON.
Great Hunting Grounds of the World. MEUNIER.
Ran Away from the Dutch. PERELAER.
My Kalulu, Prince, King, and Slave. STANLEY.

New Volumes for 1890-91.

The Serpent Charmer. By LOUIS ROUSSELET.
Stories of the Gorilla Country. By PAUL DU CHAILLU.
The Conquest of the Moon. By A. LAURIE.
The Maid of the Ship "Golden Age." By H. E. MACLEAN.
The Frozen Pirate. By W. CLARK RUSSELL.
The Marvellous Country. By S. W. COZZENS.
The Mountain Kingdom. By D. LAWSON JOHNSTONE.
Lost in Africa. By F. H. WINDER.

Low's Standard Series of Books by Popular Writers. Sm. cr.
8vo, cloth gilt, 2s.; gilt edges, 2s. 6d. each.
Aunt Jo's Scrap Bag. By Miss ALCOTT.
Shawl Straps. By Miss ALCOTT.
Little Men. By Miss ALCOTT.
Hitherto. By Mrs. WHITNEY.
Forecastle to Cabin. By SAMUELS. Illustrated.
In My Indian Garden. By PHIL ROBINSON.
Little Women and Little Women Wedded. By Miss ALCOTT.
Eric and Ethel. By FRANCIS FRANCIS. Illust.
Keyhole Country. By GERTRUDE JERDON. Illust.
We Girls. By Mrs. WHITNEY.
The Other Girls. A Sequel to "We Girls." By Mrs. WHITNEY.
Adventures of Jimmy Brown. Illust. By W. L. ALDEN.
Under the Lilacs. By Miss ALCOTT. Illust.
Jimmy's Cruise. By Miss ALCOTT.
Under the Punkah. By PHIL ROBINSON.
An Old-Fashioned Girl. By Miss ALCOTT.
A Rose in Bloom. By Miss ALCOTT.
Eight Cousins. Illust. By Miss ALCOTT.
Jack and Jill. By Miss ALCOTT.
Lulu's Library. Illust. By Miss ALCOTT.
Silver Pitchers. By Miss ALCOTT.
Work and Beginning Again. Illust. By Miss ALCOTT.
A Summer in Leslie Goldthwaite's Life. By Mrs. WHITNEY.
Faith Gartney's Girlhood. By Mrs. WHITNEY.
Real Folks. By Mrs. WHITNEY.
Dred. By Mrs. STOWE.
My Wife and I. By Mrs. STOWE.
An Only Sister. By Madame DE WITT.
Spinning Wheel Stories. By Miss ALCOTT.

New Volumes for 1890-91.
My Summer in a Garden. By C. DUDLEY WARNER.
Ghost in the Mill and Other Stories. HARRIET B. STOWE.
The Pilgrim's Progress. With many Illustrations.
We and our Neighbours. HARRIET BEECHER STOWE.
Picciola. SAINTINE.
Draxy Miller's Dowry. SAXE HOLM.
Seagull Rock. J. SANDEAU.
In the Wilderness. C. DUDLEY WARNER.

Low's Pocket Encyclopædia. Upwards of 25,000 References, with Plates. New ed., imp. 32mo, cloth, marbled edges, 3s. 6d.; roan, 4s. 6d.

Low's Handbook to London Charities. Yearly, cloth, 1s. 6d. paper, 1s.

MAC DONALD (*George*). See LOW'S STANDARD NOVELS.

Macgregor (*John*) "*Rob Roy*" *on the Baltic.* 3rd Edition small post 8vo, 2s. 6d.; cloth, gilt edges, 3s. 6d.

Macgregor (*John*) *A Thousand Miles in the* "*Rob Roy*"
Canoe. 11th Edition, small post 8vo, 2s. 6d.; cloth, gilt edges, 3s. 6d.
—— *Voyage Alone in the Yawl* "*Rob Roy.*" New Edition, with additions, small post 8vo, 3s. 6d. and 2s. 6d.
Mackenzie (*Rev. John*) *Austral Africa : Losing it or Ruling it ?* Illustrations and Maps. 2 vols., 8vo, 32s.
Maclean (*H. E.*) *Maid of the Golden Age.* Illust., cr. 8vo, 2s.6d.
Macmaster (*M.*) *Our Pleasant Vices.* 3 vols., cr. 8vo, 31s. 6d.
Mahan (*Captain A. T.*) *Influence of Sea Power upon History*, 1660-1783. 8vo, 18s.
Markham (*Clements R.*) See "Foreign Countries," and MAURY.
Marston (*E.*) *How Stanley wrote* "*In Darkest Africa,*" Trip to Africa. Illust., fcp. 8vo, picture cover, 1s.
—— See also "Amateur Angler," "Frank's Ranche," and "Fresh Woods."
Martin (*F. W.*) *Float Fishing and Spinning in the Nottingham* Style. New Edition. Crown 8vo, 2s. 6d.
Maury (*Commander*) *Physical Geography of the Sea, and its* Meteorology. New Edition, with Charts and Diagrams, cr. 8vo, 6s.
—— *Life.* By his Daughter. Edited by Mr. CLEMENTS R. MARKHAM. With portrait of Maury. 8vo, 12s. 6d.
McCarthy (*Justin, M.P.*) *Sir Robert Peel* (*Prime Ministers*).
Mendelssohn Family (*The*), 1729—1847. From Letters and Journals. Translated. New Edition, 2 vols., 8vo, 30s.
Mendelssohn. See also "Great Musicians."
Merrifield's Nautical Astronomy. Crown 8vo, 7s. 6d.
Mills (*J.*) *Alternative Elementary Chemistry.* Ill., cr.8vo, 1s.6d.
Mitchell (*D. G. ; Ik. Marvel*) *English Lands, Letters and* Kings; Celt to Tudor. Crown 8vo, 6s.
—— *English Lands, Letters and Kings, Elizabeth to Anne.* Crown 8vo, 6s.
Mitford (*Mary Russell*) *Our Village.* With 12 full-page and 157 smaller Cuts. Cr. 4to, cloth, gilt edges, 21s.; cheaper binding, 10s.6d.
Mollett (*J. W.*) *Illustrated Dictionary of Words used in Art and* Archæology. Illustrated, small 4to, 15s.
Mormonism. See STENHOUSE.
Morse (*E. S.*) *Japanese Homes and their Surroundings.* With more than 300 Illustrations. Re-issue, 10s. 6d.
Motti (*P.*) *Russian Conversation Grammar.* Cr. 8vo, 5s. ; Key, 2s.
Muller (*E.*) *Noble Words and Noble Deeds.* Illustrated, gilt edges, 3s. 6d.; plainer binding, 2s. 6d.
Mulready. See "Biographies."
Musgrave (*Mrs.*) *Miriam.* Crown 8vo, 6s.
—— *Savage London ; Riverside Characters, &c.* 3s. 6d.
Music. See "Great Musicians."

*N*AST: *Christmas Drawings for the Human Race.* 4to, bevelled boards, gilt edges, 12s.

Nelson (*Walfred*) *Five Years at Panama, the Canal.* Illust. Crown 8vo, 6s.

Nethercote (*C. B.*) *Pytchley Hunt.* New Ed., cr. 8vo, 8s. 6d.

New Zealand. See BRADSHAW and WHITE (J.).

Nicholls (*J. H. Kerry*) *The King Country: Explorations in New Zealand.* Many Illustrations and Map. New Edition, 8vo, 21s.

Nordhoff (*C.*) *California, for Health, Pleasure, and Residence.* New Edition, 8vo, with Maps and Illustrations, 12s. 6d.

Nursery Playmates (*Prince of*). 217 Coloured Pictures for Children by eminent Artists. Folio, in col. bds., 6s.; new ed., 2s. 6d.

Nursing Record. Yearly, 8s.; half-yearly, 4s. 6d.; quarterly, 2s. 6d; weekly, 2d.

O'*BRIEN* (*R. B.*) *Fifty Years of Concessions to Ireland.* With a Portrait of T. Drummond. Vol. I., 16s.; II., 16s.

Orient Line Guide. New edition, re-written by W. J. LOFTIE. Maps and Plans, 2s. 6d.

Orvis (*C. F.*) *Fishing with the Fly.* Illustrated. 8vo, 12s. 6d.

Osborne (*Duffield*) *Spell of Ashtaroth.* Crown 8vo, 5s.

Other People's Windows. New edition, 3s. 6d.

Our Little Ones in Heaven. Edited by the Rev. H. ROBBINS. With Frontispiece after Sir JOSHUA REYNOLDS. New Edition, 5s.

Owen (*Douglas*) *Marine Insurance Notes and Clauses.* 3rd edition, 8vo, 15s.

*P*ALGRAVE (*R. F. D.*) *Oliver Cromwell.* Crown 8vo, 10s. 6d.

Palliser (*Mrs.*) *A History of Lace.* New Edition, with additional cuts and text. 8vo, 21s.

—————— *The China Collector's Pocket Companion.* With upwards of 1000 Illustrations of Marks and Monograms. Small 8vo, 5s.

Panton (*J. E.*) *Homes of Taste. Hints on Furniture and Decoration.* Crown 8vo, 2s. 6d.

Peach (*R. E. M.*) *Annals of the Parish of Swainswick, near Bath.* Sm. 4to, 10s. 6d.

Pennell (*H. Cholmondeley*) *Sporting Fish of Great Britain.* 15s.; large paper, 30s.

—————— *Modern Improvements in Fishing-tackle.* Crown 8vo, 2s.

Perelaer (*M. T. H.*) *Ran Away from the Dutch; Borneo, &c.* Illustrated, square 8vo, 7s. 6d; new ed., 2s. 6d.

Perry (*J. J. M.*) *Edlingham Burglary, or Circumstantial Evidence.* Crown 8vo, 3s. 6d.

Phillips' Dictionary of Biographical Reference. New edition, royal 8vo, 25*s*.

Philpot (H. J.) Diabetes Mellitus. Crown 8vo, 5*s*.

——— *Diet System.* Tables. I. Diabetes; II. Gout; III. Dyspepsia; IV. Corpulence. In cases, 1*s*. each.

Plunkett (Major G. T.) Primer of Orthographic Projection. Elementary Solid Geometry. With Problems and Exercises. 2*s*. 6*d*.

Poe (E. A.) The Raven. Illust. by DORÉ. Imperial folio, 63*s*.

Poems of the Inner Life. Chiefly Modern. Small 8vo, 5*s*.

Poetry of the Anti-Jacobin. New ed., by CHARLES EDMONDS. Cr. 8vo, 7*s*. 6*d*.; large paper, with special plate, 21*s*.

Porcher (A.) Juvenil French Plays. With **Notes and a** Vocabulary. 18mo, 1*s*.

Portraits of Celebrated Race-horses of the Past and **Present** Centuries, with Pedigrees and Performances. 4 vols., 4to, 126*s*.

Posselt (A. E.) Structure of Fibres, Yarns, and Fabrics. Illus., 2 vols. in one, 4to.

Powles (L. D.) Land of the Pink Pearl: Life in the Bahamas. 8vo, 10*s*. 6*d*.

Poynter (Edward J., R.A.). See "Illustrated Text-books."

Prince Maskiloff: a Romance of Modern Oxford. New ed. (LOW'S STANDARD NOVELS), 6*s*.

Prince of Nursery Playmates. Col. plates, new ed., 2*s*. 6*d*.

Pritt (T. E.) North Country Flies. Illustrated from the Author's Drawings. 10*s*. 6*d*.

Publishers' Circular (The), and General Record of British and Foreign Literature. Published on the 1st and 15th of every Month, 3*d*.

QUEEN'S Prime Ministers. Edited by STUART J. REID. Cr. 8vo, 3*s*. 6*d*. per vol.

J. A. Froude, Earl of Beaconsfield.	G. W. E. Russell, Rt. Hon. W. E. Gladstone.
Dunckley ("*Verax*"), Vis. Melbourne.	
Justin McCarthy, Sir Robert Peel.	Sir Arthur Gordon, Earl of Aberdeen.
Lorne (Marquis of), Viscount Palmerston.	
	H. D. Traill, Marquis of Salisbury.
Stuart J. Reid, Earl Russell.	George Saintsbury, Earl of Derby.

REDFORD (G.) Ancient Sculpture. New Ed. Crown 8vo, 10*s*. 6*d*.; roxburghe, 12*s*.

Redgrave (G. R.) Century of Painters of the English School. Crown 8vo, 10*s*. 6*d*.

——— *(R. and S.) Century of English Painters.* Sq. 10*s*. 6*d*. roxb., 12*s*.

Reed (Sir E. J., M.P.) and Simpson. Modern Ships of **War.**
Illust., royal 8vo, 10s. 6d.
—— (*Talbot Baines*) *Sir Ludar: a Tale of the Days of good*
Queen Bess. Crown 8vo, 6s.
—— *Roger Ingleton, Minor.* Illus., cr. 8vo.
Reid (Mayne, Capt.) Stories of Strange Adventures. Illust., cr. 8vo, 5s.
Remarkable Bindings in the British Museum. India paper, 94s. 6d.; sewed 73s. 6d. and 63s.
Ricci (J. H. de) Fisheries Dispute, and the Annexation of Canada. Crown 8vo, 6s.
Richards (W.) Aluminium: its History, Occurrence, &c.
Illustrated, crown 8vo, 21s.
Richter (Dr. Jean Paul) Italian Art in the National Gallery.
4to. Illustrated. Cloth gilt, £2 2s.; half-morocco, uncut, £2 12s. 6d.
—— See also LEONARDO DA VINCI.
Riddell (Mrs. J. H.) See LOW'S STANDARD NOVELS.
Rideal (C. F.) Women of the Time, a Dictionary, Revised to Date. 8vo, 14s.
Roberts (W.) Earlier History of English Bookselling. Crown 8vo, 7s. 6d.
Robertson (T. W.) Principal Dramatic Works, with Portraits in photogravure. 2 vols., 21s.
Robin Hood; Merry Adventures of. Written and illustrated by HOWARD PYLE. Imperial 8vo, 15s.
Robinson (Phil.) In my Indian Garden. New Edition, 16mo, limp cloth, 2s.
—— *Noah's Ark. Unnatural History.* Sm. post 8vo, 12s. 6d.
—— *Sinners and Saints: a Tour across the United States of* America, and Round them. Crown 8vo, 10s. 6d.
—— *Under the Punkah.* New Ed., cr. 8vo, limp cloth, 2s.
Rockstro (W. S.) History of Music. New Edition. 8vo, 14s.
Roe (E. P.) Nature's Serial Story. Illust. **New ed.** 3s. 6d.
Roland, The Story of. Crown 8vo, illustrated, 6s.
Rose (J.) Complete Practical Machinist. New Ed., 12mo, 12s. 6d.
—— *Key to Engines and Engine-running.* Crown 8vo, 8s. 6d.
—— *Mechanical Drawing.* Illustrated, small 4to, 16s.
—— *Modern Steam Engines.* Illustrated. 31s. 6d.
—— *Steam Boilers. Boiler Construction and Examination.*
Illust., 8vo, 12s. 6d.
Rose Library. Each volume, 1s. Many are illustrated—
Little Women. By LOUISA M. ALCOTT.
Little Women Wedded. Forming a Sequel to "Little Women.
Little Women and Little Women Wedded. 1 vol., cloth gilt, 3s. 6d.

Rose Library—(*continued*).
  Little Men. By L. M. ALCOTT. Double vol., 2s.; cloth gilt, 3s. 6d.
  An Old-Fashioned Girl. By L. M. ALCOTT. 2s.; cloth, 3s. 6d.
  Work. A Story of Experience. By L. M. ALCOTT. 3s. 6d.; 2 vols. 1s. each.
  Stowe (Mrs. H. B.) **The Pearl of Orr's Island.**
  ——— **The Minister's Wooing.**
  ——— **We and our Neighbours.** 2s.; cloth gilt, 6s.
  ——— **My Wife and I.** 2s.
  Hans Brinker; or, the Silver Skates. By Mrs. DODGE. Also 2s. 6d.
  My Study Windows. By J. R. LOWELL.
  The Guardian Angel. By OLIVER WENDELL HOLMES. Cloth, 2s.
  Dred. By Mrs. BEECHER STOWE. 2s.; cloth gilt, 3s. 6d.
  City Ballads. } By WILL CARLETON. N. ed. 1 vol. 2/6.
  City Legends. }
  Farm Ballads. By WILL CARLETON.
  Farm Festivals. By WILL CARLETON. } 1 vol., cl., gilt ed., 3s. 6d.
  Farm Legends. By WILL CARLETON.
  The Rose in Bloom. By L. M. ALCOTT. 2s.; cloth gilt, 3s. 6d.
  Eight Cousins. By L. M. ALCOTT. 2s.; cloth gilt, 3s. 6d.
  Under the Lilacs. By L. M. ALCOTT. 2s.; also 3s. 6d.
  Undiscovered Country. By W. D. HOWELLS.
  Clients of Dr. Bernagius. By L. BIART. 2 parts.
  Silver Pitchers. By LOUISA M. ALCOTT. Cloth, 3s. 6d.
  Jimmy's Cruise in the "Pinafore," and other Tales. By LOUISA M. ALCOTT. 2s.; cloth gilt, 3s. 6d.
  Jack and Jill. By LOUISA M. ALCOTT. 2s.; Illustrated, 5s.
  Hitherto. By the Author of the "Gayworthys." 2 vols., 1s. each; 1 vol., cloth gilt, 3s. 6d.
  A Gentleman of Leisure. A Novel. By EDGAR FAWCETT. 1s.
    See also LOW'S STANDARD SERIES.

Rousselet (*Louis*). See LOW'S STANDARD BOOKS.
Russell (*Dora*) *Strange Message.* 3 vols., crown 8vo, 31s. 6d.
——— (*W. Clark*) *Nelson's Words and Deeds, From his Despatches and Correspondence.* Crown 8vo, 6s.
——— *English Channel* **Ports and the Estate of the East** and West India Dock Company. Crown 8vo, 1s.
——— *Sailor's Language.* Illustrated. Crown 8vo, 3s. 6d.
——— *Wreck of the Grosvenor.* 4to, sewed, 6d.
——— See also "Low's Standard Novels," "Sea Stories."

S*AINTS and their Symbols: A Companion in the Churches* and Picture Galleries of Europe. Illustrated. Royal 16mo, 3s. 6d.
Samuels (*Capt. J. S.*) *From Forecastle to Cabin: Autobiography.* Illustrated. Crown 8vo, 8s. 6d.; also with fewer Illustrations, cloth, 2s.; paper, 1s.
Schaack (*M. J.*) *Anarchy and Anarchists in America and* Europe. Illust., roy. 8vo, 16s.

Schuyler The Life of Peter the Great. 2 vols., 8vo, 32s.
Schweinfurth (Georg) Heart of Africa. 2 vols., cr. 8vo, 3s. 6d. each.
Scientific Education of Dogs for the Gun. By H. H. 6s.
Scott (Leader) Renaissance of Art in Italy. 4to, 31s. 6d.
────── *Sculpture, Renaissance and Modern.* 5s.
Sea Stories. By W. CLARK RUSSELL. New ed. Cr. 8vo, leather back, top edge gilt, per vol., 3s. 6d.

Betwixt the Forelands.	Sailor's Sweetheart.
Frozen Pirate.	Sea Queen.
Jack's Courtship.	Strange Voyage.
John Holdsworth.	The Lady Maud.
Little Loo.	Watch Below.
Ocean Free **Lance**.	Wreck of the *Grosvenor*.

Sedgwick (W.) Force as an Entity with Stream, Pool and Wave Forms. Crown 8vo, 7s. 6d.
Semmes (Adm. Raphael) Service Afloat: The "Sumter" and the "Alabama." Illustrated. Royal 8vo, 16s.
Senior (W.) Near and Far: an Angler's Sketches of Home Sport and Colonial Life. Crown 8vo, 6s.; new edit., 2s.
────── *Waterside Sketches.* Imp. 32mo, 1s. 6d.; boards, 1s.
Shakespeare. Edited by R. GRANT WHITE. 3 vols., crown 8vo, gilt top, 36s.; *édition de luxe*, 6 vols., 8vo, cloth extra, 63s.
Shakespeare's Heroines: Studies by Living English Painters. 105s.; artists' proofs, 630s.
────── *Macbeth.* With Etchings on Copper, by J. MOYR SMITH. 105s. and 52s. 6d.
────── *Songs and Sonnets.* Illust. by Sir JOHN GILBERT, R.A. 4to, boards, 5s.
────── See also DONNELLY and WHITE (R. GRANT).
Sharpe (R. Bowdler) Birds in Nature. 39 coloured plates and text. 4to, 63s
Sheridan. Rivals. Reproductions of Water-colour, &c. 52s 6d.; artist's proofs, 105s. nett.
Shields (C. W.) Philosophia ultima; from Harmony of Science and Religion. 2 vols. 8vo, 24s.
────── *(G. O.) Big Game of North America.* Illust., 21s.
────── *Cruisings in the Cascades; Hunting, Photography,* Fishing. 8vo, 10s. 6d.
Sidney (Sir Philip) Arcadia. New Edition, 3s. 6d.
Siegfried, The Story of. Illustrated, crown 8vo, cloth, 6s.
Sienkiewicz (H.) With Fire and Sword, Historical Novel. 8vo, 10s. 6d.
*Sinclair (Mrs.) Indigenous Flowers of the Hawaiian **Islands**.* 44 Plates in Colour. Imp. folio, extra binding, gilt edges, 31s. 6d.

Sinclair (F.; "Aopouri;" "Philip Garth") Ballads from the Pacific. New Edition. 3s. 6d.
Skottowe (B. C.) Hanoverian Kings. New ed., cr. 8vo. 3s. 6d.
Smith (G.) Assyrian Explorations. Illust. New Ed., 8vo, 18s.
────── *The Chaldean Account of Genesis.* With many Illustrations. 16s. New Ed. By PROFESSOR SAYCE. 8vo, 18s.
────── *(G. Barnett) William I. and the German Empire.* New Ed., 8vo, 3s. 6d.
────── *(Sydney) Life and Times.* By STUART J. REID. Illustrated. 8vo, 21s.
Spiers' French Dictionary. 29th Edition, remodelled. 2 vols., 8vo, 18s.; half bound, 21s.
Spry (W. J. J., R.N., F.R.G.S.) Cruise of H.M.S. "Challenger." With Illustrations. 8vo, 18s. Cheap Edit., crown 8vo, 7s. 6d.
Stanley (H. M.) Congo, and Founding its Free State. Illustrated, 2 vols., 8vo, 42s.; re-issue, 2 vols. 8vo, 21s.
────── *How I Found Livingstone.* New ed., cr. 8vo, 7s. 6d. and 3s. 6d.
────── *My Kalulu.* New ed., cr. 8vo, 3s. 6d.; also 2s. 6d.
────── *In Darkest Africa, Rescue and Retreat of Emin.* Illust. 2 vols, 8vo, 42s.
────── *Through the Dark Continent.* Cr. 8vo, 12s. 6d.; new edition, 3s. 6d.
────── See also JEPHSON.
Start (J. W. K.) Junior Mensuration Exercises. 8d.
Stenhouse (Mrs.) Tyranny of Mormonism. An Englishwoman in Utah. New ed., cr. 8vo, cloth elegant, 3s. 6d.
Sterry (J. Ashby) Cucumber Chronicles. 5s.
Steuart (J. A.) Letters to Living Authors, with portraits. Cr. 8vo, 6s.; ed. de luxe, 10s. 6d.
────── *Kilgroom, a Story of Ireland.* Cr. 8vo, 6s.
Stevens (E. W.) Fly-Fishing in Maine Lakes. 8s. 6d.
────── *(T.) Around the World on a Bicycle.* Vol. II. 8vo 16s.
Stockton (Frank R.) Rudder Grange. 3s. 6d.
────── *Bee-Man of Orn, and other Fanciful Tales.* Cr. 8vo, 5s.
────── *Personally Conducted.* Ill. by PENNELL. Sm. 4to, 7s. 6d.
────── *The Casting Away of Mrs. Lecks and Mrs. Aleshine.* 1s.
────── *The Dusantes.* Sequel to the above. Boards, 1s.; this and the preceding book in one volume, cloth, 2s. 6d.
────── *The Hundredth Man.* Small post 8vo, 6s.
────── *The Late Mrs. Null.* Small post 8vo, 6s.
────── *Merry Chanter,* cr. 8vo. Boards, 2s. 6d.
────── *The Story of Viteau.* Illust. Cr. 8vo, 5s.
────── *Three Burglars,* cr. 8vo. Picture boards, 1s.; cloth, 2s.

Stockton (Frank R.) See also LOW'S STANDARD NOVELS.
Stoker (Bram) Snake's Pass, cr. 8vo, 6s.
Stowe (Mrs. Beecher) Dred. Cloth, gilt edges, 3s. 6d.; cloth, 2s.
—————— *Flowers and Fruit from her Writings.* Sm. post 8vo, 3s. 6d.
—————— *Life, in her own Words . . . with Letters, &c.* 15s.
—————— *Life, told for Boys and Girls.* Crown 8vo.
—————— *Little Foxes.* Cheap Ed., 1s.; Library Edition, 4s. 6d.
—————— *My Wife and I.* Cloth, 2s.
—————— *Old Town Folk.* 6s.
—————— *We and our Neighbours.* 2s.
—————— *Poganuc People.* 6s.
—————— See also LOW'S STANDARD NOVELS and ROSE LIBRARY.
Strickland (F.) Engadine: a Guide to the District, with Articles by J. SYMONDS, Mrs. MAIN, &c., 5s.
Stuarts. See INDERWICK.
Stutfield (Hugh E. M.) El Maghreb: 1200 Miles' Ride through Marocco. 8s. 6d.
Sullivan (A. M.) Nutshell History of Ireland. Paper boards, 6d.
Szczpanski (F.), Directory of Technical Literature, Classified Catalogue of Books, Annuals, and Journals. Cr. 8vo, 2s.

TAINE (H. A.) "Origines." Translated by JOHN DURAND.
    I. **The Ancient Regime.** Demy 8vo, cloth, 16s.
    II. **The French Revolution.** Vol. 1. do.
    III. Do. do. Vol. 2. do.
    IV. Do. do. Vol. 3. do.
Tauchnitz's English Editions of German Authors. Each volume, cloth flexible, 2s.; or sewed, 1s. 6d. (Catalogues post free.)
Tauchnitz (B.) German Dictionary. 2s.; paper, 1s. 6d.; roan, 2s. 6d.
—————— *French Dictionary.* 2s.; paper, 1s. 6d.; roan, 2s. 6d.
—————— *Italian Dictionary.* 2s.; paper, 1s. 6d.; roan, 2s. 6d.
—————— *Latin Dictionary.* 2s.; paper, 1s. 6d.; roan, 2s. 6d.
—————— *Spanish and English.* 2s.; paper, 1s. 6d.; roan, 2s. 6d.
—————— *Spanish and French.* 2s.; paper, 1s. 6d.; roan, 2s. 6d.
Taylor (R. L.) Chemical Analysis Tables. 1s.
—————— *Chemistry for Beginners.* Small 8vo, 1s. 6d.
Techno-Chemical Receipt Book. With additions by BRANNT and WAHL. 10s. 6d.

Technological Dictionary. See TOLHAUSEN.
Thausing (Prof.) Malt and the Fabrication of Beer. 8vo, 45s.
Theakston (M.) British Angling Flies. Illustrated. Cr. 8vo, 5s.
Thomas (Bertha), House on the Scar, Tale of South Devon.
Crown 8vo, 6s.
Thomson (Jos.) Central African Lakes. New edition, 2 vols.
in one, crown 8vo, 7s. 6d.
—————— *Through Masai Land.* Illust. 21s.; new edition, 7s. 6d.
—————— *and Miss Harris-Smith. Ulu: an African Romance.*
crown 8vo, 6s.
—————— *(W.) Algebra for Colleges and Schools.* With Answers,
5s.; without, 4s. 6d.; Answers separate, 1s. 6d.
Thornton (L. D.) Story of a Poodle. By Himself and his
Mistress. Illust., crown 4to, 2s. 6d.
Tileston (Mary W.), Daily Strength for Daily Needs. 18mo,
4s. 6d.
Tolhausen. Technological German, English, and French Dic-
tionary. Vols. I., II., with Supplement, 12s. 6d. each; III., 9s.;
Supplement, cr. 8vo, 3s. 6d.
Tompkins (E. S. de G.) Through David's Realm. Illust. by
TOMPKINS, the Author. 8vo, 10s. 6d.
Transactions of the Hong Kong Medical Society, vol. 1, 8vo,
sewed, 12s. 6d.
Tytler (Sarah) Duchess Frances: a Novel. 2 vols., 21s.

*U*PTON *(H.) Manual of Practical Dairy Farming.* Cr.
8vo, 2s.

*V*ERNE *(Jules) Celebrated Travels and Travellers.* 3 vols.
8vo, 7s. 6d. each; extra gilt, 9s.
—————— *Purchase of the North Pole, seq. to* "From Earth to
Moon." Illustrated. 6s.
—————— *Family Without a Name.* Illustrated. 6s.
—————— *Flight to France.* 3s. 6d.
—————— See also LAURIE.
Victoria (Queen) Life of. By GRACE GREENWOOD. Illust. 6s.
Vigny (A. de), Cinq Mars. Translated, with Etchings. 2 vols.
8vo, 30s.
Viollet-le-Duc (E.) Lectures on Architecture. Translated by
BENJAMIN BUCKNALL, Architect. 2 vols., super-royal 8vo, £3 3s.

BOOKS BY JULES VERNE.

WORKS.	LARGE CROWN 8VO. Containing 350 to 600 pp. and from 50 to 100 full-page illustrations.		Containing the whole of the text with some illustrations.	
	Handsome cloth binding, gilt edges.	Plainer binding, plain edges.	Cloth binding, gilt edges, smaller type.	Coloured boards, or cloth.
	s. d.	*s. d.*	*s. d.*	
20,000 Leagues under the Sea. Parts I. and II.	10 6	5 0	3 6	2 vols., 1s. each.
Hector Servadac	10 6	5 0	3 6	2 vols., 1s. each.
The Fur Country	10 6	5 0	3 6	2 vols., 1s. each.
The Earth to the Moon and a Trip round it	10 6	5 0	2 vols., 2s. ea.	2 vols., 1s. each.
Michael Strogoff	10 6	5 0	3 6	2 vols., 1s. each.
Dick Sands, the Boy Captain	10 6	5 0	3 6	2 vols., 1s. each.
Five Weeks in a Balloon	7 6	3 6	2 0	1s. 0d.
Adventures of Three Englishmen and Three Russians	7 6	3 6	2 0	1 0
Round the World in Eighty Days	7 6	3 6	2 0	1 0
A Floating City	7 6	3 6	2 0	1 0
The Blockade Runners			2 0	1 0
Dr. Ox's Experiment	—	—	2 0	1 0
A Winter amid the Ice	—	—	2 0	1 0
Survivors of the "Chancellor"	7 6	3 6	3 6	2 vols., 1s. each.
Martin Paz			2 0	1s. 0d.
The Mysterious Island, 3 vols.:—	22 6	10 6	6 0	3 0
I. Dropped from the Clouds	7 6	3 6	2 0	1 0
II. Abandoned	7 6	3 6	2 0	1 0
III. Secret of the Island	7 6	3 6	2 0	1 0
The Child of the Cavern	7 6	3 6	2 0	1 0
The Begum's Fortune	7 6	3 6	2 0	1 0
The Tribulations of a Chinaman	7 6	3 6	2 0	1 0
The Steam House, 2 vols.:—				
I. Demon of Cawnpore	7 6	3 6	2 0	1 0
II. Tigers and Traitors	7 6	3 6	2 0	1 0
The Giant Raft, 2 vols.:—				
I. 800 Leagues on the Amazon	7 6	3 6	2 0	1 0
II. The Cryptogram	7 6	3 6	2 0	1 0
The Green Ray	6 0	5 0	2 0	1 0
Godfrey Morgan	7 6	3 6	2 0	1 0
Keraban the Inflexible:—				
I. Captain of the "Guidara"	7 6	3 6	2 0	1 0
II. Scarpante the Spy	7 6	3 6	2 0	1 0
The Archipelago on Fire	7 6	3 6	2 0	1 0
The Vanished Diamond	7 6	3 6	2 0	1 0
Mathias Sandorf	10 6	5 0	3 6	2 vols., 1s. each.
The Lottery Ticket	7 6	3 6	2 0	1 0
The Clipper of the Clouds	7 6	3 6	2 0	1 0
North against South	7 6	3 6		
Adrift in the Pacific	6 0	3 6		
The Flight to France	7 6	3 6		
The Purchase of the North Pole	6 0			
A Family without a Name	6 0			

CELEBRATED TRAVELS AND TRAVELLERS. 3 vols. 8vo, 600 pp., 100 full-page illustrations, 7s. 6d., gilt edges, 9s. each:—(1) THE EXPLORATION OF THE WORLD. (2) THE GREAT NAVIGATORS OF THE EIGHTEENTH CENTURY. (3) THE GREAT EXPLORERS OF THE NINETEENTH CENTURY.

WALERY, Our Celebrities. Photographic Portraits, vol. II., part I., including Christmas Number, royal folio, 30s.; monthly, 2s. 6d.

Wallace (L.) Ben Hur: A Tale of the Christ. New Edition, crown 8vo, 6s.; cheaper edition, 2s.

Waller (Rev. C. H.) Adoption and the Covenant. On Confirmation. 2s. 6d.

—— *Silver Sockets; and other* Shadows of Redemption. Sermons at Christ Church, Hampstead. Small post 8vo, 6s.

—— *The Names on the Gates of* Pearl, *and other Studies*. New Edition. Crown 8vo, cloth extra, 3s. 6d.

—— *Words in the Greek Testament.* Part I. Grammar. Small post 8vo, cloth, 2s. 6d. Part II. Vocabulary, 2s. 6d.

Walford (Mrs. L. B.) Her Great Idea, and other Stories. Cr. 8vo, 3s.; boards, 2s.

Walsh (A.S.) Mary, Queen of the House of David. 8vo, 3s. 6d.

Walton (Iz.) Wallet Book, CIƆIƆLXXXV. Crown 8vo, half vellum, 21s.; large paper, 42s.

—— *Compleat Angler.* Lea and Dove Edition. Ed. by R. B. Marston. With full-page Photogravures on India paper, and the Woodcuts on India paper from blocks. 4to, half-morocco, 105s.; large paper, royal 4to, full dark green morocco, gilt top, 210s.

Walton (T. H.) Coal Mining. With Illustrations. 4to, 25s.

Warner (C. D.) See Low's Standard Novels and Standard Series.

Washington Irving's Little Britain. Square crown 8vo, 6s.

Wells (H. P.) American Salmon Fisherman. 6s.

—— *Fly Rods and Fly Tackle.* Illustrated. 10s. 6d.

—— *(J. W.) Three Thousand Miles through Brazil.* Illustrated from Original Sketches. 2 vols. 8vo, 32s.

Wenzel (O.) Directory of Chemical Products of the German Empire. 8vo, 25s.

Westgarth (W.) Half-century of Australasian Progress. Personal retrospect. 8vo, 12s.

Westoby (W. A. S.), Descriptive Catalogue of 50 *Years' Postage Stamps* in Great Britain and Ireland. 8vo, 5s.

Wheatley (H. B.) Remarkable Bindings in the British Museum. Reproductions in Colour. 94s. 6d., 73s. 6d., and 63s.

White (J.) Ancient History of the Maori; Mythology, &c. Vols. I.-IV. 8vo, 10s. 6d. each.

—— *(R. Grant) England Without and* Within. Crown 8vo, 10s. 6d.

—— *Every-day English.* 10s. 6d.

—— *Fate of Mansfield Humphreys, &c.* Cr. 8vo, 6s.

—— *Studies in Shakespeare.* 10s. 6d.

White (R. Grant) Words and their Uses. New Edit., crown 8vo, 5s.

Whitney (Mrs.) See LOW'S STANDARD SERIES.

Whittier (J. G.) The King's Missive, and later Poems. 18mo, choice parchment cover, 3s. 6d.

———— *St. Gregory's Guest, &c.* Recent Poems. 5s.

William I. and the German Empire. By G. BARNETT SMITH. New Edition, 3s. 6d.

Willis-Bund (J.) Salmon Problems. 3s. 6d.; boards, 2s. 6d.

Wills (Dr. C. J.) Persia as it is. Crown 8vo, 8s. 6d.

Wills, A Few Hints on Proving, without Professional Assistance. By a PROBATE COURT OFFICIAL. 8th Edition, revised, with Forms of Wills, Residuary Accounts, &c. Fcap. 8vo, cloth gilt, 1s.

Wilmot-Buxton (Ethel M.) Wee Folk, Good Folk: a Fantasy. Illust., fcap. 4to, 5s.

Winder (Frederick Horatio) Lost in Africa: a Yarn of Adventure. Illust., cr. 8vo, 6s.

Winsor (Justin) Narrative and Critical History of America. 8 vols., 30s. each; large paper, per vol., 63s.

Woolsey. Introduction to International Law. 5th Ed., 18s.

Woolson (Constance F.) See LOW'S STANDARD NOVELS.

Wright (T.) Town of Cowper, Olney, &c. 6s.

Written to Order; the Journeyings of an Irresponsible Egotist. By the Author of "A Day of my Life at Eton." Crown 8vo, 6s.

London:
SAMPSON LOW, MARSTON, SEARLE, & RIVINGTON, LD.
St. Dunstan's House,
FETTER LANE, FLEET STREET, E.C.

www.ingramcontent.com/pod-product-compliance
Lightning Source LLC
Chambersburg PA
CBHW022049230426
43672CB00008B/1112